STRIVE

Jones Studio Adventures in Architecture

STRIVE

Jones Studio Adventures in Architecture

Marilu Knode

Foreword
by Marlon Blackwell
in collaboration with Jonathan Boelkins

OSCAR RIERA OJEDA
PUBLISHERS

CONTENTS

Foreword

Bear With Me

by Marlon Blackwell, FAIA in collaboration with Jonathan Boelkins, AIA

For many years now, I've shared what is now simply known as "The Bear Story" when I lecture. Without retelling it in detail, it involves me, as a scrawny high school teenager in Colorado, wrestling a bear, unsuccessfully. That story has been an armature for a lot of themes over the years, about being outmatched, about being adaptable, about the need for humor, the need to overcome fear. There in that makeshift ring in a rural shopping center parking lot, I found a part of myself under a sticky, warm coating of orange soda the bear regurgitated, the part that would be necessary later in life…a life in architecture. There is a kinship that comes from being in those kinds of fights, from being completely outmatched, and pressing on despite it all. That was the part of me I found, the part of me that is the bear. Over time, I found friends with that same spirit, that same tenacity, desperately trying to make meaningful architecture in out of the way places, rough places far from the centers of architectural fashion. So, it's not surprising that I had an instant affinity for Neal and Eddie and recognized their utter dedication and commitment to architecture of the highest aspirations.

We share true American landscapes of real natural beauty and constructed ugliness, mine in the Ozarks of Arkansas and theirs in the heart of the Sonoran Desert in Arizona. Out of the stark beauty of the desert, Neal and Eddie built a highly varied and intensely disciplined body of work, beautifully chronicled in this book. Books like this often convey a sense of inevitability, with designs that are so well crafted and executed that they feel weightless, like Fred Astaire gliding across the page. But when I see it, I feel the bear, sitting on my chest, panting its rancid breath in my face. I know the outright struggle it takes to do what Jones Studio has done. They have the bear in them too.

So as much as I respect the work, I have even greater respect for the people they are and the culture they have cultivated in their practice. Together with Jacob Benyi and Brian Farling and their relatively small team of people, Eddie and Neal have achieved national and international recognition for their work, building up from early house commissions to now work at the dramatic scale of national land ports of entry. Somehow, through the complexity and the significant increase in scale, the clarity and the conviction of those early projects remains.

Marlon Blackwell

Above left & right Operable shade scrim "petals" - House of Five Dreams, Paradise Valley, Arizona.

The light is what I see first in it all, that crisp, cerulean light, the blessing and the curse of the desert. At every opportunity, Jones Studio filters and sculpts the light, revealing their endless curiosity for materials and construction. Every edge is an opportunity, a place for sunlight to give way to shadow across beautifully textured surfaces so the materials become light themselves. Even weathering steel seems buoyant in their hands, floating and fine. The care they instill in every material and assembly imparts a dignity that is so rarely found in our public institutions.

Embedded in the architecture are sustainability strategies that are so thoroughly integrated, the architecture couldn't survive without them. Collecting rainwater and harvesting solar energy are celebrated, not out of pretense, but as an opportunity for architecture to gather its full potential. For Jones Studio, these are the elements of architecture, every bit the equal to columns, stairs and windows. Where so often these components and systems are applied to otherwise conventional buildings, a kind of "greenwashing," they are embedded and enmeshed, inseparable from the architecture.

What emerges is an expanded vocabulary for the discipline, one that is especially evident in the University of Arizona College of Architecture, Planning and Landscape Architecture in Tucson, Arizona. Equal parts renovation and new construction, Jones Studio's command of light, materials and systems says everything a design school needs to say. It cares for its elder, breathing new life into tired spaces, while offering airy and generous studios, the envy of any school. A feeling of effortlessness pervades, one that only comes from rigor and repetition, from knowing that the stone has been turned over and over until worn smooth.

In every case there is a clear material logic, a set of rules by which materials are selected and distributed, materials that reflect the brutality and beauty of the desert. The interrelationship of concrete and steel is a consistent source of inspiration, exploring finishes and forces. This fascination is on display in the Interdisciplinary Science and Technology Building in Mesa, Arizona, where the steel forms that shaped the perforated pattern in the precast panels were then used as an entry sculpture and wind chimes in the internal gardens. The exploration of thermal mass isn't limited to concrete alone, as evidenced by the House of Five Dreams in Paradise Valley, Arizona, where rammed earth supports an intensely detailed and delicate steel box that unfolds like flower petals, the permanence of the desert and the fragility of its flora on full display. Though dramatically different in scale and purpose, these projects sit comfortably side by side, revealing the power and versatility of a set of principles that have been thoughtfully developed and carefully refined over decades.

In each of these projects, texture and pattern are critical, sometimes cast into the architecture, sometimes cast upon it. The need for shade is forever an opportunity for articulation and exploration, as in the Mariposa Land Port of Entry in Nogales, Arizona. Here, a steel canopy gathers the entire campus, layered and feathered until it feels weightless, gesturing to welcome visitors and reaching up to the sky. Once again, the apparent lightness of the steel is read against the heft and thermal mass of the concrete, inscribed here with footprints that honor the journey so many have made between these two nations. The archetype of the cave and the forest is expanded to be an oasis through the presence of water whether natural or as a geological analogy, the lifeblood of the Sonoran Desert.

These strategies are consistent regardless of scale, having been formed and refined in the early work—the houses in particular. This dedication to articulation and composition gives every project a true sense of scale, which is another way of saying "humane." Jones Studio is also carrying on the legacy of other important architects of the desert, like Frank Lloyd Wright and Al Beadle. Beadle's work combined a Case Study sensibility with explorations of frames, patterns and deep overhangs, all worthy strategies that Jones Studio has mixed and mastered to create complex systems of articulation through aggregation. What Jones Studio adds to that already potent mix is a keen appreciation for nature, and a willingness to inject local material culture, balancing the universal nature of modernism with "the lure of the local."

Ultimately, the work of Jones Studio not only reflects the crystalline desert sky, but it also reflects them as people. It reveals their deep curiosity, their engaging humanity and a profound love for architecture. Their boundless enthusiasm and optimism are on full display in this book, which should be required reading for young architects (and perhaps old ones too), for them to see what is truly possible when you are dedicated to being from somewhere, to making your place better than it was when you found it.

Marlon Blackwell, FAIA, is an American architect and the E. Fay Jones Distinguished Professor at the University of Arkansas. Blackwell is a lifetime member of the American Academy of Arts and Letters and the recipient of the 2020 Gold Medal from the American Institute of Architects. He was a Resident Fellow of the American Academy in Rome and was inducted into the National Academy of Design in 2019 and a United States Artists Ford Fellow in 2014. His professional practice, Marlon Blackwell Architects, in Fayetteville, Arkansas, has received significant recognition including the Cooper Hewitt National Design Award in Architecture in 2016.

Jonathan Boelkins, AIA, is an architect and writer who teaches at the Fay Jones School of Architecture and Design at the University of Arkansas. Formerly the studio director at Marlon Blackwell Architects, he is a Co-Editor of a new monograph titled *Radical Practice: The Work of Marlon Blackwell Architects*. His writings with Marlon Blackwell have been featured in several books, including essays in *Shelby Farms Park: Elevating a City: The Improbable Journey of Great 21st Century Urban Park* and Brian Healy Architects' monograph *Commonplaces: Working on an American Architecture*.

Acknowledgements

by Marilu Knode

When Jones Studio approached me about telling the story of the firm, I was thrilled. Just as they relish the opportunity to test their abilities in many new arenas, writing a full-length book was a mountain I had always wanted to climb and finally, I had a firm and an ethos worth exploring. The project I organized with them at the Scottsdale Museum of Contemporary Art [SMoCA] has always been one of the most exciting of my career. At each telling of Jones Studio's risky move into the galleries, my interlocutor is inspired (as I was) by the boldness of the idea. It is that boldness that characterizes the best artists of our time. I want to thank Eddie Jones, Neal Jones, Brian Farling and Jacob Benyi for their trust and confidence in me as I sifted through the complex realities of their world and became again part of their daring plans.

In my research and interviews for *STRIVE*, I found overlapping ways of working that connect my curatorial process to Jones Studio's practice. I share with Jones Studio an appetite for learning new things and finding opportunities to express them; a passion for engaging with new people and ideas; a relentless search for intellectual landscapes for action; and the belief that artists mediate the conflicting ideas of our world, helping make sense of our present by understanding our past with an eye to the future. I am grateful to the partners at Jones Studio for sharing with me books, architects, buildings and artists who have influenced them. To that list I brought a long list of books I have gobbled up while curating in cities as diverse as Phoenix, St. Louis, Los Angeles, Milwaukee and New York, which created a rich set of ideas to frame Jones Studio's work.

My interest in architecture was fully launched when working at SMoCA, and for that I am grateful to former director Susan Krane, who introduced architecture and design shows into the mix of our programming. I also want to thank Maria and Matt Salenger for their friendship that came from our conversations at SMoCA—it has been a joy to reconnect to them, to the entire Jones Studio family and with other friends from my years in Phoenix.

In winter 2022 I flew to Phoenix to meet with Jones Studio and to conduct site visits and was disoriented by how dramatically the city had changed. In-fill shops, housing services, well-loved light rail and a vibrating street life is evidence of this desert city's growth. I hope both Phoenix and Tempe will follow Jones Studio's lead to ensure the region does not become one of the great lost civilizations found elsewhere in our desert zones. I thank friends Mary Statzer and Gene Kadish for hosting me during my trip to the glorious Arizona winter.

Gardens are another key connection between Jones Studio's work and my personal and professional interests. "Garden" seems like such a placid word, flecked with the star dust of regal landscapes created by Western imperialists to flaunt their wealth. Gardening has a reputation of being a bourgeois hobby for some, when really, gardens are radical spaces where people can feed themselves, create community, support the species in their yards and generally upend the consumer Ferris Wheel on which we dangle. Planting desert gardens restores our understanding of the unique land that forces a reckoning with the reality of place while addressing how the desert has been consumed by illogical dreams of lost horizons.

I want to thank my partner Kevin J. Miyazaki, whose sense of humor, unflagging support and own artistic exploration of family and home ensures we have art in our lives every day. His patience and feedback was invaluable as I tackled a world of ideas and language and wrestled them into this book. I am grateful to my family—mother Nina Knode, brother Tom Knode and sister-in-law Tracy Lamb—for their cheer through these locked-down years. And what do we do without our friends? They help us define who we are, showing us a mirror that is sometimes shining, sometimes cracked. I thank my extended family of friends for being who they are, and over the decades of my career, for believing like I do that art needs to be placed more fully into the center of our lives and communities.

And most of all, I want to thank all the architects, artists, curators, writers, cultural critics and art lovers who believe in the importance of interpreting the world through open-minded critical reverie.

Marilu Knode has worked as a curator and arts leader for three decades. She has supported global contemporary artists working across disciplines including video, performance, installation, sculpture, painting and other non-traditional practices in exhibitions, commissions and catalogues, and articles and reviews in national and international publications. She was the U.S. Commissioner for the 1998 Cairo Biennial, producing a site-specific installation by Nancy Spero, and co-founded the first curatorial practice program in the Middle East at the American University in Cairo. Knode served as Executive Director at Laumeier Sculpture Park, St. Louis, and returned to Milwaukee in 2016, where she was a founding team member of Sculpture Milwaukee while digging into a new range of creative projects.

Opposite page Shade trellis of brass "leaves" - Logan Residence, Scottsdale, Arizona.

Marilu Knode

Introduction

Jones Studio: The Urgency of Now
by Marilu Knode

STRIVE: Jones Studio Adventures in Architecture touches on the pivotal moments when Jones Studio's research and collaboration yields designs of meaning. Eddie Jones, founder, and Neal Jones, brother and first partner, along with new partners Brian Farling and Jacob Benyi, have built a firm, an ethos, a way of life that insists on designing beautiful buildings that open a dialogue meaningful to place. The firm's unwavering commitment to architecture fuels 40 plus years of experimentation in imagining and creating a better way to live in the desert Southwest and beyond. *STRIVE* traces Jones Studio's growth as it tackles increasingly urgent cultural and environmental changes, reacts to the ups and downs of the economy, and adjusts to the diversity of clients who provide opportunities for their work.

Readers will get a sense of the Studio's broad intellectual curiosity, the sometimes-naïve belief that time and inventive thinking always allow design resolution and a firm-wide willingness to exceed all expectations for partners, users and the public. *STRIVE* tracks the relentless commitment to risk-taking, to think beyond the obvious for surprising outcomes. The entire Jones Studio family—a literal and metaphoric word used to honor the connections, working style and bonds formed at the firm—believe in architecture's ability to transform lives and to impact culture beyond the clients they serve. Carrying a positive, give-us-a-chance, always, every time attitude is the unique elixir of Jones Studio's success. They fight fearlessly to find the right solution to technical issues and human needs. By sharing the speed bumps in the multiplex pursuit of making architecture, their intellectual honesty will be clear throughout this book.

The themes in *STRIVE* are based on the pillars of Jones Studio's design work: using nature as a partner to generate design solutions; meeting and exceeding each building's program goals through innovative, interrelated and sustainable spaces; and mixing history and politics, place and imagination that allows for a high level of creative achievement. *STRIVE* explores 37 projects, three public art works, five unbuilt concept structures and two exhibitions that showcased Jones Studio's experimental work boiling with ideas. *STRIVE* enumerates Jones Studio's work in education,

Above top to bottom Saguaro National Park - Tucson, Arizona; Haboob - Phoenix, Arizona; Desert rain - Mohave Desert, California.

performing arts, government, nature centers, homes, sports and spiritual structures, creating new visual and functional vocabularies for each. The scale and scope of the diverse buildings created by the small team—a stable fourteen but ranging from three in the beginning and upwards to twenty-two in response to project demands—is astounding. Jones Studio's design discipline is a synthesis of many art forms, where time is an active agent as buildings mature and evolve. While these elements may seem self-evident, keeping them balanced and in the air at the right time and in the right proportion is not.

> We have the most fun finding those essential conceptual seeds that can become meaningful with respect to making something new, substantial, and that impacts lives.
> Brian Farling[1]

The fruits of architecture are the most visible and long-lasting signs of culture, though architecture is perhaps the least understood art form, rooted in deep human need but today governed by the rules and regulations of our overwhelmingly intricate, regulation-managed world. Architects shape how we live, how we interact, how we are included or excluded from society and neighborhood. To understand how architecture gets made we must peel back the overlapping and often contradictory demands placed on designers and their buildings. To understand how one of the country's most exemplary mid-size firms that consistently punches above its weight works is at the heart of *STRIVE: Jones Studio Adventures in Architecture.*

Architects, as designer Bruce Goff (see page 21) once said, "often work against or beyond their own experience."[2] Jones Studio is energized by the possibility of new building typologies, each with unique needs necessitating new forms—the firm does not create cookie cutter buildings. They are willing to consider off-the-shelf materials by twisting them out of the context for which they were intended, often befuddling manufacturers and construction teams but always with the goal of architecture in mind. Jones Studio couples an audacious aggressiveness with high project aspirations and an (almost) cultivated unknowing—sometimes not having experience with a system allows them to generate a new template.

The office environment at Jones Studio is focused on the shared experience where their daily work routines are organized around one long common table. This "Family Table" facilitates an open environment that has allowed the team to grow, shift and adapt in natural ways. Their use of the Socratic method of questioning is spread broadly across the team so that everyone is pulled forward through learning. The culture of Jones Studio is predicated on collaboration and discussion, the push-and-pull of ideas that produce those seeds of design to meet the goals of each project.

Jones Studio's foundational purpose—for being, for designing, for contributing to our time—is to "help people live better."[3] *STRIVE* will explore this core thought, and the ways in which Jones Studio honors and learns from the land and from those who came before while establishing a direction for those who will come after. Jones Studio's seeds of exploration, planted at the firm's beginning, continue to grow and flourish in the glorious desert Southwest.

What is the "urgency of now" in this examination of Jones Studio's far-ranging catalogue of projects? After four decades of work, evaluating their past is critical to the firm's future success. It also comes at a time when we as a culture, as a species, can no longer close our eyes to the impacts of human-driven climate change, and building, tearing down and re-building are *ür* representatives of these human impacts. We have seen how population growth gobbles up land. While the entire country is not yet covered with Monopoly-like single family homes, the board is groaning with the weight and consequences of this building. Eddie founded Jones Studio after learning to read the beautiful, harsh, explicit messages of the Sonoran Desert, and each family member since has learned to interpret the mutually impactful interactions between nature and culture. Jones Studio imagines and designs for place, whether developing a unique desert aesthetic because of their position as cultural insiders, or through their deep research practice when immersing themselves in other types of environmental, social and political climates.

We understand the building industry's impacts are based on its material extractions, and iron, cement, stone and wood are permeated with and sheathed by the chemical fabrications of industry. However, it is the less durable materials of Earth and sky that dominate desert-sensitive design. Water is the least abundant resource in the desert and sun is its superabundant twin. Ancient peoples designed to manage these two resources; Arizona's first peoples used the Earth itself for life. Jones Studio too focuses on these elements, to ground their work in place and to take good care of this land.

Just as Arizona has a unique ancient history, it also has a modern architectural patrimony that is impossible for designers to ignore. Frank Lloyd Wright trained with noted architect Louis Sullivan in Chicago, taking from Sullivan a commitment to an American vernacular rooted in native landscapes as the only proper way to create an "organic" architecture, one of place, materials, history and people. Wright first visited the Sonoran Desert in 1928. He planted Taliesin West in Scottsdale, at the far Northeastern reach of Phoenix in 1938, leaving a long legacy of buildings and students behind. Wright's one-time apprentice Paolo Soleri too was inspired by the desert. His home, Cosanti, in Paradise Valley, and on-going sustainable utopian city, Arcosanti, 70 miles north of downtown Phoenix, mirror Wright's dream of creating an architecture of place. Both ancient and modern architects have left their fingerprints on the Arizona landscape, creating a diagram of the past while Jones Studio forges a path into the future.

The Sonoran Desert, Jones Studio's base of operations and primary inspiration, is not an island isolated by its landscape and history. Instead the region is connected to that "stripe around the Earth where we all share the same sun doing the same things."[4] The desert—defined as a lack of access to water, which also includes ice caps and glaciers—links the Sonoran Desert, the lushest desert on Earth, to other parts of the world.[5] The Sonoran Desert puts Jones Studio into a global narrative of desert exchange, desert aesthetics and desertification that requires deep analysis for an informed architectural response.

Above Bavinger House, Norman, Oklahoma - Bruce Goff. **Below** Taliesin West, Scottsdale, Arizona - Frank Lloyd Wright.

Above Grape orchards with Camelback Mountain in background - Phoenix, Arizona, early 1900s. **Following spread** Salt River Valley Hohokam canal map - Arizona, 1929.

The Desert Condition

> Form…is from nature…Design [is] the human response.
> Louis Kahn[6]

Before we explore how Jones Studio interprets the desert landscape for our contemporary world, I want to draw a quick line through the country's past 500 years or so to understand how immigrants to the American desert fundamentally changed its culture. In his book *The Big Muddy: An Environmental History of the Mississippi and Its Peoples from Hernando de Soto to Hurricane Katrina*, Christopher Morris explores one aspect of the many irreparable consequences of European colonization: Europeans tried to make the wet Mississippi delta dry to make it useful to empire. And naturally, they tried to make the dry desert Southwest wet to support themselves while siphoning off its riches.[7]

The white settlers violated all the rules nature set out for this land. The colonizers grafted their ideas about the commerce and utility of land, and their habit of brutal human subjugation, onto a continent with its own diverse civilizations and histories.[8] The desert had no identifiers or lacked recognizable meaning, "no sublime or picturesque" from a European point of view.[9] Noted historian of the west Patricia Nelson Limerick relays that what Easterners wanted and needed from the West was arable land, safety from others, and "a Promised land for surplus men" to become Thomas Jefferson's ideal (and pliable) yeoman farmer. Europeans believed the "empty" desert was clear for projection, ready to accept the enslaved, the indentured and the disenfranchised from Europe and its client states.[10]

Furs, timber and minerals were extracted to support economic growth in Europe and the East coast. Mining reshaped the land and upended its ancient human communities, using each technological innovation to siphon off more treasures. By the late 19th century, environmental and social trauma were written in the ruts and forts and reservations that lay scattered across the country. The desert in particular was to be tamed and refashioned into a fantasy image of somewhere else. The invention of the American desert "underpins the invention of America itself."[11]

Today, we think contemporary desert living is an exercise in controlling the sun, maybe even the dust that uniquely constitutes the Sonoran Desert.[12] The most important element that links humans to land however is water, its management, preservation and purification. In some ways, the white settlers were right: they *would* need more water to conquer this exquisitely resistant landscape.

In *Savage Dreams: A Journey Into the Landscape Wars of the American West,* Rebecca Solnit writes about how humans have always managed their landscape, even in the desert.[13] The Hohokam, first inhabitants of the Phoenix region, managed water by creating a canal network (see pages 24, 25) nearly 500 miles long and serving 50,000 inhabitants. This network, the largest in North America, required collaboration and coordination along the length of the Salt River (*Rio Salado*), the lifeblood of Phoenix.[14] Community clusters along the river directed the resource, proof that Arizona's Indigenous peoples cooperated to create their vibrant civilization layered with social and political networks. The Hohokam lived for nearly fifteen hundred years carefully striking an ecological balance for survival.

Why the Hohokam disappeared in the mid-fifteenth century is unclear. In *Collapse: Why Societies Choose to Fail or Succeed,* Jared Diamond outlines how cultures from New Mexico's Chaco Canyon to Chile's remote Easter Island collapsed due to political infighting and over-exploitation of natural resources among other causes that are hauntingly familiar to us today.[15] Even the most wildlife abundant and verdant natural environment can be turned to dust by the hubris and selfishness of its people. European settlers recognized the need to harness the power of the desert's water sources, but they did not heed the warning of the Hohokam's disappearance.

With so much evidence of desert civilizations, or civilizations that became deserts, wiped off the landscape by political or natural disasters, what can Phoenicians expect as the city's population explodes, making it one of the fastest-growing cities in the country and thus the most likely to over-exploit its finite resources? The modern City of Phoenix, founded in 1881, was named in acknowledgement of the area's past inhabitants, the city's 19th century "discoverers" sure that *this* iteration of an American desert outpost would *not* disappear.[16] Still, Phoenix, or the Valley of the Sun as it is known to the inhabitants of this wide bowl through which the Salt River meanders, is haunted by the Indigenous groups forced from view, their homes and canals traceable if barely perceptible, their lessons (see page 26) waiting for a broader reconsideration in our era of resource scarcity and global warming.

Phoenix continues to be shaped by the technical businesses that boomed post-World War II, including manufacturing, military, mining, aerospace, technology, government, education, agriculture and leisure industries. Each stakes a claim to one of Arizona's five C's: cattle, cotton, citrus, copper

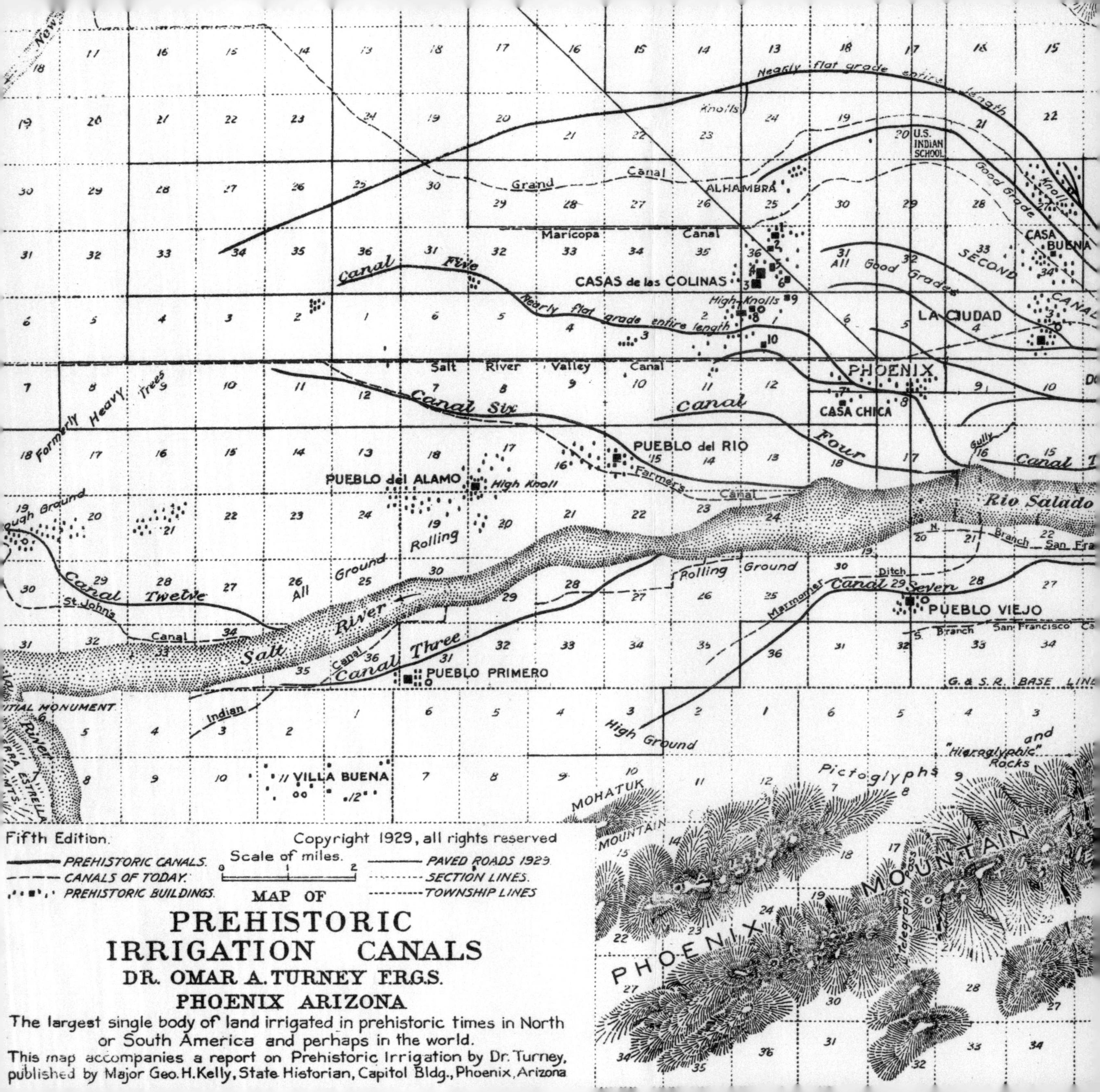

Nearly flat grade entire length
Knolls
U.S. INDIAN SCHOOL
Grand
Canal
ALHAMBRA
Good Grade
Knolls
Maricopa
Canal
CASA BUENA
Canal
Five
All Good Grades
SECOND
CANAL
CASAS de las COLINAS
High Knolls
Nearly flat grade entire length
LA CIUDAD
Salt
River
Valley
Canal
PHOENIX
Formerly Heavy Trees
Canal Six
Canal
CASA CHICA
PUEBLO del RIO
Four
Gully
Canal
PUEBLO del ALAMO
High Knoll
Farmers
Canal
Rough Ground
Rio Salado
Rolling
N. Branch
San Fra
All Ground
Rolling Ground
Ditch
Canal Twelve
All
Marmonier
Canal Seven
St. John's
PUEBLO VIEJO
Canal
Salt
River
S. Branch
San Francisco
Canal Three
canal
PUEBLO PRIMERO
G. & S.R. BASE LINE
INITIAL MONUMENT
Indian
High Ground
and
"Hieroglyphic"
Rocks
River
VILLA BUENA
Pictoglyphs
MOHATUK
MOUNTAIN
ESTRELLA
MTS.
PHOENIX MOUNTAIN
Telegraph Pass
Fifth Edition.
Copyright 1929, all rights reserved
PREHISTORIC CANALS.
Scale of miles.
0
1
2
PAVED ROADS 1929.
CANALS OF TODAY.
SECTION LINES.
PREHISTORIC BUILDINGS.
TOWNSHIP LINES
MAP OF
PREHISTORIC
IRRIGATION CANALS
DR. OMAR A. TURNEY F.R.G.S.
PHOENIX ARIZONA
The largest single body of land irrigated in prehistoric times in North or South America and perhaps in the world.
This map accompanies a report on Prehistoric Irrigation by Dr. Turney, published by Major Geo. H. Kelly, State Historian, Capitol Bldg., Phoenix, Arizona

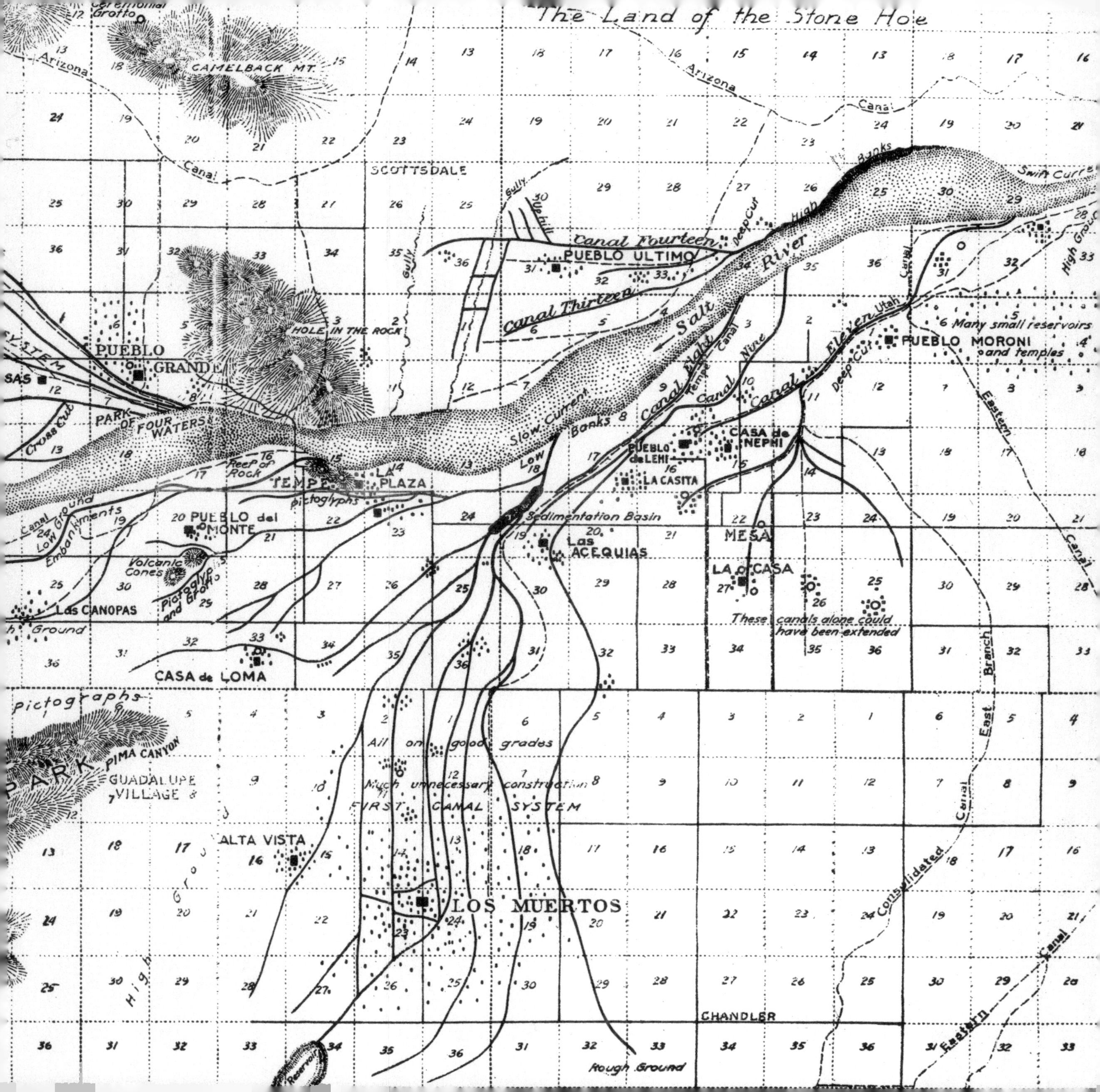
The Land of the Stone Hoe
Ceremonial Grotto
CAMELBACK MT.
Arizona Canal
SCOTTSDALE
Gully
Up hill
Canal Fourteen
PUEBLO ULTIMO
Deep Cut
High Banks
Swift Current
High Ground
Canal Thirteen
Salt River
HOLE IN THE ROCK
PUEBLO GRANDE
SAS
SYSTEM
Cross Cut
PARK OF FOUR WATERS
Slow Current
Low Banks
Canal Eight
Tempe Canal
Canal Nine
Canal Eleven
Utah Canal
Deep Cut
PUEBLO MORONI
Many small reservoirs and temples
Eastern Canal
Reef of Rock
TEMPE
LA PLAZA
pictoglyphs
PUEBLO de LEHI
CASA de NEPHI
LA CASITA
Canal
Low Ground
Embankments
PUEBLO del MONTE
Sedimentation Basin
Las ACEQUIAS
MESA
LA CASA
Volcanic Cones
Pictoglyphs and Grotto
Los CANOPAS
Ground
These canals alone could have been extended
CASA de LOMA
East Branch
Pictographs
PARK
PIMA CANYON
GUADALUPE VILLAGE
All on good grades
Much unnecessary construction
FIRST CANAL SYSTEM
ALTA VISTA
High Ground
LOS MUERTOS
Consolidated Canal
Eastern Canal
CHANDLER
Reservoir
Rough Ground

Above left Grand Canal - Phoenix, Arizona, 1923. **Above right** *Arizona Republic* cartoonist Reg Manning's cautionary tale of water scarcity in the West - 1947.

and climate, only the latter two being of place, the rest requiring extraordinary amounts of piped-in Colorado River water to prosper. With great weather and booming industries, the city saw a population spike in the 1950s, and again in the 1990s. In 1995 the *Arizona Republic* estimated one acre of desert was torn up for building per hour.[17] Phoenix, which is less dense than Los Angeles, chews up desert like a hungry dog and spits out cheap architecture. From a regional population of 221,000 in 1950 to approximately 4.6 million in 2022, Phoenix provides a landing pad for those hoping to capitalize on the modern-day wild Wild West.[18]

Marc Reisner recites John Wesley Powell's mid-19th century predictions about water in *Cadillac Desert: The American West and Its Disappearing Water*, and details with insistent clarity how mistaken ideas about the West and water fostered a rush of dam and canal-building (see page 28) that have fueled the Southwest's population explosion.[19] The conditions that triggered Powell's alarm in the 19th century—resident surge, water limitations and a desert landscape resistant to our English gardens—exist today. Residents and leaders willfully ignore the desert's tough love lessons at their own peril.

The desert condition is one rife with metaphor but also of truth—of the limits of natural resource extraction and the consequences of population growth amidst climate change. Valley fever is an occasionally deadly virus spread in the Southwest's dust, particularly with all the new construction that tears the land apart. This is a metaphor for how development's omnivorous appetite pollutes both our natural and cultural environments. Economic volatility leaves underwater homeowners isolated in the sprawl of cities like Phoenix, cut off from public transportation, jobs and community. Sprawl means more than eating up the land—it means eating up people too. Deserts are canaries in the landscape coal mine; as goes the desert, there goes its civilization.

Repairing Place

Jones Studio is a leader in creating sustainable architecture, working against a go-go desert economy that drinks water as if living by a Great Lake. If the taps still run, if pools can be filled and lawns can be watered then there must be no problem...right? And yet there is. Jones Studio heeds the claxon of water shortages blaring across the western United States, accepting the region's arid nature and grappling with its realities. Inspired by the traditions of Indigenous people who lived in harmony with the Sonoran Desert's limited water and bountiful sun, Jones Studio is forging a new relationship with the precious resources of their home. With every design project, the studio wants to remind their clients of water's scarcity, and with a dedicated focus on water recycling and reuse, offer respite by integrating landscapes that seek to "return the desert to itself." Jones Studio has built a foundation on listening to the land, pioneering a new course for living sustainably in our world.

The phrase "desert garden" appears throughout *STRIVE*. A garden in the desert is different than our conception of "garden" brought by Europeans: imposing, imperial spaces built by the aristocracy to exalt their economic hold on global trade. In *Radical Gardening: Politics, Idealism & Rebellion in the Garden*, George McKay explores gardens as spaces of resistance and repair.[20] Desert gardens are not places for gamboling or lawn bowling. Desert gardens recapture the identity of place, honor the peoples who first managed its gifts and share in the glory of the desert's green forms. The desert ecosystem includes the animals, insects and plant-life that evolved through millennia of climatic change. Today the desert's flora must respond quickly to the dramatic water squeeze conditions. Interlocking, precisely designed desert life forms have created world class biodiversity; remove one element and the system lurches. Remove its underlying wellspring of water and the entire system might collapse.

These unique forms tell stories about survival and evolution that shout to those who listen. Design inspiration from these natural forms is free for the taking, but few understand that humans too need to adapt to this home. Jones Studio keep their eyes and minds trained on the land. There are opportunities to address this fundamental resource conundrum, and Jones Studio proceeds to do that one building at a time.

Cultural Landscape

Cultural landscapes are fashioned by groups living in nature where "culture is the agent, the natural area is the medium, the cultural landscape is the result."[21] Architecture, drawn from nature and its materials, is how humans survive in this unique climate. Architecture mediates our human relationship to landscape, and without nature and all of her resources, the "cultural" part of the landscape disappears.[22] Despite evidence of the diverse Indigenous building typologies found at first contact, most American architecture is an import "except Native American or Taos Pueblo" building.[23] Architecture is a persistent if fragile marker of the complex cultural landscape humans

Above Colorado River at Lake Mead from Hoover Dam, Arizona - October 2021.

have created out of necessity, and continues to announce our successes and failures in understanding the dramatic impact we have had on the Earth.

In an article from 2002 that first named the Arizona School, including Neal and Eddie, Lawrence W. Cheek notes that Frank Lloyd Wright was the first modern architect to "interpret the land itself into the architecture."[24] In *Modern Architecture Since 1900*, William J. R. Curtis notes that different architectures used nature-reference of structure, "poetic perceptions of underlying order" sometimes in context of "organic" models of culture.[25] Jones Studio is part of a global design tradition that uses local resources that shelter and protect its inhabitants. Each set of local design responses are international in *fact*, and of habit, not just by aspiration. Jones Studio reflects the global in the local and brings their local to a global discussion.

It is not surprising that Eddie and Neal have grounded the firm in honor of the peoples and places that raised the Jones Studio family. In their reverent honor of ancient customs—living *with* the land, using its resources appropriately and effectively and considering the future changes caused by their actions today—Jones Studio foregrounds ancient architectural and social lessons that are relevant today. We therefore share the Land Acknowledgment from the City of Tempe as an expression of gratitude for the opportunity to dream about the next iteration of life in this complex landscape. Land Acknowledgements are but a first step in recognizing the communities that pre-date European arrival.

Arizona is unique in that many of the First Nations listed below are leaders in the state's civic life. Native Nations are finally part of the urgent calculations regarding the Colorado River waters. Only with the diverse Indigenous communities of Arizona can we fashion social structures to ensure Phoenix does not once again collapse into ashes. Jones Studio is committed to acknowledging the past, and the inhabitants of this landscape, through all their work.

> Jones Studio wishes to respectfully acknowledge that our office in Tempe is on the homeland of the Native people who have inhabited this landscape since time immemorial. Anthropological studies document large and advanced Ancestral O'Odham settlements located throughout the entirety of present-day Tempe and recognize the ancestral lands of the O'Odham (known as the Pima), Piipaash (known as the Maricopa), and their ancestors as extending far beyond our community. This land continues to be spiritually connected to the O'Odham of the Salt River Pima-Maricopa Indian Community [SRP-MIC] and Gila River Indian Community [GRIC]. The SRP-MIC and GRIC, located northeast and south of Tempe, respectively, are confederations of two unique groups with their own languages, customs, cultures, religions, and histories: the O'Odham and the Piipaash. Both the O'Odham and the Piipaash are oral history cultures.
>
> The landscape is sacred to the O'Odham and Piipaash and reflects cultural values that are central to their way of life and their self-definition. Their oral history and song culture are indelibly tied to tangible places that are associated with specific historic, cultural, and religious values. Settlement patterns, advanced irrigation practices, and other lifeways driven by a deep understanding of and respect for the landscape are directly attributable to the ancestors of the O'Odham and Piipaash and served as the template for the establishment of Tempe. We accept the responsibility of stewarding those places and solemnly pledge to consider this commitment in every action.[26]

STRIVE allows Jones Studio to demonstrate their commitment to place, and to those leaders and residents who want to see it thrive.

Jones Studio: The Early Years

Roots: Growing Up in the Middle

> I was born in the middle of the century in the middle of the country to middle class parents…where the houses and yards were neither huge or tiny, neither old or new… nobody was rich and nobody was poor.
>
> Kurt Andersen[1]

It is revealing that Eddie Jones's first words written to launch *STRIVE: Jones Studio Adventures in Architecture* are from Kurt Andersen's deep dive into the roots of the contradictory American character. The extremes of American politics and culture date not from the 1960s, when Eddie was a young teen, but closer to the 1660s, according to Andersen. The conflicts between nature and culture, owner and owned, between forests and desert or wet and dry, were firmly planted as the continent was colonized with alien ideas grafted onto tap roots of the old.

The middle of the 20th century, when Neal and Eddie were children, saw a country-wide questioning of European Enlightenment ideas triggered by the brutality of two world wars and ongoing conflict in Southeast Asia. Every part of American society contributed to the war effort, and as a result, every group—particularly women and people of color—wanted more say in their daily lives. New strains of cultural behavior were cobbled together from the scattered bits and pieces of the American puzzle, while ancient philosophical traditions, such as Buddhism, began their own spread across the country. New ideas about America's growth, immigration, diversity, equality, economic equity, food access, health and environmental integrity were unleashed as a result.

Generational struggle over ideas and narratives in American life would shape the character of baby boomers, born between 1946 and 1964. Post-war prosperity and a population tidal wave triggered a building boom and an unfortunate architectural homogenization of our cities and towns. Despite efforts in California to design a modern housing type that could mitigate the cliché of home, lenders and construction companies would block architectural efforts to find a crisp, modern typology for a broader public to enjoy. Amid this social tumult, Kurt Andersen's middle seemed like a safe place to grow up, to weigh your options and to capture creative condensate from the confetti rain of the culture wars of mid-century America.

Eddie Jones was born in 1949 in Fort Worth, Texas, and moved as a child with his folks and older brother Tommy to Oklahoma City. He was also a middle child, with Lyn Ellen arriving four years later and Neal coming along two years after Lyn Ellen. His father Tom was a petroleum engineer. (Eddie spent a lot of time at oil rigs and knows how to weld.) Mother May worked in the home raising her kids and bringing America's prosperous post-war dreams to life.

Eddie found his calling when he was six years old. Tom had bought the 15-volume *Compton's Pictured Encyclopedia* from a door-to-door salesman to help the kids start their school careers. Eddie consumed the books—mainly the pictures—starting at A and working to Z. He paused at the Wright Brothers to marvel at their no-holds-barred, part engineer, part madcap scientist, part philosophical quest to defy nature in their efforts to fly. But it was images of a home floating above water that fired his imagination. Frank Lloyd Wright's Fallingwater (see page 34), 1937, in tiny, grainy, black and white images, mesmerized Eddie. Wright's unique building forms and materials of place inspired Eddie to pursue architecture. Mid-century America's architectural experiments were also expressed in more popular culture outlets; May's subscriptions to *Good Housekeeping* and *House Beautiful* included features on post-war modernist homes, with low-pitched roofs and lots of glass. Eddie would try to match inside and out of these structures in his own drawings, adding his circular walkways that burble up in his work decades later.

Tom and May supported Eddie's, and later youngest son Neal's, interest in architecture. An odd home going up in Oklahoma City became a magnet for the family's Sunday drives. The "screwy" house, the imaginative name the brothers used, was Bruce Goff's Pollock-Warriner House (see page 35), completed in 1955. The nine jumbled rectangles with a green fiberglass canopy buried in a garden jungle was an astounding sight, further fueling Neal and Eddie's ideas of what a building could be. In Goff's Bavinger house, also completed in 1955 and designed for colleagues at the University of Oklahoma where Goff was an influential teacher, the architect suspended the rooms in a spiral hanging from an oil field drill pipe. The Bavinger home embodied Goff's belief in "people, place, time, materials and spirit," and expressed the specifics about the here and now.[2] Eddie and Neal's reverence for history of place took root from Wright and Goff's commitment to an American style of architecture that springs from the landscape.

Eddie graduated from Oklahoma State University [OSU] into a tumultuous social environment in 1973. Demands for civil rights, an appreciation for our multi-cultural society, feminism and a recognition of the effect of immigration on America's Indigenous peoples created new narratives. Many of these movements would influence the obligations and goals of architectural practice in general, and Eddie's ethical practice in particular. From the first Earth Day on April 22, 1970, solar power research and the environmental justice movement to Ray and Charles Eames's 1959 World's Fair pavilion in Moscow and Buckminster Fuller's 1967 Montreal Expo geodesic

THE WORK OF A GREAT AMERICAN ARCHITECT

These pictures show examples of the work of Frank Lloyd Wright, world-famous master of functional design. They illustrate his theory that architectural beauty should be created out of the essential engineering elements of a building—its skeleton framework, its supporting beams, its structural materials of wood, stone, brick, or concrete. He cried out against decorative features applied to a building without definite relation to its underlying structure. At the left is Fallingwater, a home at Bear Run, Pa. It seems a very part of its wild, rocky setting. Reinforced concrete, in cantilever construction, was used for this "extension of the cliff beside a mountain stream."

Above Fallingwater as shown in *Compton's Pictured Encyclopedia*, Bear Run, Pennsylvania - Frank Lloyd Wright.

dome biosphere, ideas of social and environmental equity permeated the field. Scientists at Los Alamos, New Mexico, having to pivot from their war-time military research activities, were conducting high tech/low tech experiments on solar adobe housing forms, reviving interest in one of the most ancient building materials on Earth.[3] Every corner of American society was up for reconsideration, to reorder priorities and uncover histories long buried by the myths America holds of itself.

Counter to the material experiments and social demands of the 1960s and '70s was the urgent need for quick and cheap housing for the country's growing population. Suburbs began to grind up agricultural and natural lands, facilitated by freeways and the ubiquity of cars. In the 1930s, roads were "the architecture of our restlessness," a way for folks with different ideas to flee rigid social structure in small town America.[4] In the 1960s, roads were the route back into suburbia's rigid hierarchies, reinscribing ethnic and economic segregation in the face of a changing world.

Top left Oil derricks, Burkburnett, Texas - 1920. **Top right** Pollock-Warriner House, Oklahoma City - Bruce Goff. **Above** Arcosanti, Arizona - Paolo Soleri.

Because of the eras' unmoored expectations and flowering of new opportunities, in 1966 the phrase "new regionalism" was coined to describe a generation of architects who, like Glenn Murcutt of Australia, were reconsidering how to live in place with the grace of its first occupants while using contemporary technologies.[5] Finding a balance between the past and future was taking shape within the architecture community.

Given these complex competing forces, where could a young architect go to start his own experiments? Eddie wanted to risk new design solutions by integrating architectural history fermented in a mixture of new ideas. Frustrated with his stiflingly conservative state, Eddie looked to the West, and specifically Arizona, for those opportunities. Frank Lloyd Wright had chosen the Sonoran Desert for his winter field of dreams, and Paolo Soleri was designing his own sustainable desert city. Eddie had seen several issues of *Arizona Highways* magazine, one of the Southwest's most brilliant promotional devices. Pages of stunning sunsets and the photographs

Above White House ruin - Canyon De Chelly, Arizona. **Below** Hopi house rendering - Eddie Jones.

of plant life attracted the young mid-westerner. In 1973, at age 24, Eddie and wife Mary loaded up their '67 Volkswagen Beetle with their possessions and two-year-old son Christopher, checked the oil and headed West in search of a chance to dream. Eddie never looked back.

Once he landed in Phoenix, Eddie cold-called architecture firms, got five job offers and took the one from Lescher & Mahoney, the oldest architecture firm in the state (Eddie reports Leslie Mahoney's Arizona architecture license was #3). Lescher & Mahoney was bought by Dana, Larson, Roubal, of Omaha, whose specialty was government housing for Housing and Urban Development [HUD], particularly homes for Native American residents. Eddie was hired to drive around the state and the greater Four Corners region to document Indigenous architecture to begin his career.

The ambitious young architect was inspired by what he learned and saw. He connected with Hopi architecture, where homes merged with surrounding mesas, ancient and modern at once. Lessons from the Anasazi, Sinagua and Hohokam showed how orientating buildings to create deep summer shade, with rock or other material overhangs that allowed in sun during the cooler months, were practical heating and cooling strategies.[6] Eddie was intrigued by the round Diné hogan, whose design is deeply symbolic but also retains heat efficiently. Walls of rammed earth and adobe bricks, made from hyper-local materials, controlled light and provided passive heating and cooling. To Eddie, this was "real" architecture—one material, inside and outside, monolithic, the essence of simplicity. Other regional influences were from the Spanish, whose internal courtyards kept homes cool while providing privacy and security. Eddie would use these methods and materials for building in this desert "stripe of earth," showing his commitment to the environmental and social movements of America's youthquake. Eddie's paid education grounded him in his new home.

Eddie estimates thousands of his designs were built during his six years working on HUD housing. The firm would receive a commission with a new regional group, and he would design three or four variations on a house, and then 300, or 500, would get built. His unique design strategies borrowing traditions from the Native Nation he was designing for were often "value engineered" out to meet minimum standards or were rejected by the Native American families who saw Western housing as "superior" to their own traditions. Every now and then Eddie can spot one or two of his houses off in the distance while on a road trip. He wonders if the design and materials have held up over time.

After six years of this work Eddie reviewed what he had done and was…disappointed. He was a progressive thinker and had what Louis Kahn described as a "semi-mystical and yet utterly concrete notion about the relationship between the natural and the manmade, the perceived and the created, the outer world and the inner one."[7] Eddie wanted to search for his "authenticity" that would uniquely express what was true to his time and place and unleash his artistic passion for architecture.[8] On June 8, 1979 (coincidentally both Frank Lloyd Wright and Bruce Goff's birthdates), Eddie quit to follow his own path and founded Jones Studio.

Shingle on the Door

Before he quit, however, in 1976 Eddie had started moonlighting in his spare bedroom on the solid oak Hamilton drafting table his dad bought him for college. He received several smaller commissions and helped architect friends with drawings for their projects. In 1977 Eddie's graphic designer wife Mary lost her job, so the couple had to sell their youthful splurge, a convertible Jensen-Healy sports car, to make ends meet. While they were closing the car's sale with Chuck Tatham, Chuck said to Eddie "by the way, you say you're an architect?" Eddie had passed the hard parts of the multi-day architect's exam in 1976, but he had flunked the design portion, so technically he was not a licensed architect. But he said yes to Chuck and Joyce anyway. This would be Eddie's first opportunity to begin his architecture of place, testing his ideas against the inspirations around him and the first of many calculated chances he would take throughout his career.

After a year of moonlighting at home, and a year when the project was put on hold, Eddie had construction drawings, an architect's registration stamp and a building permit for the site. To stay on budget Chuck decided he and Eddie should build the house themselves, with Eddie playing the role of general contractor. Eddie quit his job when they began the two-year process of building the Tatham House, sustaining Eddie with extra cash flow and lots of "essential personal growth."

Opposite page Pauson House ruins - Phoenix, Arizona, Frank Lloyd Wright.

Alta Vista Park Neighborhood: Tatham House and Pauson Chimney

Phoenix, Arizona, 1977-1981

The scrabbly Phoenix landscape holds dear its ancient stories and unique plants. Eddie recognized and accepted the challenge to follow the desert's guidance on preserving its lifeforms, and to enhance our appreciation for nature's logic and concise engineering. For the Tatham House, his primary goals were to preserve the desert landscape of this rapidly gentrifying eastern edge of the City and cradle the modern home against the rocky slope, nestling it so it would become an irreducible element of the site.

The house lounges on the stepped site in the Alta Vista Park neighborhood, its H-shaped form opening to vistas and light. The red brick floors, laid by teen son Greg Tatham, and the lustrous wood shiplap ceiling both run inside and out, tying the building together. The simple concrete block and wood structure cocoons its inhabitants, orienting them towards the solar-grade glass walls, some flat, some sawtooth in shape. The views are the main act in this performance of elegance on a budget.

Because of Eddie's lack of construction experience he had not learned how to mix mortar, so he dry stacked the entire house, including the 13-foot-tall concrete block retaining wall whose aggregate was dug from the site. As always, Eddie's reaction to a personal limitation was to improvise, and the wall has maintained its integrity ever since. Emboldened by his success, Eddie created his own minimal sculpture inside, a dry-stacked cinder block fireplace that provides a dynamic focal point between the living room and kitchen. This is first time we see Eddie using the material noted Tucson architect Judith Chafee called "the adobe brick of our time," Eddie intuitively celebrating a material both ancient and new.[9] Finally, Eddie exploited the desert's most abundant resource. Light permeates the house, popping up in geometric slices overhead or in discreetly recessed windows that lighten corners and connect residents to the desert outside.

Opposite page Tatham House perspective drawing with Pauson ruins in background - Eddie Jones.

Above left Eddie Jones and Pauson House chimney at Alta Vista Park. **Top right** Pauson House ruins - Frank Lloyd Wright. **Above right** Pauson House - Frank Lloyd Wright.

Jones Studio would be part of an architectural tradition that celebrates the landscape, not just bulldozes it, leaving behind a chicken pox pattern of homes as was happening in suburban areas across the country. The edges of landscape and building would bleed into one another, allowing the building to recede. He had not quite grasped the concept of an architecture "of the garden." That would come later. But he did return the desert to itself by taking advantage of the natural contours and materials of the site, by using water harvesting strategies both modern and prehistoric and by employing the unique diversity of Arizona's native plants to welcome visitors to the site.

This ethos—celebrating the desert, its resources and its other inhabitants—underpins Jones Studios' moral commitment to sustainability. As Eddie explained to architect and professor Chad Schwartz, "It wasn't just about designing for a desert climate, it was about being resourceful enough to do something that was as much a result of the climate as it was a product of my

Above Tatham House with Piestewa Peak in background.

limitations, tight budget, inexperience."[10] Jones Studio's sensitivity to opportunity and site would guide the firm for decades to come.

While Eddie was working on the Tathams' home, in 1980 he was hired by their neighbors in the Alta Vista Park neighborhood to design an entry feature for the community. He had the opportunity to create an informal piece of public art using one of the area's 20th century ruins: a chimney from the Frank Lloyd Wright Pauson House.

Wright had visited Arizona in 1928 to consult on several projects, and in 1938 established a year-round western outlet for Taliesin's Apprenticeship program, the labor force that helped with his prolific output. Wright completed the house for the Pauson sisters in 1942. The house tragically burned down within six months, leaving behind a remarkably beautiful ruin, commonly

Above Pauson Chimney drawing at Alta Vista Park, Phoenix - Eddie Jones.

referred to as "Shiprock." The Pauson sisters abandoned the property that would later become the Alta Vista Park community's common property. The City of Phoenix later bought the land to connect two major roads to accommodate the region's growth. Much to Eddie's dismay, the road was slated to run right through the "Shiprock" ruins. Eddie was determined to honor them by incorporating the monolithic south Pauson chimney into the neighborhood's new entry feature. The commission became his excuse to "pay back" his hero Wright.

This small project would be funded by the $15,000 pay-out from the City to the neighbors' group as compensation for taking over the hilltop property. Eddie would have to work quickly to not interfere with the road construction schedule. Stepping into a meeting between the road builder and City staff, Eddie overheard a remark about "some knucklehead architect thinking he would save the ruins." The naysayers would be surprised by Eddie's persistence.

Eddie knew he needed a level footprint at the Alta Vista entrance for the displaced chimney. He had watched others use heavy equipment but had no actual experience operating them himself; this gap did not matter to the equipment rental company a few miles down the road. Eddie paid the rental fee and was given the keys to a backhoe. Eddie bounced back and forth adjacent to the street traffic, meeting his construction challenge with joy. The work was not fast, but he managed.

After a few days, Eddie stumbled onto a one-inch pipe where the chimney would sit. The road builder confirmed all utilities had been disconnected or rerouted, so Eddie used the backhoe to jerk the pipe out of the gravel, resulting in a hook-shape of metal hanging 10 feet above the ground. It had been a long day, so Eddie called it a night. The following morning, he returned to discover multiple public utility vehicles, amber lights flashing, surrounding the pipe. Eddie didn't make eye contact with anyone and discreetly turned around and headed back home. He would later learn that the road builder had missed this one live gas line; luckily there was no damage to people or vehicles. Eddie reflects that there is something to say about living under the right cloud.

With the chimney site prepped, Eddie hired a house mover whose $15,000 price tag took the entire construction budget, including Eddie's fee for the design work. This would not be the last time Eddie would give himself away to implement a great idea. The relocated chimney would stand sentry for another 32 years before finally collapsing in 2012, returning to the ground from whence Frank Lloyd Wright drew it. This gesture of passion for the past was another element in Eddie's commitment to an architecture of place. Since Eddie did not create the original chimney, this could be considered his first act of public art in honor of the histories hidden in the landscape. He was awarded a Valley Forward environmental award for "Art in Public Places" for the project.

Eddie's Tatham House and Wright's Pauson Chimney serve as conceptual and spiritual guideposts for Jones Studio. They show Eddie's reverent posture towards the land and a sensitivity to the shifts in cultural opportunities around him. The Tatham House also put Jones Studio into an informal "capsule collection" of modern and contemporary architects who have built in the Alta Vista Park neighborhood, including: Frank Lloyd Wright; Bennie Gonzalez, one of the first architects of color to work in the region; James Elmore, Arizona State University School of Architecture's first Dean and a major force in the region; Bob Nevins, a legendary University of Arizona educator; George Christianson, whose buildings spread across the region; Will Bruder and Marwan Al-Sayad, colleagues named by Lawrence W. Cheek as part of the Arizona School; and Tod Williams and Billy Tsien, who completed the addition to the Phoenix Art Museum in 1996.[11] The unique topography of Alta Vista Park drew discerning clients with budgets to create unique homes that stand tall against the shabby structures that blemish the glorious landscape. The Tatham House announced Jones Studio as a part of the next generation of architects experimenting with the desert landscape.

First Home: Alfred Newman Beadle and the Twelfth Street Office Building

Phoenix, Arizona, 1984

In 1984 Eddie began looking for a space in downtown Phoenix for an expanding Jones Studio, partially to get out of his spare room, mainly to put forth a serious face for the firm. Eddie was very interested in renting a small portion of the top floor, with the hope of slowly "borrowing" more space over time, of Hanny's, a four-story, 1950's International Style building near downtown. It was the rooftop terrace and the other elegant details that attracted Eddie to the high-end men's department store, but the building had been condemned and was thus unavailable. Another possibility was a small structure on the roof of the Hotel San Carlos. The mini cabaña was in great disrepair, requiring investment beyond his means. Eddie finally chose a 1978 office building designed by Al (Alfred Newman) Beadle. Beadle, originally from Minnesota, was largely self-taught. He volunteered for the Navy during WWII where he worked in the Construction & Building division, or Seabees, making all manner of building types on the fly using materials cobbled together from what was at hand. He moved to Phoenix after having experienced the warm climates of the South Pacific, and despite licensing and funding issues, was a prolific designer and builder for a city that would grow 800% over the forty years Beadle lived there.

Like the Europeans who developed the International Style after the devastations of World War I, and believing that everyone deserved aesthetically pleasing, cost-competitive housing, Beadle set out to produce buildings of all sizes and for all types of clients, not just single families, to prove it was possible. His Boardwalk Apartments elevated the approach to affordable housing in the desert by using a garden as the social fabric that linked the 34 two-bedroom units together. Beadle's deliberate blurring of architecture and landscape would be a reoccurring influence for Eddie and the studio team.[12]

The Twelfth Street Office Building, of simple glass and steel, was commissioned in 1978 by Dave Schuff of Schuff Steel. Beadle partially bermed the building with a grass scarf to create half-sunken shaded spaces and gardens. The Miesian Beadle fixed the "inherent discombobulation of glass boxes" with a garden office concept to create refuge from visual chaos outside.[13] Its "captive landscape," a "cool, shaded, luxuriantly planted" garden was accessible to all employees and visitors to the building.[14] As at the Boardwalk, Beadle was able to inject into his rigid orthogonal the positive

Above Twelfth Street Office Building, Phoenix, Arizona - Al Beadle. **Below** Boardwalk Apartments, Phoenix, Arizona - Al Beadle.

environmental and social benefits resulting from integrating the architecture with a garden, cooling and shading the building from the inside and out. Beadle's highly refined sculptural vocabulary earned him the honor of having the only non-California building—the Triad Apartments in Phoenix—included in the influential Case Study House program sponsored by *Arts & Architecture* magazine from 1945 to 1962.[15] Inspired by Wright and Beadle, Eddie would expand his focus on the natural environment around and inside his buildings. Nothing resists the grid of a city like the unique forms of the desert; the desert would emphasize the contours and philosophical intentions of Jones Studio's work.

Another of Eddie's design muscles was being exercised in the Beadle. He realized architecture was not just mechanics and materials. It was the poetics of architecture, and its ability to address heart as well as mind, that proved to him that architecture is a spiritual endeavor, enriching, uplifting, delightful. By living and working in the Beadle he could feel, not just think about, how architecture can change our lives. Eddie believed that architecture gives back more than it takes. He still believes that architecture makes us who we are.

Halas House

Paradise Valley, Arizona, 1985

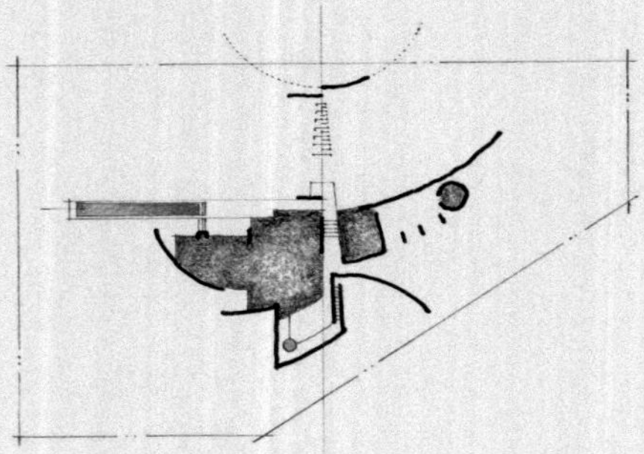

Eddie's next home crystallized his commitment to using water as a design driver. Celia and Mike Halas's project came to Eddie—rather like the Tatham House—through personal circumstance. Mary was seeing Celia, a well-respected psychologist specializing in issues faced by women in a changing social climate. Eddie was surprised when Celia invited Eddie home to meet Mike. They wanted his help designing a home to be perched on the side of Camelback Mountain, a key geological feature in central Phoenix. (Mike mentioned his Uncle George during their discussions. When Eddie asked sports-enthusiast Neal who that was, Neal's jaw dropped. Former football star and coach George Halas was one of the co-founders of the National Football League, an incidental detail that would have great resonance once sports stadium-savvy Neal joined Eddie in Phoenix the following year.)

Eddie had to grapple not only with the composition of Camelback Mountain, but the drainage pattern required to sluice water away from the house. Eddie's opposing curves of the main roof, and the translucent entry canopy, were meant to echo the form of Camelback Mountain's weathered granite outcroppings, creating a valley gutter to manage water from summer monsoons. Eddie channeled, dropped and directed the water to three Palo Verde trees left untouched during construction and that now obscure the home from the street. He slowed water down so it might seep back into the aquifer so nature could recharge herself. This was Eddie's first foray into water harvesting—a phrase he had never heard before, and that was not yet part of mainstream architectural vocabulary—but that made sense in this landscape. The Halas House would be Eddie's second attempt at returning the desert to itself.

Eddie took a big gamble in the Halas design: to avoid interrupting the view from the 24-foot-tall north-facing living room, he designed compression fittings to hold six pieces of glass in place without a distracting mullion structure (before the now more common glass mullion spider fittings were available). He built a full-scale cardboard mockup to give to Connie and Jim Knight of Glass Line, fearless glazing contractors with whom Jones Studio would work for decades, to help him solve

Above Plan diagram - Eddie Jones. **Opposite page** View south with Camelback Mountain in background.

Opposite page Main entry at dusk. **Above** Perspective rendering - Eddie Jones.

the problem. As Eddie says of this design innovation: "No testing, no calculations, no permit, no permission. We just did it." The glass wall held in place by glass mullions and custom steel fittings is still there—and still beautiful.[16]

While designing the house, Eddie met Australian architect Glenn Murcutt, who was driving an appreciation for architecture linked to regional traditions and materials during his first trip to the United States and years before he won the Pritzker Architecture Prize in 2002. Murcutt spotted a flaw in Eddie's drawings: the soaring barrel vault of the living room trapped the spatial energy where it intersected with the vertical bulkhead. Eddie quickly designed stub columns to lift the vault four inches above the bearing point. The resulting "saber" of light from above transformed the space, becoming a frequent design element in Eddie's work. The elegant masonry retaining walls and glowing wood interiors demonstrate Eddie's adroit use of materials that create enveloping spaces.

In a slick effort to reduce interest rates, Phoenix-based Western Savings and Loan collapsed in a financial crisis instead. Celia got a call that they had lost the money they had intended for construction, so it took longer than planned to finish the home. The Halas House won *Sunset* magazine's 1988 Home Award, confirming Eddie's growing expertise and confidence finding design solutions integrating common materials performing uncommon feats.

Neal Jones: Make It a Family Firm, 1986

Neal Jones knew he wanted to be an architect at age nine, in third grade, because of his big brother Eddie. Neal too loved to draw, which trained him on the way real objects translated into two-dimensional drawings. Even though going into the oil fields is what many of their classmates did, Neal and Eddie had other dreams. From an early age, the brothers planned to have their own architecture firm.

Neal also graduated from OSU's architecture program but realized either he or Eddie had to pursue business training. Neal "drew the short straw" and with the encouragement of his faculty advisors, enrolled in one of the first combined Master of Architecture and Master of Business Administration programs in the country, at the University of Illinois at Champaign-Urbana. As he neared graduation in 1980, Neal identified five market sectors to begin his career, sent out 222 resumes and spent his last semester flying around the country to see where he'd like to land. He chose to work for Heery International in Atlanta, a firm of 450 people and one of the country's leading full-service architecture and engineering firms that pioneered integrated construction services. Working for Heery would also enable Neal to get his license faster. Heery was incredibly important to Neal's learning the business of architecture. He had great mentors; Bob Edney, Scott Braley, Bob Eskew, Skip Yauger and Fred Krensen allowed him to be involved in business and marketing decisions. Heery designed dozens of sport facilities, which would help Neal lay the groundwork for Jones Studio's growth.

It was the jolt of their older brother Tommy's sudden passing that made Neal and Eddie realize they'd better get on with their dream of working together. Tom and May were worried the brothers would fight and break the family up, but despite the occasional disagreement, Neal and Eddie's partnership has inspired client and colleague confidence for over 40 years because of their unified passions and goals.

On June 1, 1986, Neal started his first day at Jones Studio. No computers, no fax machines, no cell phones, just graphite, colored pencils, markers, press-on letters and parallel bars. Neal notes there was also no work and no paycheck; the brothers certainly had made a big leap into the unknown. Neal incorporated Jones Studio and joined as a full partner. From the start, Neal and Eddie knew they

Above left to right Tommy, Eddie & Neal Jones; Neal's first day at Jones Studio; Eddie and Neal holding Halas House model.

would always push themselves to try new building types with all the programming demands and client personalities that come with it. They were confident they could handle big jobs, calculating where they should take their most ambitious risks. Their plan was to make buildings that would evoke an emotional response in the user that would be meaningful, significant and enduring.

Neal's first order of business was to get the firm on as many municipal, county and state job lists as possible. After receiving a Request for Qualifications [RFQ] in the mail, he would attend the pre-proposal meetings and introduce himself to the clients afterwards. Neal learned about the competition, too, and how they assembled their proposals and marketed themselves. He spread his card around like butter, smoothing the way to getting the brothers' first job together.

Neal's wife Lexie played a significant role in the early years, working late into the night preparing responses to those early RFQ's on a Brother typewriter. She also helped put together invoices while the couple's daughter Kelsey was in grammar school and daughter Taylor was in preschool. In December of 1989, Lexie was working at the front desk while pregnant with their third child. One day, she exclaimed that she might need to go to the hospital given her frequent contractions. Neal responded alright, but don't we need to finish up these invoices? Lexie replied yes, absolutely, they needed the money. Lexie finished those invoices and on the way to the hospital, dropped them off at the post office. A few hours later, Xane entered the world. What a way to mix business with family life. About a year later, the couple's fourth child Cayter was born, Lexie and Neal agreeing their own family growth would stop here. Eddie's family, however, would shrink; he and Mary split, Mary eventually moving to California with their son Christopher. Neal and Lexie provided continuity for the family firm.

Over the years, Neal's skill at putting together great teams—whether working with Jones Studio's family or consultants—and keen business deftness have helped the firm grow. He considers one of his special talents is to "help people be better." He continues to guide the firm in learning new skills and is willing to answer questions from colleagues across the Valley looking for advice. In a changing and competitive environment, that generosity remains an astounding part of how Jones Studio supports their entire community.

Homolovi Ruins State Park Visitor Center and Support Facilities

Winslow, Arizona, 1987

Homolovi Ruins State Park is Arizona's only archaeological park, located near the Hopi Indian reservation in Winslow, Arizona, in the Northeastern part of the state. Homolovi is Hopi for "place of the Little Hills," and is centered around a network of seven pueblos occupied during the late migration period from the 1200s to late 1300s. The stepped constructions rise along the hills, following 20 miles of the Little Colorado River on the high desert grasslands of the austere Colorado Plateau. The enormous complexes, two with over 1,000 rooms of varying ritual and living use, speak of an evolved culture. Once the Hopi ancestors abandoned Homolovi, the buildings began to slowly collapse under the weight of the desert's shifting sands.[17]

Arizona's architecture field was changing in the late 1980s. Rather than sliding along the greased wheels of the good ol' boy network, Neal and Eddie got an RFQ for the Homolovi project in the mail. They applied and won their first job together. The Park staff wanted something beautiful, not just "on time and on budget." Eddie and Neal worked closely with the Parks staff, members of the Hopi reservation and area residents to create a building that would sit gently on the land like the ancient pueblos the site honors and be self-sufficient and sustainable.

To design for the complex if modest program that included site utilities, exhibit space, maintenance, training and workshop space, signage and separate spaces for the campground restrooms and outside interpretive ramadas, Eddie and Neal started pinning imagery to the wall of their conference room. They were inspired by a rusty coffee can buried in the dirt and the site's strata of decomposing granite. They landed on a design with rusting steel walls that would age like the landscape, and emphatic banding in a contemporary take on the geologic layers of landscape. A farmer donated local stone for the building, rooting the facility with ancient materials. To lay the stone, Eddie found out there were four incarcerated masons in a prison near Winslow, so he negotiated with the prison warden to allow these masons to visit the site for paid work. Jones Studio ensured natural ventilation and daylighting for human comfort, and water harvesting strategies to keep the tiny oasis as green as possible during hot desert summers.

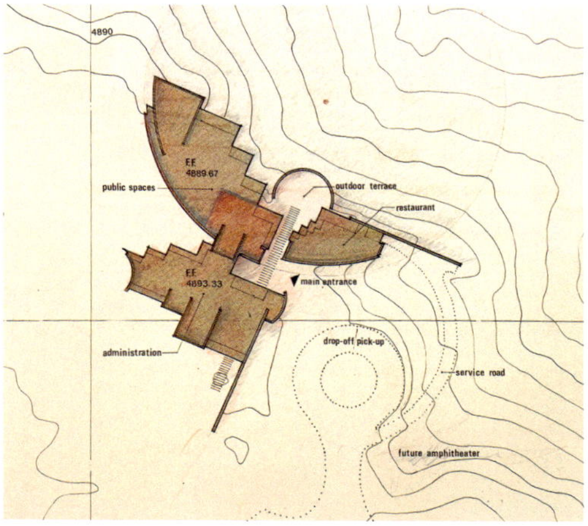

Opposite page Perspective rendering - Eddie Jones. **Above left** Master plan drawing - Eddie Jones. **Above right** Model. **Below** At construction completion. **Following spread** 34 years after completion.

In a natural gem-like structure such as this, reflecting the desert beneath it, we see Jones Studio's grounding in Indigenous customs mixed with a regional consciousness that elevates a sense of place. There is an intimacy to the facility, burrowed into the site like an ancient Hopi shelter. The building is a variety of shapes—round, square, horizontal and vertical—capturing the exuberance of a child at play. The textures are smooth and rough, clean and rubbly. Homolovi lives up to Eero Saarinen's three principals: "function, structure, being part of our time through materials."[18] Homolovi is an important touchstone of the formal and contextual concerns in Jones Studio's work, laying the groundwork for elevated connections to nature.

Arizona Cardinals Corporate Headquarters and Training Facility

Tempe, Arizona, 1988

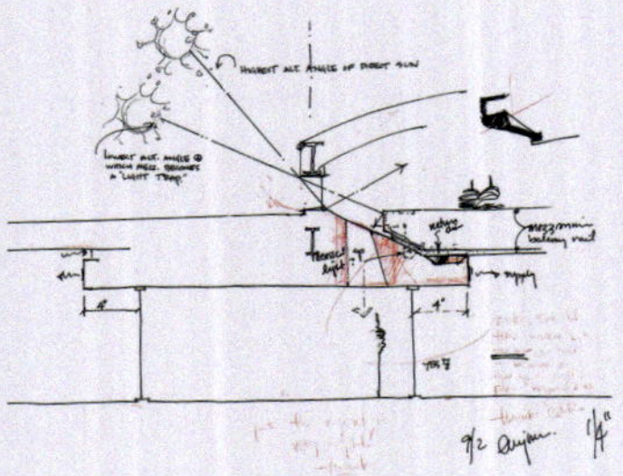

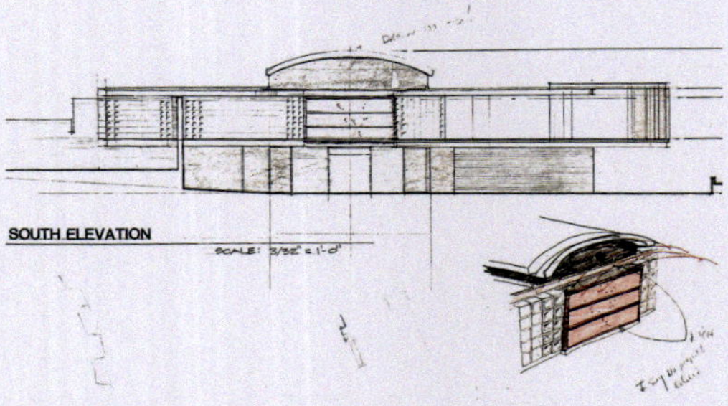

From its founding, Jones Studio has expanded its design skills and capacity by tackling projects of different sizes and diverse users for vastly different outcomes. While private homes had provided the designers many opportunities to capture the hearts of their clients, Homolovi had the responsibility to honor ancient peoples and their deeply connected relationship to the land while educating the public on contemporary modes of living lightly on the Earth. Their next big break was a distinct departure from their previous work: they jumped into the sports arena, one of modern-day America's most rabid obsessions. Jones Studio would craft a building that embodied their commitment to a sensitive sustainability while learning to juggle the diverse interests and egos associated with big business.

Jones Studio wrangled its way into the closed application for the new Arizona Cardinals (at the time known as the Phoenix Cardinals) Corporate Headquarters and Training Facility in Tempe, a suburb abutting Phoenix to the east. Eddie and Jones Studio's first employee Mike Whalen were eager to use Neal's professional sports design experience to secure the training facility job. This was a leap for the firm into a new typology and a much-expanded budget. They partnered with Tempe-based Kenyon Architects and included sports consultant Milton Babbit, who had been involved with the development of the Dallas Cowboy's Training Facility, to pursue the Cardinals RFQ. Curt Mosher, the Cardinals executive responsible for the architect selection, had previously been with the Cowboys during that team's training facility design, so having Babbit on the team resulted in a winning strategy: Jones Studio and Kenyon got the job.

Cardinals team owner Bill Bidwill was interested in Southwest architecture, although the green grass of the fields was far from a native landscape. The facility had to be high functioning to support the heavily used set of interlocking parts. Jones Studio's goal was to create an efficient, sustainable and light-filled home for the team. This would be the first big expression of Eddie's "compound of complex forms," combining European Modernism with adaptations to the desert.[19] Eddie set up

Above Detail study sketches - Eddie Jones. **Opposite page** Entry ramp approach from parking lot.

Above West elevation at dusk.

zoning diagrams with a sensitivity to site, creating a visionary design that would add intangible human-centric qualities to the spaces.

There were many site constraints. The Cardinals' two football fields, carved from a 10-acre alfalfa field, had to be dead level to simulate the conditions of game day. Jones Studio enlisted the building itself to capture runoff water to keep the fields vibrant while saving on water bills. Opening the building to this micro climate took advantage of the natural evaporative cooling effect inherent in wet turf.

For their biggest design move, Jones Studio shaded the building from a beating west sun with a 300-foot-long wall of fireplace chimney flue tiles stacked horizontally as a sunscreen (see page 63), a practical use of a material designed to protect from heat. The wall created a 10-foot-wide corridor

break between the floor-to-ceiling glass walls, providing a buffer zone or thermal break—a phrase Eddie and Neal didn't know at the time—and reducing costs for cooling and heating. This western corridor allowed light to flood into spaces on every floor, from the head coach to accounting offices, sharing light democratically.

The Cardinals building was at the forefront of the sustainable building movement. The facility received numerous awards from the City of Tempe, the Arizona American Institute of Architects [AIA], and the Western Mountain Region AIA. The Cardinals' facility was also twice Jones Studio's next largest project budget, a pattern of growth that would continue for the next several decades. The Cardinals Training Facility proves Jones Studio's ability to draw from a wide range of approaches and solutions with the same level of invention and experimentation, and apply them to projects large and small, public and private.

Above Public entry. **Below** West elevation. **Opposite page** Chimney flue tile sunscreen wall. **Following spread** Glowing chimney flue tile sunscreen at night.

Black Canyon Hiking and Equestrian Trail
New River, Arizona, 1992

The trail winding between Phoenix and Prescott, Arizona, was used by ancient peoples for travel, trade and moving flocks of sheep between grazing lands. In the 19th century, the Pony Express route was dominated by stagecoaches and mining concerns. Black Canyon is rustic and remote, requiring the structures to be self-sufficient and sustainable.[20] Jones Studio won the commission to create new structures through a public call by the U. S. Department of the Interior Bureau of Land Management [BLM]. As with Homolovi, a reverence for the architectural typologies of the region's succession of cultures allowed Jones Studio to use nature as a partner. Although located in a remote landscape far from any population center, this small outpost would receive the same rigorous conceptual consideration as the team's more urban projects.

Black Canyon Trailhead consists of a 400-square-foot outhouse, picnic shelters and an informational kiosk with a map and other information for visitors. At the South trailhead, launching point for 60 miles of horse trails, Jones Studio built naturally ventilated and illuminated self-composting rest rooms. The studio used concrete block, weathered steel siding, galvanized corrugated roofing and photovoltaic solar power to run lights, an exhaust fan and to charge the battery for nighttime illumination. Several shaded picnic ramadas with barbeques and a 360-degree view of the surrounding landscape provide space to rest. Jones Studio's decomposed granite paths would allow for users of different abilities to access the site. Black Canyon gave Jones Studio the chance to charge the compact spaces with outsized design ambitions.

Black Canyon Hiking and Equestrian Trail received numerous awards for design and energy efficiency and responsiveness, leading to larger opportunities. In the early 1990s, they received so many commissions in the parks and recreation field with clients like the BLM, the National Parks Service, the National Forest Service and the Arizona State Parks system, Neal and Eddie started referring to themselves as "Park-a-tects" doing "Park-a-tecture."

Above Vernacular design influences. **Opposite page** Shade ramadas and restrooms.

Opposite page Collection of shade ramadas and restroom structures in the desert. **Above** Perspective drawing - Eddie Jones. **Below** Shade ramada.

In the 1990s, the architecture and construction industries were starting to pivot. Budgets and schedules started over-shadowing design leadership for projects. Jones Studio would deftly manage the changing environment of project planning and management to ensure the firm's growth.

Arizona Public Service Environmental Showcase Home
Phoenix, Arizona, 1994

Warnings from the environmental movement were slowly permeating public and corporate consciousness. Citizens were increasingly aware of the negative results of industrial pollution on their lives and livelihoods, demanding that politicians and industries address the multiple crises happening across the country. Architects too would need to develop "ecocentric and technocentric" approaches to understanding environmental problems, goals already at the heart of Jones Studio's work.[21] Noted environmentalist, poet and farmer Wendell Barry said that "sustainability can only be understood through localized values," and Jones Studio was committed to integrating both ancient and new best practices to ensure their architecture would model news ways to live in the desert.[22]

In response, local utility giant Arizona Public Service [APS] hosted a state-wide design competition for a modern suburban home featuring systems and appliances more sustainable than those in a typical "McMansion" in the choker of towns surrounding Phoenix. APS was one of the first public utilities to address conservation through this type of exercise. With their recent buildings at Homolovi and Black Canyon Trail, Jones Studio was one of four short-listed firms for the APS Home; thanks to their track record of sustainable experimentation, they won the project.

There is a long history of building fairs pre- and post-WWII in the United States and Europe. These were partly trade expos showing off new building processes and materials, and partly sales jobs to entice the growing bourgeoisie into modern (almost always) single-family homes.[23] APS's five target communities were "production and custom builders, financial lenders, environmental leaders, the media, and the homebuying public."[24] APS's goals were to show how a regular tract home could be water and energy efficient using the newest mechanical systems and design products available. Jones Studio's goals included pushing the limits of sustainability through great design, and substituting the public's, lenders and construction companies' addiction to ungainly homes, that achieve only the basest requirements for comfort and efficiency, with a taste for real, sustainable architecture.

Above Overall home at night. **Opposite page** West shade trellis over private patio.

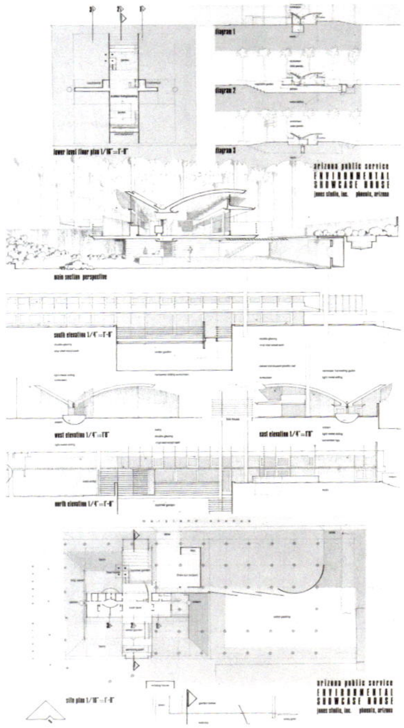

Above left Site plan rendering - Julian Clark. **Above right** Original competition winning entry drawings - Eddie Jones.

Eddie had been inspired by the cooling effect of desert washes during his hikes, so his entry design featured a sunken garden and riparian pond with a waterfall to help cool indoor and outdoor spaces. Jones Studio's team designed a sawtoothed butterfly roof with photovoltaics to support rainwater harvesting and distribute light which would lower electric costs. Jones Studio used recycled or renewable materials wherever possible. The roof's shape mirrored the hills that surround Phoenix, pulling the mountains into the paved city.

While the application of the new HVAC, water harvesting and other systems fulfilled APS's goals, the design did not resonate with the focus groups. The winning design, although logical, innovative and beautiful, was not recognizable to the construction professionals or, in their estimation, would it be to the general house-buying public. As a result, Jones Studio returned to the more culturally familiar pitched gable roof profile to maximize the prototype's influence while retaining all the strategies needed to make it efficient and affordable. Rooms flowed seamlessly from indoors to out, surrounded by a native landscaping with the solidity of a shelter's embrace. Even the soft green palette seemed radical at a time when flavorless beige was everywhere.

Central to the APS House's success was Tom Hahn, another early Jones Studio family member. Tom was relentless in his research focused on environmentally responsible design, predating the rise of LEED [Leadership in Energy and Environmental Design] and the broader focus on sustainability

Above left & right Rain water collection and scupper details. **Following spread** View from street at night.

of the early 2000s. Tom would later become a highly regarded sustainable design consultant.

The APS House remains another keystone project for the firm, elevating their celebration of nature through sustainable building. It received numerous awards for its interior design, use of concrete and masonry, overall design, environmental excellence, lighting, beautiful environment and for marketing, an increasingly important part of any successful design firm's equation. While the building was advanced for its time, it was rendered technologically obsolete quickly while the ancient strategies—building orientation, water harvesting, shading and massing—retained their value. Jones Studio's design produced the greatest savings; getting the public, clients and construction firms to embrace innovative design would underpin the studio's work.

Brian Farling, future Jones Studio partner, was attending architecture school at the University of Arizona [UofA] in Tucson while working for Les Wallach at Line and Space, one of the four finalists for the APS House competition. Inspired by Jones Studio's winning ideas, Brian reached out to Eddie, hoping he would be a mentor on Brian's fifth year Capstone project. Brian joined the firm four years later. Jacob Benyi, another future Jones Studio partner, studied and visited the APS house during a class while in architecture school at Arizona State University [ASU] in 1999. He too was influenced by the firm's sustainability strategies. Both later joined Jones Studio to help further the firm's environmentally sensitive design.

Arizona State University Karsten Golf Course Clubhouse

Tempe, Arizona, 1994

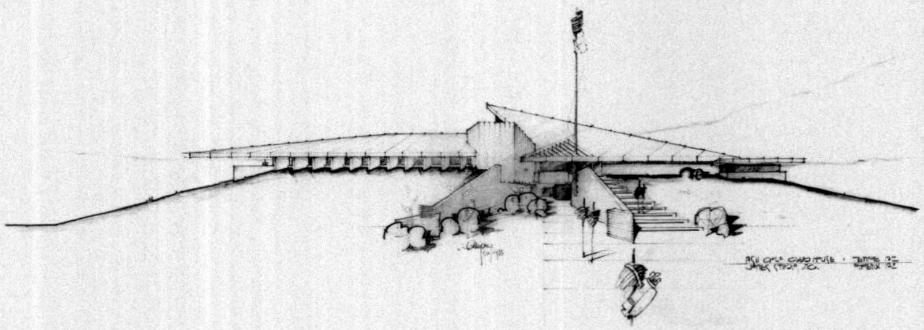

A building is a struggle, not a miracle, and the architect should acknowledge this.
Louis Kahn[25]

076 The success of the APS House, which set a new benchmark for design quality and ethical sustainability, paralleled the completion of the Karsten Golf Course Clubhouse, the first of many projects for ASU. Yet getting this commission was far from easy. The competition was opened only to those architects with experience in golf clubhouse design, a conundrum that seemed intended to support older firms who had cornered the market. Jones Studio did not have any experience in this typology, and Eddie specifically did not play golf, thinking it to be a huge waste of time, an attitude that might have bled into their early conversations with the client. Not surprisingly, Jones Studio did not receive an invitation to participate in the design competition.

But given Neal's experience in sports architecture, he would not, *could* not let go. He convinced the competition organizers they had nothing to lose by letting Jones Studio spin their inexperienced wheels putting together a submission. That determination paid off and Jones Studio was granted permission to submit an entry to the competition. Eddie immediately started visiting the many clubhouses sprawled across Phoenix and Scottsdale. One of his biggest takeaways was that the architecture was mediocre. Just because he didn't golf didn't mean those who did had to dwell in unremarkable spaces. Approaching the design challenge with fresh, unspoiled eyes allowed an unconventional diagram to quickly emerge.

Eddie understood that college students were often hard-pressed to pay green fees, which caused a rash of non-paying visits. In recognition of this truth, and with the goal of integrating the existing elements of the site—all entry and exit points, first tee and last green, parking and bag drop security—the team designed a triangular building with the cashier located in the apex to exercise 360-degree visual control. Eddie assumed this design solution was so self-evident that everyone in the competition would have the same solution—they did not. During their presentation, Jones Studio demonstrated how traditional orthogonal proposals blocked an effective and functional flow for security personal as well as users. Jones Studio won the project.

Above Perspective drawing - Eddie Jones. **Opposite page** Views from golf course.

Karsten was designed with expansive daylighting that exploited the region's ubiquitous natural asset. An elevated water harvesting system fed the golf course, and locally sourced and produced materials reduced costs and building waste. Rather than fight the non-desert grass, the designers used it to berm against the building, insulating the facility for greater utility savings. Grass is the opposite of Jones Studio's "desert garden" principle, but its green would be admitted to their materials palette for the clubhouse.

Nearly 26 years later, and despite many accolades, Karsten was caught up in the fast-paced redevelopment environment in Tempe. In 2016 Neal lobbied ASU to stop them from decommissioning the building. The University sold it to a developer who was going to put up office buildings. Karsten, unloved with weeds growing around it, was finally demolished (see image below) in 2021, a shocking end to a ground-breaking facility designed with flexible future uses in mind.

Louis Kahn's observation about the struggle associated with building was particularly true with Karsten, but the APS House taught the team lessons as well. Both facilities pre-figured the current promotion of a "regenerative" economy, growing from the scientific disciplines that flourished in the 1960s.[26] Despite incorporating repurposed and locally sourced elements to allow for future adaptations, Karsten ended in a sad loss for the Earth that gave up its materials for naught. In an era where landfills are at capacity and the public bemoans the devastation natural resource extraction leaves behind, destroying a building not yet 30 years old seems shortsighted. Jones Studio's original design for the APS House brought great invention to the typical suburban home model unsuited for the climatic conditions of the desert. With the rapid evolution of sustainable technologies and a timid audience, the house would not have its hoped-for impact. It has been repurposed so it escaped Karsten's fate, but it would not fulfill APS's primary intention to transform how single-family homes could be desert-efficient.

Architects have an obligation to be gentler on the planet, but so do the manufacturing industries who relish the planned obsolescence of their unrecyclable products. Luckily, Jones Studio retained all the passive and active design lessons that express sustainability in their future work for much better outcomes.

Opposite page Envelope at exterior patio. **Above left** Patio view from dining. **Above right** Same view looking east after demolition. **Following spread** Exterior patio at dusk.

River Legacy Parks Living Science Center

Arlington, Texas, 1996

Neal continued his dogged work looking for new opportunities. He got Jones Studio on a list for the River Legacy Living Science Center Project in Arlington, Texas, and with their history of site responsive design, Jones Studio was awarded the project. River Legacy's land, south of the West Fork of the Trinity River, was scarred by a huge gouge left by a road project to level Green Oaks Boulevard atop the site's hill. During a visit, Eddie and Neal discovered a children's fort made of nature's debris in the woods, constructed without architectural precedent, no building permit needed. The voice of the forest spoke to Eddie through the children's construction; it would have a profound influence on the form and material of the future nature center. Jones Studio would repair and restore the site and create a building that would magnify the Center's educational goals. The building was a permission slip to celebrate the connection between the forest and its human stewards.

Nature is woven through and across the building. The exuberant roofline resembles feathers of the area's birds. Warm woods and cool stones are flooded with dappled light from the building-length roof skylight. Stacked stone walls resemble ancient ruins, clean of line and colorful with fossils from the past. The borrow pit gash was transformed into a riparian habitat, the studio returning the forest to its original inhabitants.

The building process gathered together a village of support: the Texas Rangers baseball team donated trees torn down to make way for a widened road in front of their facility, a local farmer hauled away the tree trunks for them and a neighbor stored them until needed. Boy Scouts earned badges by debarking the trees that were then used as the support columns for the curved ridge beam. Some unconventional fundraising helped bring the building to life. In the "Nuts About Nature" capital campaign, a chance to square dance with Eddie was sold for $1, and Girl Scouts sold pickle juice, a well-known regional tonic. Neal and Eddie once cornered former Dallas Cowboys quarterback Troy Aikman in an elevator and coaxed a donation from him.

Above Children's fort precedent structure found on site. **Opposite page** West roof canopy overhang at dusk.

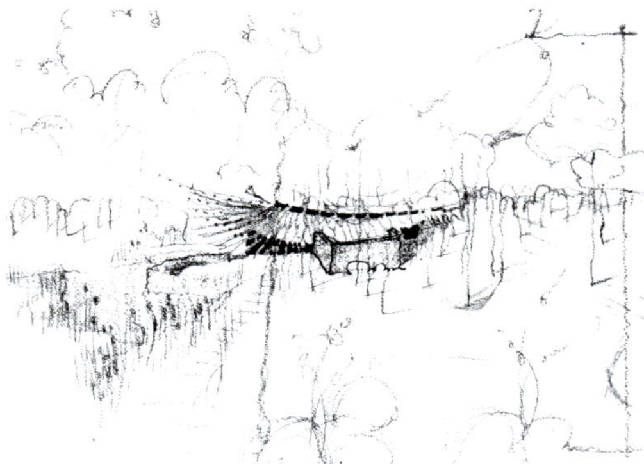

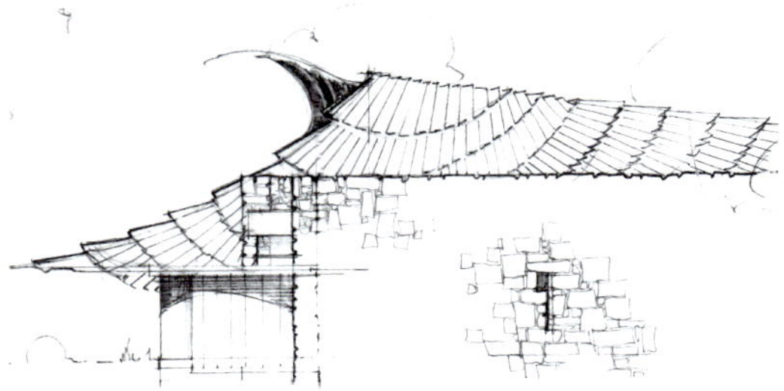

Opposite page Public entry approach. **Above & below** Study sketches and perspective rendering - Eddie Jones.

At River Legacy, Jones Studio created a beautiful modern building that embodied a reverence for nature. As always, the team started from scratch with this new building typology and lets the materials, site, history and nature help design it. Many of the children who were students in the Center's school have become teachers or have their own children enrolled in programs today. This continuity of care is part of Jones Studio legacy to the people and landscape of Arlington. It took a community, a close partnership between the designers, client and contractor and inspired originality to make the project one of the best centers of its kind in the country.

Opposite page View north with wetlands in foreground. **Right** Lobby, ridge skylight, and tree trunk columns. **Following spread** West canopy glowing at night.

NAI Horizon Corporate Office Building

Phoenix, Arizona, 2000

Phoenix retains the look of a city tossed up quickly in a war-time effort with as little aesthetic interest as a staff sergeant might muster. The beige style continued to spread across the region through the various booms and busts of the region's gyrating economy. When Jones Studio was approached by friend and colleague Scott O'Connor, son of Supreme Court Justice Sandra Day O'Connor, to design an architecturally distinguished and energy efficient office building for the Alva Corporation and their international partners, the designers were interested in trying a new formula: what if they could demonstrate that "good architecture also makes good business," defying the sergeant's aesthetic? [27]

The central idea was to wrap a glass building in a horizontal lattice work to provide a 45-degree solar cut off to reduce heat gain. Although the resulting design concept resembled a lobster trap, Eddie and Neal were confident when they arrived at the client meeting. Their presentation was in English, but the Belgian developer spoke Dutch. His body language during the presentation gave off a positive vibe, but the following Monday morning, Scott O'Connor said the developer thought the proposal was ugly and "there is no way that building would be built." How could Jones Studio bridge the gap between the developer's resistance to the non-traditional aesthetic of the building and the designer's goals to prove that a well-designed, light-filled, environmentally friendly building would draw tenants while reducing overhead costs?

Jones Studio was given another chance to prove that responsible, viable, site appropriate buildings are attainable with conventional sources of finance and would be profitable for the open-minded investor. Neal and Eddie brought the developer back on board by couching all the unique design elements in energy and cost savings, such as a reduction of tonnage for the mechanical systems by 50% and a reduction in electric lighting costs because of all the natural light. Having produced the operational savings data combined with a full-scale mockup, the Belgian developer relented and gave the design a green light.

Above Perspective drawing - Eddie Jones. **Opposite page** Interstitial space between sunscreen and building envelope.

Opposite page East sunscreen. **Above left** Installation of modular sunscreen. **Above middle** O'odham dwelling and ocotillo spine ramada. **Above right** Japanese Kare-sansui zen garden as sunscreen inspiration.

Inside, the 28,000-square-foot building features polished concrete floors, exposed duct work, warm wood built-in furniture, brightly colored walls, custom carpets designed by Eddie, glass walls, an interior glass clerestory and translucent panels. A sense of light flows throughout the spaces, allowing for connection and conversation. Each upper-level window is operable, allowing employees to take advantage of cross breezes during the desert's gloriously temperate months.

The most unique design element was the sun-shading, horizontal scrim around the second floor. The recycled sawdust infused with plastic polymers was a cost-effective way to protect the upper story from light using weatherproof materials. Jones Studio wanted to use the product to shade the building, inspired by the Tohono O'odham's use of cactus spines (see image above) to shade their outdoor spaces, but in a non-traditional way. The manufacturer refused to sell them the material they needed. Even the main supplier refused to sell to them despite the fact that the non-traditional use was encompassed within the manufacturer's specifications. Jones Studio bypassed the recalcitrant supplier and ordered 10,000 lineal feet from a different distributer out of Tucson, had it cut into the dimensions they wanted, and shipped the material to Phoenix. Despite the threat of a lawsuit that never materialized, and hoping, naïvely, that the composite lumber supplier would discount their product in this chance to break into a new market (they did not), Jones Studio was able to bypass roadblocks to install the material as designed.

NAI Horizon has been almost fully leased since it was built, proving that good architecture *does* make good business. Jones Studio continues to battle the developers, suppliers, manufacturers and bureaucrats who suppress positive changes in the construction industry one building at a time. Perverse persistence has always been a valuable Jones Studio asset.

Above West shaded entry. **Below** Conference room, balcony and striated light. **Opposite page** Zen garden influences in sunscreen. **Following spread** West elevation at night.

Coconino Community College Lone Tree Campus

Flagstaff, Arizona, 2002

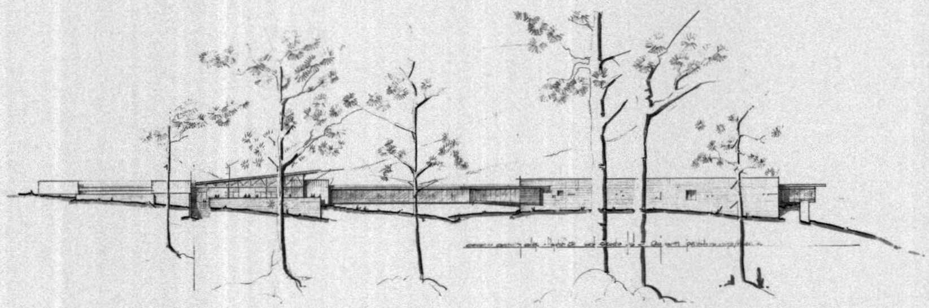

“Learn and grow” could be the Jones Studio motto. Their daring had bred a taste for bold action and investigative design forays, so when they received their first commission for an educational institution, they hoped to inspire students through the buildings where they would spend their college years. This type of facility would transform citizens for decades to come, extending Jones Studio’s design zeal into the community.

Coconino Community College [CCC], founded in 1991, is one of 20 two-year colleges in Arizona, serving the residents of Coconino County, the second largest county by acreage in the country. CCC services a largely female adult population, which helped drive some of Jones Studio’s design decisions.[28] Getting the project was a throwback to Jones Studio’s earliest days scrapping to break into the state’s nascent RFQ system. Jones Studio was hired to do programming but not the entire job. Eddie and Neal talked the school’s leadership into allowing them to pursue the competition to build a new campus from whole cloth, and they won.

The original campus was in a strip mall on the eastern edge of Flagstaff. To create the new Lone Tree Campus, they evaluated 90 pristine acres on a knoll owned by the College and accessed by a single dirt road. They partnered with Wyatt/Rhodes Architects and Christy Ten Eyck Landscape Architecture, another long-term collaborator, to understand the site and find its most elegant resolution. To protect the unique natural setting, Jones Studio created a campus that was “dancing in the trees” of the woody northern Arizona landscape. The 128,000-square-foot building wraps around the knoll at the center axis point of the 90 acres, flaring around the access road and parking lot to make the building visible and accessible to students of multiple abilities.

There are four legible zones within the building: the central student commons area, a computer commons, administrative offices and classrooms, all of which benefit from skylit corridors with views

Above Elevation drawing - Eddie Jones. **Opposite page** Bus drop off at main entry.

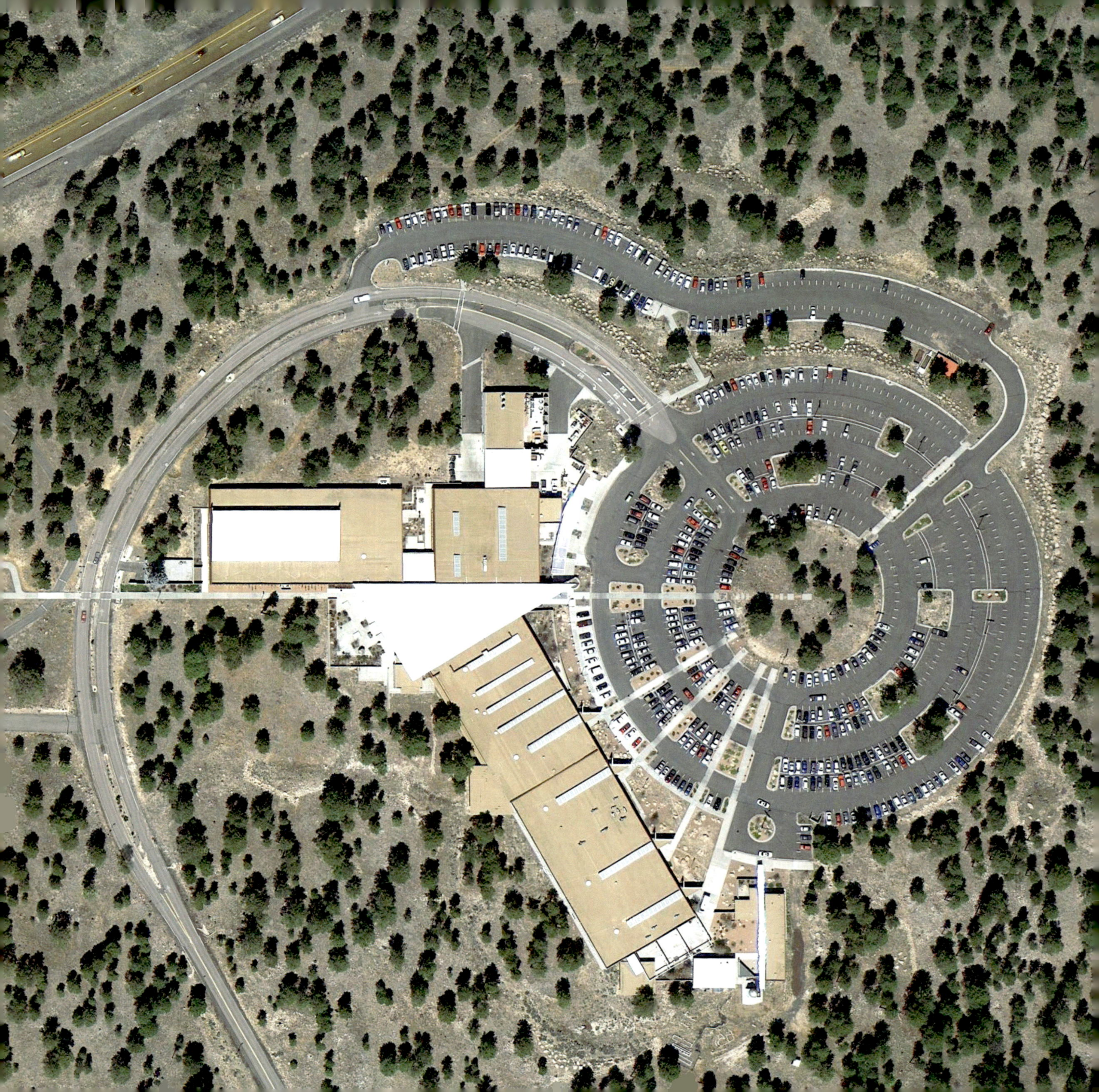

Opposite page Overall campus aerial. **Above** Student commons at operable glazing wall. **Following spread** Nestled with the Ponderosa Pines.

of the woods punctuating the spaces. The kit of materials included polycarbonate panels to bring daylight into every space, rusting metal siding and sand-blasted concrete block that reflect the rugged landscape and require minimal maintenance. Jones Studio designed tables and chairs, rather than desks, to accommodate the accoutrements hauled around by working adults.

Like any architecture firm, Jones Studio constantly deals with new systems and regulations, changing delivery and procurement processes, and opaque political and economic drivers, finding ways to overcome obstacles to realize their design dreams. At Coconino they grappled with unknown site conditions, change orders from the contractor and unreliable subcontractor skill sets, but none of this derailed a great outcome. Coconino is an important building block in Jones Studio's progression, twice the size of the next biggest project to date with a new range of design successes. It taught Jones Studio how to ensure all its partners have matching priorities and an aligned design sensibility. Despite its size, Coconino continues to provide inspiring lessons for much larger design challenges.

Growing the Family

With a growing catalogue of varied and significant projects under their belt and several underway, by the late-1990s Neal and Eddie needed to grow the team. In 1998, capitalizing on the initial connection with Eddie after the APS competition, Brian Farling, originally from Harrisburg, Pennsylvania, joined Jones Studio. His early interactions with Eddie left an undeniable impression; Brian could see a clear connection and feeling of like-mindedness about not only architecture, but the broader world. He saw Jones Studio as an optimistic leader in the field committed to designing for the Sonoran Desert and jumped at the opportunity to join the team.

Like Eddie and Neal, Brian grew up in a middle-class family. Throughout his early years, he discovered a love of drawing and excelled at making things, always getting A's in his creative classes. As high school graduation approached, Brian realized he needed a path to facilitate his passion for art and decided to enroll in the National Guard as a means to pay for college. It was later at art school where he discovered architecture. A sculpture professor at Millersville University in Pennsylvania suggested Brian investigate the field based on the way he approached and executed his projects. He attended the College of Architecture at the UofA after falling in love with the desert while visiting a cousin in Tucson.

Brian speaks of UofA's focus on "critical regionalism," the discipline of interpreting landscape as the grounding for architecture advocated by the school's professors, particularly Judith Chafee. Chafee, who spent part of her early life in Tucson and returned after many successful years on the East Coast working at some of the most important architecture firms of the time, was inspired by the ancient architecture of the Tonoho O'odham, the courtyards of Spanish colonists, but most particularly, she revered the reality of place.[29] Just as the field was evolving to focus broadly on environmental issues, "regionalism" became a more lauded ethos in architecture schools. Architectural historian William J.R. Curtis legitimated Chafee's work by admitting that: "At its best regionalism penetrates to the generating principles any symbolic substructures of the past then transforms these into forms that are right for the changing social order of the present..."[30] Chafee, like other designers working outside a homogenized, corporatized architectural vocabulary, was finally being recognized for developing buildings relevant to

Opposite left Perspective drawing of 5th year Capstone project: Center for Arizona Architecture - Brian Farling. **Opposite right** Blackwell House by Judith Chafee - sketch by Brian Farling. **Above** Self Portrait over life drawing collage - Brian Farling.

their social and natural landscapes. Brian's practice would be rooted in the idea that only by understanding the history of place will meaningful architecture emerge.

Brian's maneuver to get to college came back to bite him while in his first semester at UofA: he was called up for active duty and relocated to Saudi Arabia as part of Desert Storm. (In only one way was this timing lucky. Melissa Farling, an architect who has worked for and collaborated with Jones Studio, was completing her master's degree and was scheculed to be Brian's studio teaching assistant, which would have precluded their dating. The couple married in 1994.) While stationed in Saudi Arabia, Kuwait and Iraq, Brian spent time in extreme temperatures, observing the brutal conditions and beautiful austerity of the dry desert. He would sketch the shifting sands, understanding how light sun and shadow played an important role in survival. These lessons, and his preoccupation with water, were passions that would coalesce at Jones Studio.

Also joining Jones Studio in 1998 was Rob Viergutz. Originally from the Washington, D.C. area, Rob visited the desert Southwest with his folks during vacations. Rob enrolled at ASU, enjoying the great wood shop and studio spaces where he and his cohort could experiment. Rob remembers particularly the influence of ASU President's Professor Max Underwood, whose breadth and depth of knowledge about architecture and culture allowed students to experiment and find their own style.

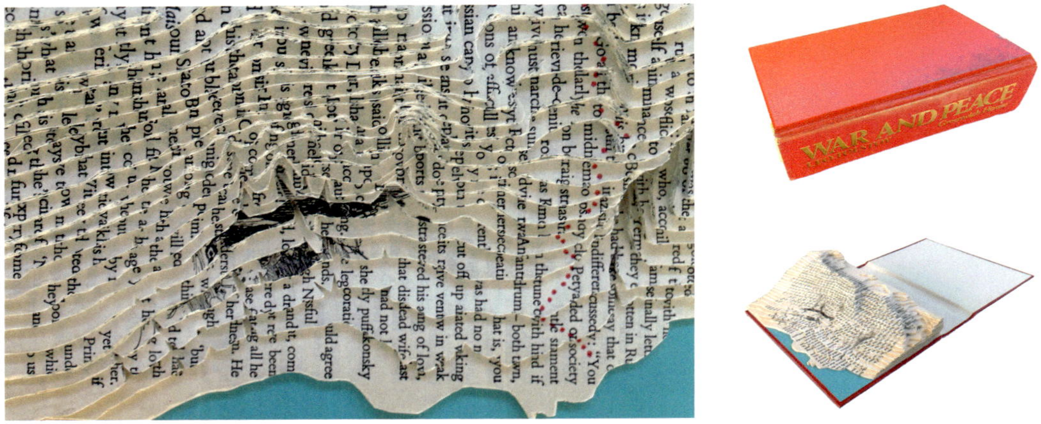

Above War & Peace book art project - Maria Salenger.

Rob believes that, because there is much less architectural tradition in Arizona, the region's political and business leaders are more open minded around experimentation, although battling against conservative bureaucrats takes up much of the firm's time. Rob relishes the diverse work of an architect and the need to pivot quickly, one minute deep into code books, the next moment experimenting with materials. This capacity to multi-task is particularly important for a mid-sized firm, where testing ideas allows every family member to contribute ingenious solutions. Rob's flexibility and expertise would allow him to contribute to the firms' growing success.

Maria Salenger, *née* Pensiero, received her undergraduate architecture degree at the UofA where she met Brian, gaining a broad interest in sculptural practice as well as a respect for site, daylighting and raw materiality. After graduation she worked in Phoenix while pursing sculpture classes at ASU so she could make things rather than just do drawings for colleagues. In 1996 she did some moonlighting gigs for Jones Studio and met her future husband Matt Salenger there. Interested in pursuing a Master's in Fine Art outside of Arizona, Maria ended up in London in the fall of 1999 while Matt pursued graduate studies at London's Architectural Association. One of her most formative professors at the Slade School of Fine Art at the University College London was artist Phyllida Barlow, whose conversations pushed Maria to develop a deep, conceptual research process that she applies to her work at Jones Studio. Maria joined the firm full-time in 2000.

Maria has been a witness to the dramatic changes in Phoenix. Her childhood home, once at the edge of the city is now in the middle. She avoided the desert as a kid but returned deliberately to take advantage of the design opportunities that would come with its growth. Maria observes it took Phoenix 50 years to do what it took other cities hundreds of years to develop more slowly over time, so pressing a culture of good design into the ecosystem would be important for the city and its residents. Through her work at Jones Studio and coLAB, the public art and architecture studio she co-founded with Matt in 2004, Maria has a particular focus on the natural species of Arizona. She elevates the structures of native life as well as the ethical responsibility we humans have to the Earth across her projects.

The next long-term family member to join Jones Studio was Jacob Benyi. Jacob grew up in Phoenix, and was influenced by his art historian aunts and by his journalist grandfather's library that allowed him to explore global art, architecture and history. Jacob was most attracted to castles, cathedrals, bridges and Indigenous architectures from around the world, particularly big construction projects that changed the cultures that produced them. His interest in maps and mapping as means of controlling and conveying information would also come in handy for his chosen career.

Jacob knew in junior high school that he wanted to become an architect and was part of the first generation of designers using now-ubiquitous computer programs to design. He studied architecture at ASU, where during an intro class he watched a documentary on Jones Studio's APS house with a follow-up site visit. Dr. Nan Ellin invited Eddie to give a guest lecture to Jacob's class on "Architectural Programming," and Tom Hahn, a former Jones Studio family member, used Eddie's rammed earth home as an example of sustainable design in his "Construction Systems" class. Jones Studio's work was threaded throughout ASU's curriculum.

ASU ran a lottery to place students into a required "Professional Practice" internship at a regional firm, and luck of the draw, Jacob got his internship at Jones Studio. He joined the team on May 15, 2002. Over that summer Jacob worked on Jones Studio's Lattie Coor Hall project at ASU, and in the fall, continued to work for Jones Studio performing construction administration on Lattie Coor while finishing out his final year of classes. Jacob graduated from ASU in 2003 and started working at Jones Studio full-time. In the firm's culture, everyone is afforded the opportunity to participate fully in a project. Where many firms would stick an intern with mundane tasks, Eddie and Neal instead wanted everyone to experience and contribute to projects. Jacob recalls attending a client meeting on his second day of work. He describes those early days as "drinking from the fire hose" so great were the opportunities and challenges to think and act.

In fall 2007 Jacob moved to New York to pursue a graduate degree in architecture at Columbia University, returning over winter and summer breaks to work on the Mariposa Land Port of Entry project. He returned full-time to Jones Studio in July 2010 to jump into the deep end of Mariposa.

Like Maria, as a native Phoenician Jacob has seen first-hand the climatic changes that would drive his interest in making water more visible in the desert environment. As the late summer monsoons changed, and as fire became a more frequent weather event, Jacob knew designing for a desert climate would be an ever-more urgent concern. He advocates communicating the goals of designing for water, bringing clients along on the journey for water conservation. Jacob is also the firm's *de facto* historian. His continued perceptive attention to Jones Studio's history allows them to understand lessons from each project and to use that information to forecast where they are going next.

With this new cohort in place, a group that would cohere and provide a strong backdrop for the firm's work, Jones Studio continued to integrate changing water systems and an evolving artistic sensibility into their commissions.

Moonlighting Architecture

In a PBS documentary on Louis Sullivan, Sullivan reports he fired Frank Lloyd Wright for moonlighting. Wright said he quit.[31] Wright defended himself by saying that Sullivan and partner engineer Dankmar Adler were too busy inventing a new American architecture to take on private houses, so Wright brought the battle into the domestic realm.[32] Funny enough, Frank Lloyd Wright fired Taliesin Apprentice Paolo Soleri for working on the Dome house in Cave Creek, Arizona, with Taliesin colleague Mark Mills. Wright demanded the right of unimpeded, uncompromising self-expression but did not support that right for others.[33] Sullivan and Wright were not alone in their attitude. Moonlighting on outside projects is typically discouraged in architectural firms—except Jones Studio.

By embracing moonlighting—it's only fair since the firm started with Eddie's own moonlighting gigs—Jones Studio demonstrates a flexibility that spreads into each family member's life. For those with the stamina, the extra work provides additional income, experience and the weight of personal responsibility. Although the list of moonlighting projects designed by the studio family is long and varied, some of the best examples are personal dwellings designed with site conditions, family changes and the drive to invent new ways to live in the desert in mind. Elements of these private projects occasionally pop up in the firm's work—it is impossible to segregate ideas and images when there is so much overlap between the personal and professional. One of the moonlighting projects, Vol'ume[s]: a bookstore on design, exemplifies how Jones Studio's family gives back to the dynamic design community in the region.

Opposite page Vol'ume[s]: a bookstore on design - Melissa Farling, Jennifer Parette, Donna Barry, Brian Farling, Burt Little and Rick Labonte.

vol' ume [s]

Farling House

Tempe, Arizona, 1994-2002, 2003, 2009

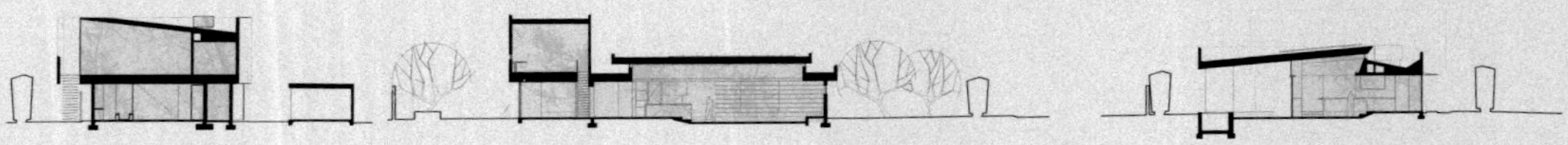

Soon after Brian and Melissa were married, and while Brian was finishing his final semester at the UofA, the couple decided to invest in a home and studio. Their search criteria consisted of three primary elements: first, they believed in the inherent value and optimism of reuse—of transforming something old and cast aside into something new; they wanted to be centrally located in the Valley of the Sun with quick access to ASU, downtown Phoenix and the freeways that connect to Tucson, Flagstaff and Los Angeles. Finally, they wanted to find an existing home with "good bones," something they could occupy and gradually transform with a long-term master plan.They wanted to "dig-in" and rebel against the consumer driven concept of a starter home. In spring 1994 they purchased a 1950s one-story masonry ranch house with an east-west solar orientation and located just south of ASU in Tempe for $84,000.

Through "sheer force of will," and with limited resources and time, they worked on the first phase of the house renovation between 1994 and 2002. Brian and Melissa were inspired by the resourcefulness of mentors such as Judith Chafee, Will Bruder and, of course, Eddie, all of whom stretched tight budgets by elevating simple materials and construction techniques to something elegant and truthful. With this first renovation, the pair made minor upgrades: connecting interior spaces, chopping in skylights, planting trees and ripping up carpet. This phase of work might have gone more quickly had Brian and Melissa not partnered with two other architect couples to open Vol'ume[s]: a bookstore on design.

In 2003 the couple was expecting a baby. The next phase of the master plan included adding a bedroom and upper-level aluminum clad studio, a contemplative space that opens to the north with a 14-foot-tall glass wall that captures indirect light and views of the distant mountains. Brian was his own general contractor with a few subcontractors and friends pitching in. Another big goal was to rework the main living space so that it could accommodate family and friends for large social gatherings.

Above Section drawings - Brian Farling. **Opposite page** Yia-Yia pavilion patio.

Opposite page Aluminum sheet clad volumes. **Above** Upper level studio with north light. **Following spread** Indoor-outdoor Yia-Yia pavilion at night.

Melissa and Brian were committed to not adding extra interior square foctage that would require additional air conditioning in the hot summer months. The desert appropriate response was inspired by Melissa's Greek grandmother, or Yia-Yia, who loved large family gatherings. The Yia-Yia pavilion would shelter an equal amount of interior and exterior space flexing from regular day-to-day use into party mode thanks to a 22-foot-wide, nine-foot-tall sliding glass wall. With a continuous concrete floor and no door track, the room feels whole when the glass wall is pushed aside, connecting the volumes and bringing the climate in. The space dances with the shimmering, reflected light from the small, shaded plunge pool at the south edge of the property.

Melissa had joined Jones Studio in 2007 to work on Mariposa while she and Brian completed their newest addition. With the economic collapse of 2008 occurring just as the Yia-Yia pavilion began construction, Brian and Melissa were able to hire out-of-work concrete craftspeople and woodworkers to help realize the project. Walls that were designed to be masonry and countertops that were unresolved all became concrete, putting those remarkable talents to work and creating a space defined by only a few aesthetically rich materials.

It is important to underscore the support Neal and Eddie provided while Brian and Melissa were doing this major remodel work. Jones Studio's unwavering commitment to making architecture allows the family's experimentation to shine.

Opposite page Main entry. **Above** Indoor-outdoor Yia-Yia pavilion. **Below** Process plan study drawing - Brian Farling. **Following spread** Upper level studio.

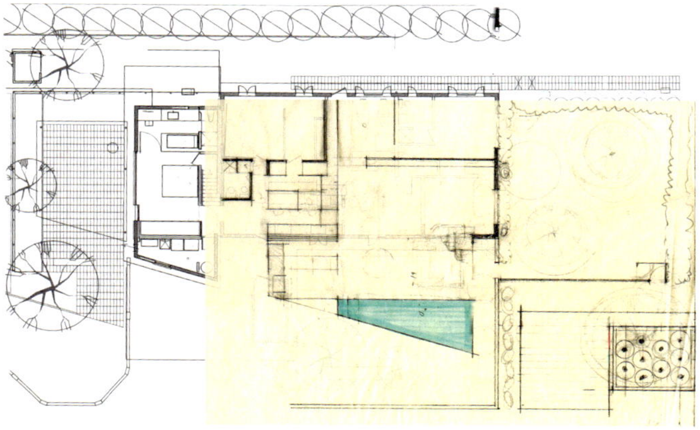

Johnson Jones House

Ahwatukee, Arizona, 1998

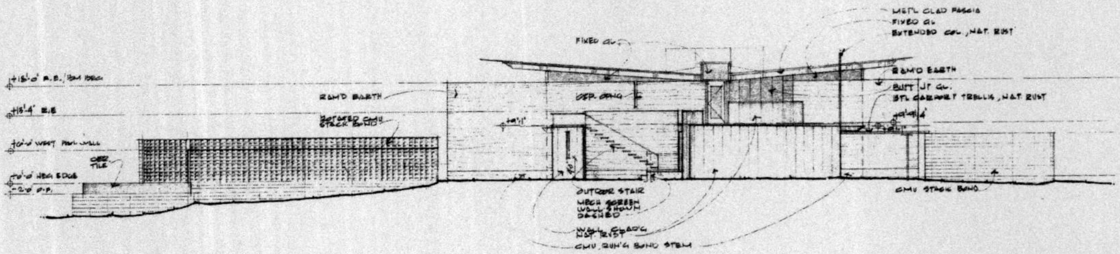

In 1992, just after Eddie had just completed his competition presentation for the APS House, he flew to Toronto on an industry junket. Also on the tour was Lisa Johnson, who owned the sole distributorship for Knoll in the Phoenix area and had worked with Eddie on the Cardinals headquarters. Sparks flew between the pair, and after a necessary intermission to allow for disentanglements before they could entangle, the newly blended family knew they wanted a place of their own.

Lisa's family lived in Ahwatukee, on the south side of South Mountain, one of the largest municipal parks in the country, and wanted to stay there so Kara and Kurtie Johnson could stay in school with their friends. Eddie and Lisa found an irregular site adjacent to where Frank Lloyd Wright had designed the San Marcos in the Desert resort. Begun in 1928, San Marcos was brought to a halt by the Depression.[34] On the parcel instead was the Ahwatukee community's enormous round water chlorination tank. Because every other buyer saw the tank as a negative, the asking price for the land had been significantly reduced. The owner admired Eddie's work and was easily motivated to sell to the couple.

Although the giant tank was not a problem for Eddie, living in the suburbs was. The only way he could live in the architectural nightmare of faux but expensive housing was to block the suburbs out. In *Landscape in Western Art*, Malcolm Andrews describes Jay Appleton's "habitat" theory. Ancient peoples wanted landscape that helped them see but not be seen by enemies and prey.[35] Eddie would use numerous design strategies to mask the buildings around him by an almost complete blurring of home and garden. The riotous exterior, designed by landscape architect Bill Tonneson and fed by water harvesting systems, screens the building from the street. Eddie's rugged rammed earth walls block out the monoculture of Ahwatukee while preserving views of the sky and desert. Eddie would celebrate the poetic meaning of dirt, the most ancient of materials, to counter the perpetual newness of suburbia.

Above Elevation drawing - Eddie Jones. **Opposite page** Rammed earth walls set against lush desert landscape and South Mountain Park.

Opposite page Re-purposed wood door from Homolovi. **Above** South Mountain Park, water tank and the edge of suburbia.

From the south we see Eddie's experiments with geometric shapes as they mass together, juxtaposed as they are at Homolovi Ruins State Park. Eddie's eight-foot-square, three-inch-thick wood clad door, activated by a hydraulic pivot, was originally used at Homolovi. When Homolovi's management declared the door a hazard to visitors due to its weight, Eddie grabbed it, storing it for nine years until he was able to use it in his own home.

Inside, the building opens to the northeastern flank of South Mountain. Light pours in from the glass wall of the two-story living room. A glass, second story walkway distributes light throughout the home with a horizontal skylight that throws parallel beams of sun and shadow, creating a rhythmic stability for the transparent passageway. Eddie often uses glass as a literal and symbolic representation of the desert sun; an indoor-outdoor crushed-glass garden connects the conditioned and unconditioned spaces. A live tree planted in the living room's glass garden is framed against the sky, its green lungs providing fresh air for the family. Striations of the rammed earth wall, eight inches of dirt pounded down to four, create an EKG pattern of the planet's life, animating the home's central gathering space.

The Johnson Jones home is dense and translucent, smooth and rough. Energy is compressed and released. Eddie uses high end systems to make the home sustainable and comfortable, but it is his deeply sensitive touch that has created a private retreat in the middle of the city.

Construction Zone [CZ], a construction firm led by architects who understand the nuance of real design (co-founders Richard Fairbourn and Andy Byrnes each worked at Jones Studio at one point), helped bring Eddie's vision to life. Burt Little, a key CZ team member, first heard Eddie speak at the UofA, where he was one year behind Brian and Maria, and was inspired by Eddie's ardor for making architecture. Burt's joy in bringing Eddie's personal home to life prompted him to join Jones Studio, where he would contribute his design and construction skills to the success of many Jones Studio projects. Burt was also central to one of Jones Studio's secret weapons—the Family Table—the enduring connector and anchor for the close-knit team.

Above Double height living space with view to South Mountain. **Opposite page** Upper level skylight over glass bridge circulation. **Following spread** Glowing living space and exterior garden at night.

Vol'ume[s]: a bookstore on design

Phoenix, Arizona, 1999-2001

At a gathering of friends in downtown Phoenix and inspired by some shots of tequila, Melissa Farling and fellow architects Donna Barry and Jennifer Parette found themselves discussing the baffling lack of an architectural bookstore in the region. They wondered how they might address that gap, and the next day began laying out a path towards that goal. All three had partners who were architects—Brian Farling, Rick Labonte and Burt Little—and together they schemed to create that space.

Melissa, Donna and Jenn developed a business plan, gathered municipal support and secured a loan. The team developed a concept design inspired by turning a Noguchi paper lamp inside out and lining the walls with back lit fabric, and they made a flexible space for books, exhibitions and lectures by putting bookshelves on wheels. They picked an accessible location on Central and McDowell, near the Phoenix Art Museum, Will Bruder's Central Library and the downtown cultural and business cores. Brian and Burt would leave Jones Studio at five p.m. every day to meet Rick and work late into the evening, renovating the empty 1940's commercial space. In November of 1999 Vol'ume[s]: a bookstore on design opened with a celebratory party with hundreds of guests. One of Brian's favorite lectures was by ASU's Max Underwood, who talked about his time working with Ray and Charles Eames and their relentless approach to solving problems with enthusiasm and inquisitiveness.

Against the aspirations of the award-winning cultural space was the economic reality of running a bookstore. Melissa, Donna and Jenn did a balancing act of running the store alongside their day jobs, constantly looking for the right balance. Unbeknownst to the architects, the property owner of the high-profile corner had plans to sell the cluster of buildings for commercial development (eventually a CVS drugstore moved in). Melissa's lawyer uncles had advised a "no demolition" clause in the lease that forced the landlord to buy them out. The group broke even, paying off the loan but was unable to muster the resources or time to start all over.

Above Stainless steel bookmark and membership card. **Opposite page** Main bookstore, gallery, and flex lecture space.

ARATA ISOZAKI

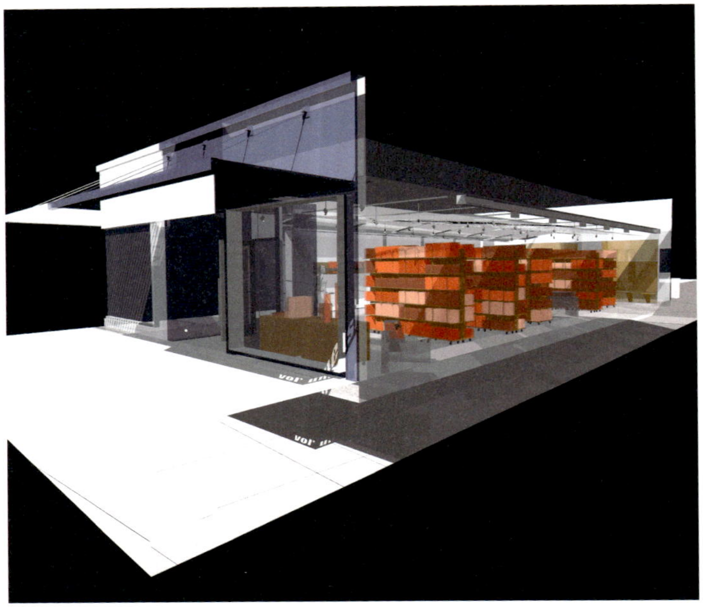

Jones Studio was emotionally supportive of Brian and Burt's time and donated financially to the cause. They were cheerleaders for the group's entrepreneurial dedication and design experimentation, understanding the bookstore's value for the entire architectural community.

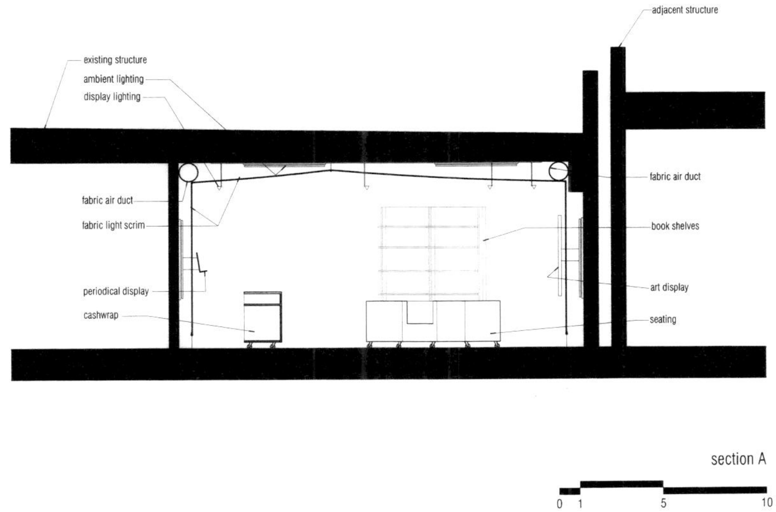

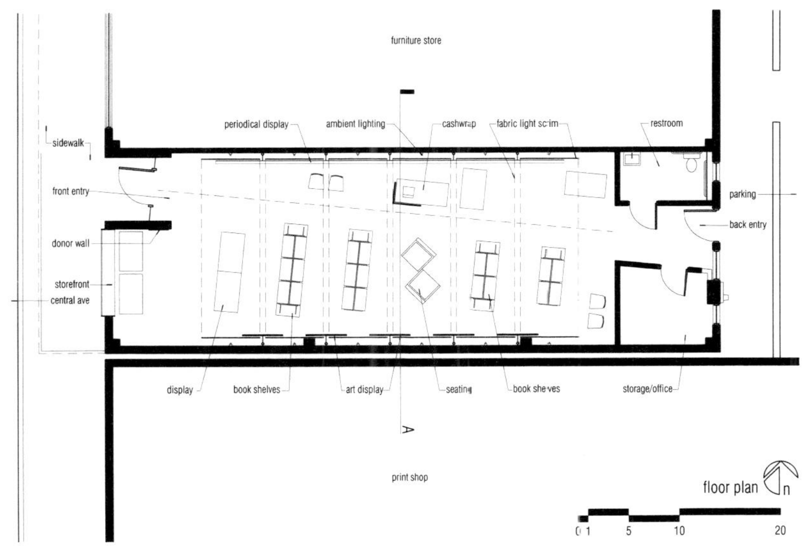

Opposite page Study renderings - Brian Farling. **Above** Plan and section drawings - Brian Farling. **Following spread** Interior views and details

a+t

AA files 38

FRANK LLOYD WRIGHT AND JAPAN
THEORIES AND DOCUMENTS OF CONTEMPORARY ART
A SOURCEBOOK OF ARTISTS' WRITINGS
streamlined
A Metaphor for Progress
Milan
Istanbul

a+t
a+t
ARTFORUM
CITY
THE ART OF MODERNISM
STARCK
MORGAN
Bystander
A History of Street Photography
beadlearchitecture
PHAIDON

Salenger House

Tempe, Arizona, 2000-2004, 2009-2010

Maria and Matt owned a one-story 1950s masonry home close to Brian and Melissa's house in Tempe. Like the Farlings, Matt and Maria wanted to use their property as a playground for experimentation. In the first design iteration they tested the relationship between public and private by deconstructing and gutting the house for one large space with a kitchen, dining room and studio. They built two sleeping "pods" in the back yard for a closer relationship to nature: each pod was wide enough for a bed and long enough for an outdoor deck and garden enclosed inside translucent walls. Maria and Matt did most of the construction work themselves while at Jones Studio.

In 2007, when the couple was expecting, they realized they had to re-establish the more traditional functions of the home. A third "baby pod" was a possibility, but they decided to poll friends and family to help drive the design. The surveys came back: if resale value was key, then a great room was the priority. If resale was not of concern, then including a courtyard or atrium was preferred. Maria and Matt accomplished both.

The two pods were dismantled and reconfigured into covered walkways to create a courtyard connection to a new addition, consisting of a rectangular space that mirrors the shape of the original home. The house was renovated with sleeping spaces while the elegant new structure would hold a great kitchen, dining and living room and a studio behind a mobile bookshelf that cradles the treasures of daily life. High windows on the north wall became a gallery of art by friends and family. The grassy interior courtyard enfolds son Oscar and his pals in their play. Both buildings have large spaces as flexible as possible with moveable partitions so the next major life event wouldn't require significant design demands. Maria and Matt achieved a space with social *and* future resale value.

Above Section drawing - Matt Salenger. **Opposite page above** Courtyard and great room living space. **Opposite page left** Deck and garden end of sleeping pod. **Opposite page right** Bedroom end of sleeping pod.

American Institute of Architects Gallery, *Moonlighting: Jones Studio Employee Projects Off-the-Clock*

Phoenix, Arizona, 2003

When the Phoenix Chapter of AIA invited Jones Studio for an exhibition, the designers chose to do the unexpected: they would feature off-the-clock projects by Jacob Benyi, Patricia Chen, Brian Farling, Aaron Forbes, Eddie Jones, Burt Little, Maria Salenger, Matt Salenger and Rob Viergutz. The team suspended 16-inch diameter cardboard cylinders used for casting concrete columns horizontally at eye height, moving room-to-room through the AIA spaces in a giant rectangle. On the inward facing side of the tubes were mounted project documents—interpretive site sketches, presentation documents, in-process images and pictures of the resulting buildings—hidden from the casual visitor to the space, just as moonlighting is often furtive, completed at night and concealed from workplaces for fear of reprisal.

Eddie reports that visitors to the exhibition were incredulous that Jones Studio "lets" their team members experiment on their own time. (This makes an outsider wonder how much control architecture firms think they have over the minds, souls and spare time of their employees.) Jones Studio's *esprit de corps* supports everyone's efforts to change the built environment for the better. It takes experimentation and sometimes failure to sharpen one's intellectual and practical skills. By presenting outside projects each architect declared their willingness to have their personal efforts be seen outside of the moonlighting shadow.

Opposite page Moonlighting exhibit opening event.

Family Table #1

Birth of the Family Table

Jones Studio had seen a lot of change during their early years in the Beadle building. Comings and goings and ups and downs kept the firm changing and improving. Theirs was a spirited culture but the office layout did not support the pace of exchange that made the firm successful. Family Table #1 grew from this realization.

Burt Little took on modifying the Jones Studio space in the Beadle to make space for and to build Family Table #1. Only Neal chose to have a semi-private office—financial record-keeping requires administrative isolation. The suite was transformed into an open space with a conjoined worktable that would hold the projects and personalities of the workplace. Family Table #1 was an inventive solution and a solid business decision that allowed for continued growth and evolution.

While "open concept" offices have long been a fixture in the corporate environment, it is Jones Studio's dedication to collaboration and debate that distinguishes the role of the Family Table. Sharing a table is easy; making it a vibrant social space for discovery is harder to do. Creating a true family through the table's use is again a rare thing, but it has been a constant across the changes in family composition and studio site, adding to the firm's success.

Above 12th street office building - Al Beadle. **Opposite page top** Family Table #1 image collage. **Opposite bottom** Floor plan of Jones Studio office and Family Table #1. **Following spread** Family Table #1 in action.

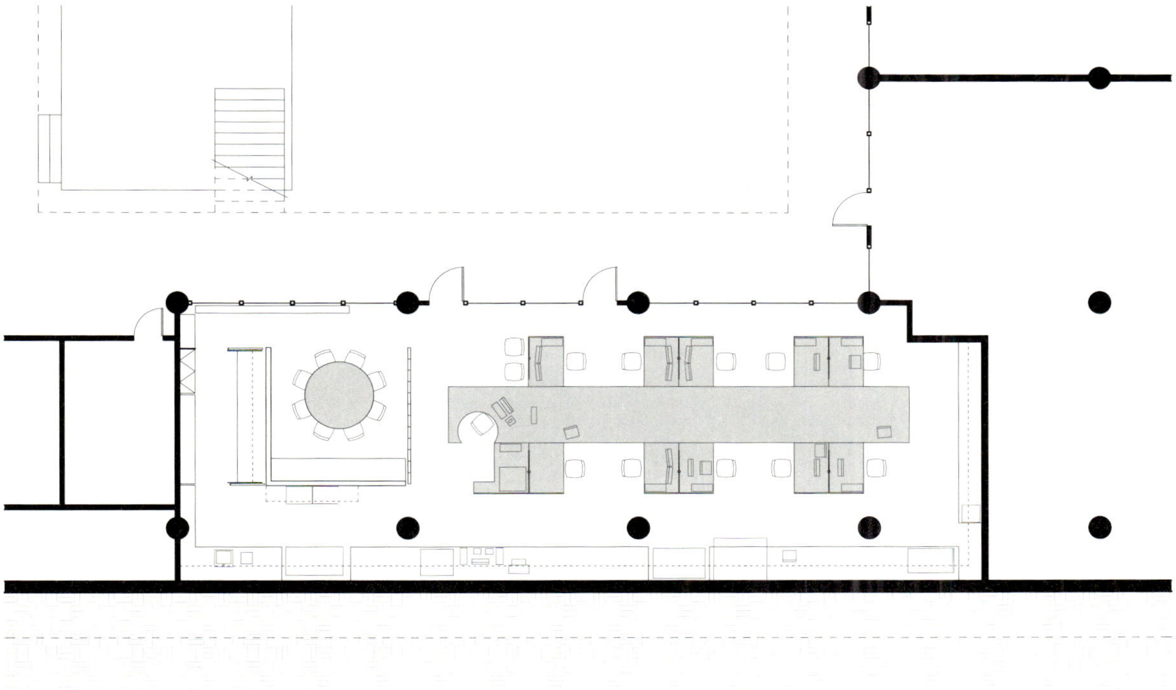

Higher Education in the Desert

America's educational landscape has been built over two centuries of cyclical investment driven largely by the influx of new citizens and economic booms in local economies. Outside of the oldest universities on the east coast, most American states saw their first institutions of higher learning founded after the Civil War, typically with land set aside by state legislatures to begin schooling immigrants from other parts of the world. These investments helped establish the idea of citizenship while also training the newest arrivals on how to grow food, produce objects or provide services in their new country.

America saw another influx of resources for higher education after World War II, which was a particularly vibrant time in Arizona. The tenor of these institutions was shaped by bottom-up social movements demanding more equity, access and inclusion, while business and tech leaders were looking for the next generation of employees, inventors and entrepreneurs. Whatever strategies or motivation drove government or private investments in schools of law, business or the arts, leaders saw the importance of using these brain trusts to develop new technologies, pioneer new fields of study and generally supplement training found at the technical schools that play an equal role in forming our society.

Jones Studio has been fortunate to be part of Arizona's flush of educational investment in the first two decades of the 21st century. School buildings allow for design to influence citizens over generations, sensitizing students from across the region or the globe to the spirit of learning through architecture. University and colleges often embrace an ethos of research and discovery, making them great clients for Jones Studio's experimental approach to design.

Opposite page Interdisciplinary Science & Technology Building 3 - Arizona State University Polytechnic campus.

Arizona State University Lattie F. Coor Hall

Tempe, Arizona, 2003

When Jones Studio received the ASU Lattie Coor commission, it was the largest project they had received to date. The existing conditions of ASU were radically different from Coconino—urban versus rural, major research university versus commuter college, a budget and building more than twice the size—with appropriately different outcomes. About 70% of the office worked on Lattie Coor, which suggests the importance of the project for the firm. To tackle this project, Jones Studio teamed with the Santa Monica office of Gensler, who at the time was the world's largest architecture firm based on number of employees. Jones Studio would need to be mindful of how their two cultures would mesh.

Lattie F. Coor Hall, named after ASU's 15th president, would include state-of-the-art mediated classrooms, open computer labs, research and special purpose facilities and staff and faculty offices. Goals for the facility were layered: Lattie Coor was to be a flagship building announcing a new era of growth and ambition for the University, and the building would need to preserve the circulation pattern on campus while welcoming ASU's neighbors at the University's western gateway. Jones Studio would grapple with the diverse intellectual disciplines living in the building, from contemporary to historical, from global to local, from intensely conceptual to professional training programs. Accommodating the different departments would be a stimulating challenge.

Lattie Coor was designed as three interconnected buildings: a cast-in-place concrete structured office tower clad in ice cube blue glass, hovering above a transparent computing commons area and a precast concrete classroom building. The classroom building took only about a week to assemble after its pre-cast concrete elements were brought on site. This configuration of material allowed the General Contractor the time needed to construct the cast-in-place structure of the tower, later quickly completing the classroom building below.

Above Perspective sketch - Eddie Jones. **Opposite page** Volume and material layering.

One of the biggest successes of the building was the consistent distribution of sunlight. Every architect in Arizona must "acknowledge the sun and light—creatively, defensively, or provocatively."[1] Jones Studio had prioritized consistent daylighting since the Tatham House and Lattie Coor would raise the stakes. *Every* occupied room in the building's 275,000-square-foot interior would have access to natural daylight. The glazing on the building was designed to cast light into the lower levels and upper corridors by harvesting light from one room and passing it into the next. Stippled glass was used to create privacy while allowing surfaces to glow. Jones Studio expressed the joy of Arizona's sun while taming its impact. Unfortunately, a water feature planned for the main classroom corridor was budgeted out of the project. The team would resurrect the idea of allowing water to perform in the desert to great effect in numerous subsequent projects.

Jacob led a double life during the construction of Lattie Coor; he attended on-site meetings and interfaced with the construction teams on behalf of Jones Studio while finishing his undergraduate degree a few buildings away. Discussions could turn into arguments when trying to clear up design and construction issues. Eddie would be brought in to resolve any problems, keeping the discussion real, not personal, about what the problem wanted in order to be solved. Listening is a key skill set in these negotiations. The construction team nicknamed Eddie the "Snake Charmer" for his ability to reconcile differences and get the teams moving in the same direction again.

As part of ASU's Percent-for-Art program, ASU commissioned Chicago-based artist BJ Krivanek to reflect on the complex Tower of Babel that is any university. Early concepts for the project would wrap the tower's façade in phrases and quotations pulled from the scholarship of the many academic disciplines in the building. Getting committees of administrators and faculty to agree on which quotes to select proved problematic. A second, simplified proposal contemplated using simple inspirational words to provide encouragement to the thousands of students who would pass through the classrooms. This too resulted in controversy.

After many discussions about the hierarchy and value of language, the hegemony of English in global culture and other issues of relevance for the faculty and staff, Krivanek chose illegible fragments and phrases that were etched forward and backwards into the sky blue-tinted glazing. Krivanek used abstracted characters from Latin-based, Native American and Asian languages, as well as numbers and punctuation marks to "represent the universal potential of language" while recalling the disciplines inside the building.[2] This eliminated arguments about authority in cultural formation and suggested instead the astounding array of symbolic systems humans use to communicate. In addition, a bold "EXPLORE" sign was added to cast a shadow and reflect a distinct perspective.

The blue façade distinguishes the building from everything else in the area. Blue was chosen for its feeling of ice, of cool and depth, a welcome relief and sly visual snap in the Arizona sky. When looking up, the building fades away, a lovely metaphor for how languages and civilizations can be lost to history.

Above Integrated public art by BJ Krivanek at curtain wall with "EXPLORE" sign and reflection above.

Several significant transitions occurred in the architecture field during the completion of Lattie Coor. Construction drawings were now all CAD-based, although Jones Studio still used some hand sketches to address construction issues. The firm transitioned from the use of fax machines to communicate information to email, generating less paper waste but requiring the same high level of tracking. The project pushed Jones Studio's expanding skills base, tested their reflexes in a fluid and changing marketplace and remains a sentinel of change for ASU's Tempe campus.

ARIZONA STAT
LATTIE F.

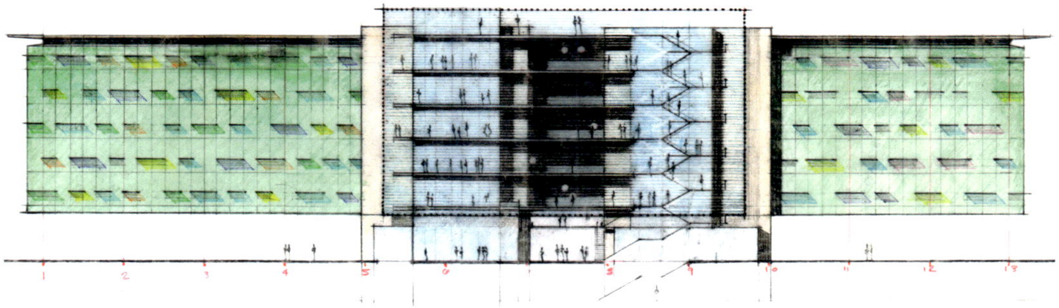

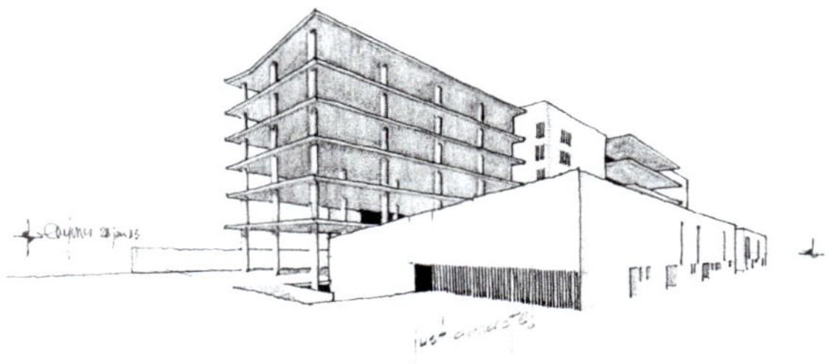

Opposite page Primary student circulation path under building. **Above** Study drawings - Eddie Jones. **Following spread** Overall composition in context at dusk.

EXPLORE

South Mountain Community College Performing Arts Center

Phoenix, Arizona, 2003

Architecture is always a frame for performance. It can provide enlivened social space and facilitate scripted and non-scripted interactions between friends, colleagues and strangers. Every culture has its own traditions and histories for the performing arts, from dance and song to storytelling and poetry. A performing arts center allows points of contact across traditions, helping us to share emotional connections through body and voice. Jones Studio was eager to try this typology that so clearly reflected their commitment to pushing boundaries.

Publicly funded higher education institutions fulfill the purpose of our shared social contract through equitable access to education, gathering community across borders, allowing for guided self-discovery and self-definition so citizens can contribute to their society. South Mountain Community College [SMCC] is in an underserved area of Phoenix; 56% of the student body have Central or South American backgrounds, 70% attend school part-time.[3] Through a regional bond program that provided funding for a new performing arts center, it was immediately understood by the College leadership, faculty and staff that this facility could be an ambassador to the South Mountain community. There would not be a "town and gown" relationship with the residents, rather a "neighbor meets neighbor" environment creating partnership and connection. SMCC's commitment to celebrating the area's histories *via* its new arts facility in a growing part of the metropolitan area would do the hard work of distributing the arts across the class and ethnic divisions of the region.

Brian and Neal presented the firm's work to the SMCC Performing Art Center's team using a 35mm slide projector (amazing how quickly technology changes). The staff and faculty appreciated Jones Studio's thinking and hired them to design their Performing Arts Center [PAC]. The facility should be a state-of-the-art teaching facility and performance space and a beacon to the surrounding South Mountain neighborhood—in other words, it should nurture a feeling of shared ownership and pride. To ensure the building would participate in the life of the area, Jones Studio pulled the building

Above Concept rendering - Brian Farling. **Opposite page** Self-shading metal cladding with rust patina. **Following spread** Lobby lantern, performance hall and fly tower massing.

STOP

away from campus and towards 24th street, a major north-south thoroughfare connecting the city's neighborhoods. This left space for an outdoor green amphitheater for the SMCC community, with room for graduation ceremonies, impromptu performances or lunchtime picnics.

Inspired by the self-shading characteristics of a saguaro cactus, the building was wrapped in a pattern of eight simple drip flashing shapes, falling away at the lobby to let light emanate out like a 40-foot-tall lantern. Tucson-based glass artist Tom Philabaum was commissioned to create a work; his pyramid of colorful blooms titled *Baseline Bouquet* honors the Japanese American flower farms that had been arrayed along Southern Avenue, at the campus's front door, before World War II.

The arid nature of the climate allowed for the use of raw black iron sheet metal and steel detailing without a fear of rust becoming a problem. Instead, this "desert patina" has aged with time, its durable coating becoming visually rich while protecting the metal. In contrast to the tough exterior envelope of steel and glass, the interior was conceived as a delicate musical instrument inspired by Maria's childhood violin (see page 163). When opened, her instrument's hard black case revealed the sinuous and carefully crafted wood violin nestled in a rich bed of purple velvet. These simple contrasts would guide the architecture.

The faculty and staff at the SMCC PAC continue their commitment to helping students achieve their highest potential. Their jewel box of a building inspires and engages each generation of student as well as their families and friends. Jones Studio applied their artist-driven aesthetic so culture would be produced and enjoyed outside the city's traditional core. Jones Studio realized that creatives may be their best clients: they have a shared sense of discovery and are willing to take chances that might inspire something completely new and transformative for the building's users.

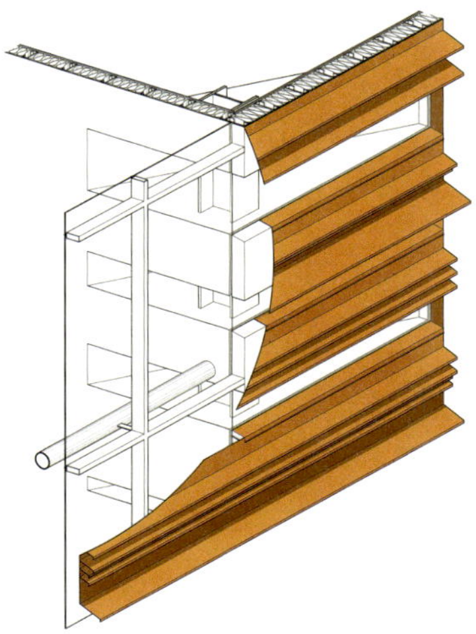

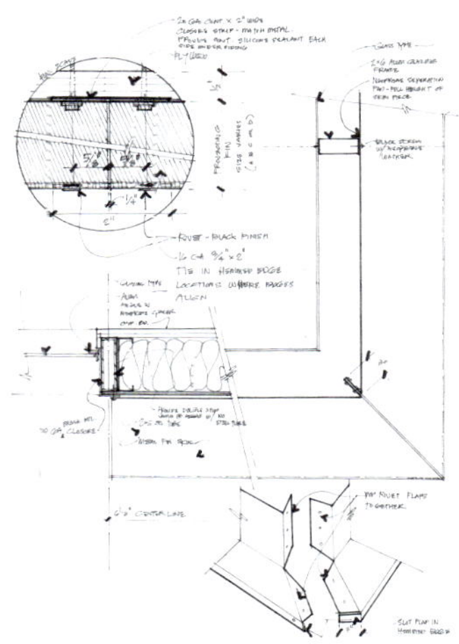

Opposite page Inside lobby with *Baseline Bouquet* - Tom Philabaum. **Above** Detail drawings and sketches - Brian Farling. **Following spread** Elevated, exterior lobby and shade ramada.

Family Table #1

Opposite page Section perceptive rendering - Brian Farling. **Above** Eucalyptus "violin" wall in performance hall. **Below left** Maria's childhood violin and case. **Below right** Model photo. **Following spread left** Lobby lantern glowing at night. **Following spread right** Translucent glazing and shade scrim at dusk.

Arizona State University Polytechnic Campus

Mesa, Arizona, 2003-2006

During World War II, Phoenix had two air force bases: Luke Air Force Base on west side and Williams Air Force Base on the east, both built in 1941. In 1993 the Clinton administration began reducing military spending, closing many bases across the country including Williams. The Williams airfield was converted into a small public airport, but with lots of land and surplus buildings from the 1940s and '50s, ASU and the community college system claimed Williams for their various expansions.

ASU East (now Polytechnic) was disconnected from the original campus located in Tempe. ASU East had its own selection committees, facilities departments and procurement processes. Although Jones Studio had to apply like everyone else for each of their five projects on that campus, the close relationship the designers developed with the staff made the process less stressful than a normal application presentation. Jones Studio would roll gently between projects in the dry and isolated fields of the east Valley.

Because Jones Studio was among the first designers to begin ASU's Williams transformation, they had the responsibility of recognizing what the campus could be. Polytechnic was part of incoming ASU President Michael Crow's goal to swell the school's capacity to educate at the scale of the country's population explosion. Mike Whalen had rejoined Jones Studio and worked with the team on the four Williams remodeling projects that included the renovation of Sutton and Wanner Halls, each three-story former barracks buildings. The primary goal was to open up the structures and breathe life into them for staff offices. The designers used camouflage colors inspired by the lining of Air Force combat jackets in green and blue, in honor of the buildings' previous inhabitants (see page 169).

The studio re-fashioned The Base Exchange's commissary and converted it into the Morrison School of Agribusiness, whose various functions had been dispersed across the campus. The renovation provided open, accessible space for groups to work and learn together, along with labs, equipment storage, outdoor staff offices and gardens for informal gatherings. Among its most unique features

Opposite page "Main street" hub in Morrison School of Agribusiness.

ARIZONA STATE UNIVERSITY
WELCOME
AGRIBUSINESS CENTER

EXIT

Opposite page Colored glazing in Morrison School of Agribusiness. **Above left** Existing holes filled with colored glazing at Sutton & Wanner renovation. **Above right** Interior volumes at Morrison School of Agribusiness. **Below** Renovated former Air Force barracks - Sutton Hall.

were a stock market trading lab, a golf swing simulator and an interior "main street" to provide students with a pleasant place to relax between classes. The building was retrofitted with modern technologies for water harvesting and electricity reduction. An expressive color palette was drawn from the desert flowers slowly reclaiming the flattened campus.

Jones Studio expanded the spaces of the "Bee Lab," or the Field Research facility for the School of Life Sciences researchers, adding habitat greenhouses for beehive management, growth and experimentation. The Bee Lab's focus on biodiversity deepened Jones Studio's commitment to help the landscape recover and thrive, giving them another tool to support the vibrant desert beneath them.

Arizona State University Polytechnic Interdisciplinary Science and Technology Building 3

Mesa, Arizona, 2005

Landscaping conditions at Williams were a challenge as Jones Studio considered how they would design the brand new Interdisciplinary Science and Technology Building 3 [ISTB3]. ISTB3 would attract world class scientists to the research opportunities in the departments of Applied Biological Sciences, the Arizona Biodesign Institute, the Applied Cognitive Sciences Institute and the Healthy Lifestyles Institute, but the site was sub-optimal for scientists with many competing opportunities in much prettier landscapes. Jones Studio applied their sharpened focus on the unique environment of the Sonoran Desert to inspire and enliven the work on this still-developing campus. ISTB3 illustrates Jones Studio's work to create a healthy building, tightly integrated with gardens to celebrate the site.

ISTB3 was Jones Studio's first collaboration with landscape architect Chris Winters, who applied his deep knowledge of the desert's sensitive systems to support Jones Studio's design work. The building's technical demands allowed Jones Studio, with laboratory consultant RFD of San Diego, to harness the condensate of the lab mechanical equipment and channel it to a 10,000-gallon tank that provided irrigation for the nature reintroduced to the barren site. Jones Studio also captured the clean wastewater byproduct of the hydrogen fuel cell next door, reducing that technology's environmental impact while bringing benefit to the grounds. ISTB3 used sustainably harvested wood, materials with recycled content and other contemporary products made of renewable Earth-friendly products to reduce toxins in the building.

To promote cross-disciplinary interaction between experts, and to focus attention away from the hardscape of the base, laboratories were organized around three interior garden oases and shared circulation paths that recall traditional Mexican courtyard architecture. Jones Studio wrapped the building around the gardens to fulfill the goals of the facility but also to concentrate the effect landscape has on the human mind and body. ISTB3 became one of the many successful

Above Persepctive drawing - Eddie Jones. **Opposite page** Precast concrete panels with "negative invert" panel of steel forms in foreground.

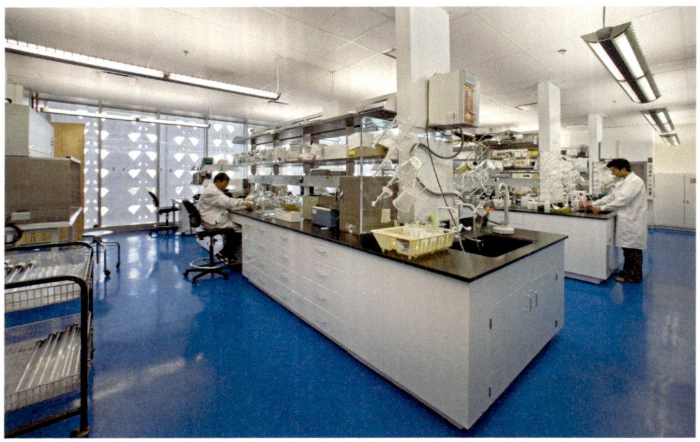

buildings Jones Studio has created where the landscape brings nature to occupants while highlighting the matchless glory of the Sonoran Desert.

Finally, Jones Studio created a flexible, modular interior laboratory zone to support evolving research needs of today and for the future. This planning strategy would allow research units to expand and contract as funding permitted, maximizing the University's investment and ability to serve changing scientific research, much of which is geared towards sustainable fuel sources and air and water remediation. Jones Studio was the perfect match to visualize this research path.

A special design element of ISTB3 was inspired by Frank Lloyd Wright's collection of buildings at Florida Southern College.[4] Into giant concrete building blocks Wright cast slots and squares then filled with different tones of cast glass. ISTB3 too used factory pre-cast concrete panels because of its lower cost and construction efficiency. Eddie designed a series of small inserts to perforate the walls so the gardens might visually "breathe" into the building. The forms were inspired by the ribcage of a classic Cosanti bell by Paolo Soleri but also resemble bones of an ancient dinosaur or the steel framework of a building where the concrete has melted away. As these panels wrapped the building perimeter, they would sometimes serve as a perforated site wall around gardens, while in other cases they would transition to become the building envelope itself, where the openings would be infilled with glass.

Jones Studio turned again to Connie and Jim Knight, the daring team at Glass Line who helped solve technical issues at the Halas House, the Cardinal's Corporate Headquarters and the Johnson Jones Residence, to pull off this design detail. Connie and Jim did what the glass contractor on the job would or could not: produce the hundreds of custom cut pieces of glass that would fill out the concrete panels' many small holes. At the building's main lobby, light and dark colored stained glass was inserted into the openings, making the interior surfaces shimmer with points of color. These pinpoints are activated by the sun, changing the atmosphere of the building throughout the day. In an act of public art, and to preserve these forms, Eddie wove them into a hanging sculpture, one that welcomes visitors to the building, the rest serving as wind chimes in the garden courtyard spaces. ISTB3 was the first building on ASU's Polytechnic Campus to achieve LEED Gold Certification, an important recognition of Jones Studio's commitment to aligning their buildings with nature's needs.

Opposite page top Main entry shade trellis. **Opposite bottom left** Interior lab with private garden beyond. **Opposite bottom right** Interior stained glass at precast openings. **Following spread left & right** Interior collaboration space and private courtyard.

174

Family Table #1

Above Perforated precast panel. **Below** Section through labs and courtyards - Eddie Jones. **Opposite page** Experimental research garden. **Following spread** Exterior of experimental research garden at dusk

University of Arizona College of Architecture, Planning and Landscape Architecture

Tucson, Arizona, 2007

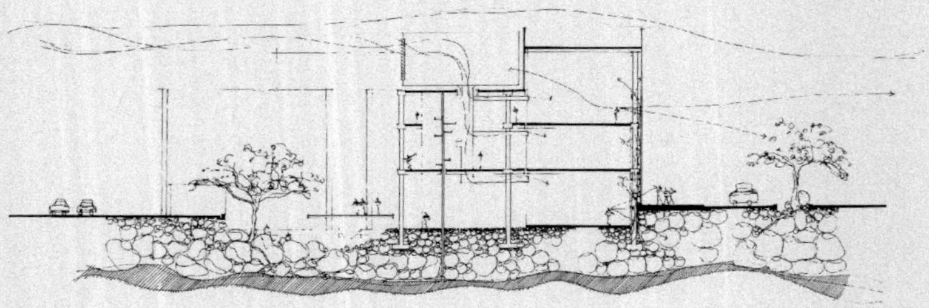

In 2004, the University of Arizona wanted to merge the programs for Architecture, Planning and Landscape Architecture into one shared college, with a much-needed renovation of the existing College of Architecture building for administrative offices. By cementing the strong connections between the three disciplines, the University's goal was to be a global leader in design and sustainability in arid and semi-arid regions.[5] In the 1980s, the best architecture schools increasingly acknowledged that including considerations of "topography, site, ecology, and geography" was key in designing buildings.[6] Merging the three schools allowed UofA to write the next chapter in educating creatives to design appropriately for our global desert zones.

The most important conceptual goal for the project was rooted in the pedagogical mission of the newly merged CAPLA: to create a facility that expressed the symbiotic relationship of the disciplines. The building's tectonic expression would be a teaching tool where all systems and structure were clearly legible, creating an aesthetic composition of its essential parts. Interweaving the building and the landscape would dissolve the lines where the building stops and a series of embracing gardens would begin.

> ...landscape has the capacity to critically engage the metaphysical and political programs that operate in each society, that landscape architecture is not simply a reflection of culture but more an active instrument in shaping of modern culture... Landscape reshapes the world not only because of its physical and experiential characteristics but also because of its eidetic content, its capacity to contain and express ideas and so engage the mind.
>
> James Corner[7]

Given its focus on landscape, CAPLA would also be Jones Studio's premier expression of the scarcity of water, and the power of harvesting rain and spent building water to halt resource loss. Working again with landscape architect Christy Ten Eyck underscored the design team's intention to sensitize

Above Conceptual section drawing - Maria Salenger. **Opposite page** North glazed curtain wall.

182 **Above** Abdu'l-Baha quote sandblasted into garden steps (young landscape). **Below** Section through studios, water harvesting tank and south living sun screen.

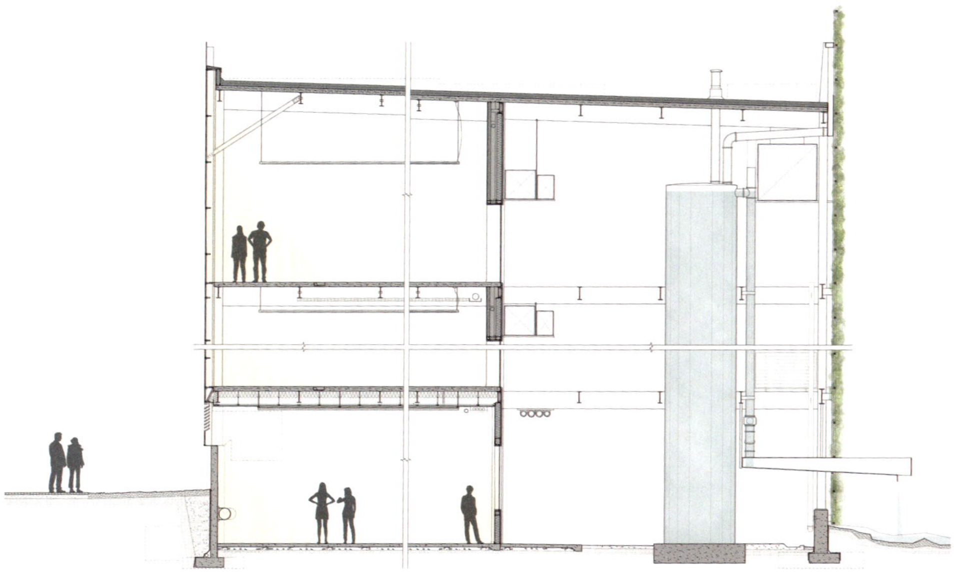

generations of practitioners to the importance of integrating sustainable values in their work. Nature would be celebrated as the third partner in bringing the building alive. The review team from the University, with their diverse backgrounds, interests and goals, immediately understood the conceptual poetics and pragmatic solutions of the team's design, giving them the green light to test their design integrating the building with its landscape.

In contrast to gardens encircled by the ISTB3 building, the CAPLA Underwood Garden instead wraps the building. The southern elevation of the 34,000-square-foot expansion is shaded by a living sun screen. This vertical garden of native perennial yellow orchid vines has slowly covered the façade and is irrigated by a water harvesting system that provides a set of emphatic visuals for the building. Condensate from the mechanical systems and captured rainwater are channeled into a visually expressed 11,600-gallon, three-story-tall fiberglass tank that is nestled in the structure's footprint, with a scupper diving board that allows water to spring into a sunken pool. The architecture captures the water to irrigate the garden and in turn, the garden grows to shade the building.

Beyond the south facing living wall, an outdoor landscape classroom demonstrates the five Arizona ecosystems and provides a cool microclimate respite from the intensive heat of an Arizona summer. Educational signage diagrams the systems and details the design's cumulative water savings. UofA's calculations reveal that CAPLA recycles 80-90% of its recaptured and recirculated water, providing inspiration for the rest of the university. This would be the first time Jones Studio would capture so much water and in such an elegant way.

Ten Eyck lined the stairs of the sunken demonstration garden with a quote by Abdu'l-Baha:

> At the gate of the garden some stand and look within, but do not care to enter. Others step inside, behold its beauty, but do not penetrate far. Still others encircle this garden inhaling the fragrance of the flowers, having enjoyed its full beauty, pass out again by the same gate. But there are always some who enter and, becoming intoxicated with the splendor of what they behold, remain for life to tend the garden.[8]

In Abdu'l-Baha's writing, the garden is a metaphor for life; he exhorts us to enter its swim, whether through our profession or through our personal inspirations. In his writing about "radical gardens," George McKay explores how gardens are "mundane and magic, public and private." They are not just about a garden's users but about the public sphere.[9] Jones Studio has demonstrated how the teaching at CAPLA can spread far beyond campus and into the swim of life. Generations of students will take this metaphor with them as they fulfill the school's promise.

The north half of the 34,000-square-foot expansion is defined by transparency which connects the studio spaces to the distant Catalina Mountains. This three-story wall of almost interruption-free glazing along Speedway Boulevard puts the building on display—it is the University's calling card to the community. Daylighting pushes and pulls light into every crevice of the building, allowing students and faculty to live naturally through the day's cycles while learning how to amplify those cycles through their

own work. This celebration of Arizona's most abundant natural resource was a constant source of joy to Rob Miller, CAPLA's Director of Architecture from 2010-2022. Rob often recruited Brian, Maria, Eddie and other Jones Studio family members to teach at CAPLA and share in the experience of growth and change embodied in the project's design.

The presence of nature as partner, as buffer, as client for the building forces us to see the important inter-relationship between inside and out. CAPLA's new building will continue to change over time, and its uses will too since demands of the field will force adaptations unimagined today. CAPLA set the tone for Jones Studio's work with water consciousness and planting buildings in a garden. The building influences the pedagogy—its spaces, gardens and balconies feed a respect for expertise in each field and showcase the power of design. Together these capture the different time and space scales of human industry.

Building and landscape are inextricably intertwined, and capture James Corner's hopes that landscape becomes a more visible partner in the creation of culture. In discussing CAPLA Brian notes that time has become a design element for his work, and the connection with gardens its most obvious expression. The desert's cycles run at a different speed from our frenzied post-industrial world; it's no wonder gardens are an effective way to focus our attention. We rarely think of time as an element in architecture, although it takes time to design, to build, to use, to appreciate and to neglect.

There are lovely echoes between ISTB3 and CAPLA: ISTB3 is a building wrapped around interior gardens, while CAPLA is a garden wrapped around a building. One set of gardens is private, the other public, both designed to facilitate connection and creation. Jones Studio's work on these dissimilar building types with overlapping timelines allowed for cross-pollination, a dynamic percolation of design ideas with radically different outcomes. Nature constantly asserts herself as a key building block in Jones Studio's work, becoming a constant across the firm's *oeuvre*.

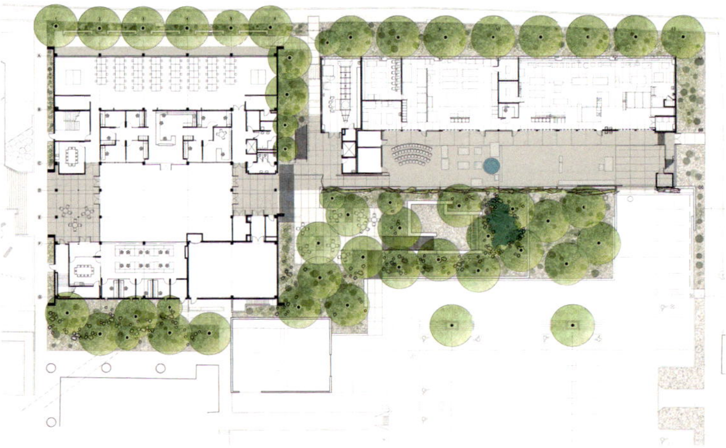

Opposite page Underwood Garden plaza. **Above** Underwood Garden site plan.

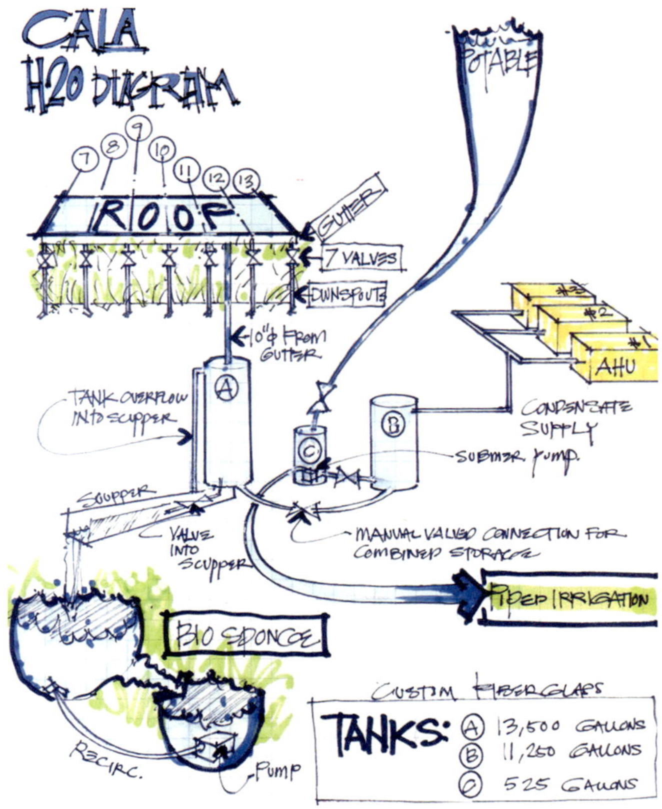

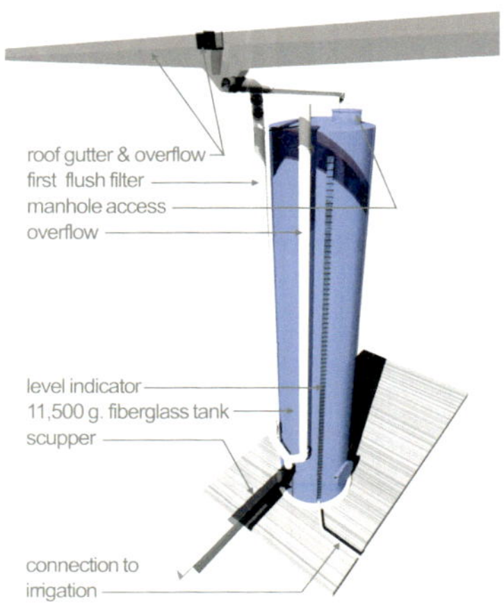

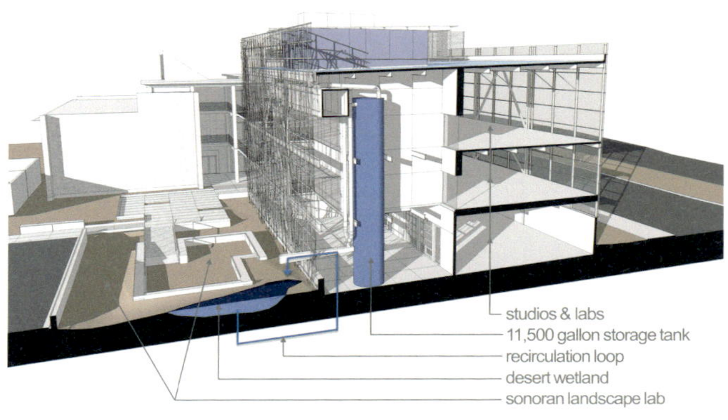

Above & opposite page Water harvesting integration - sketches, diagrams, under construction and complete.

Opposite page Architecture and landscape blurring together. **Above** "After" view of garden with 5 years of growth. **Right** "Before" view - same as above from former parking lot. **Following page** Mature garden view from above tree canopy.

Left above to bottom Studio; Interior and exterior shop. **Opposite page** Breakout room. **Following spread** North elevation with studios at night.

Home Is Where the Art Lives

> ...art remains a means for paying attention—to ourselves, to the world around us, and to the relation between the two.
>
> Barry Schwabsky[10]

Private homes are often where architects express their most refined aesthetic ideas. In the large body of private spaces produced by the team at Jones Studio, whether for themselves or for clients, the designers infuse living volumes with their aesthetic sensitivities that create moments of spiritual uplift and conceptual clarity.

These aesthetic sensitivities are heightened when the demands for a private home are also driven by the art objects of a world class private collection. In two private "galleries" that also function as homes, Eddie was given a passport to respond to the works chosen carefully, and delicately, over decades by the collectors. In these homes Eddie established the container's spatial vocabularies to reflect the diversity of artistic expression of the contained, creating an embodied experience for residents and visitors alike.

Opposite page Gallery - Logan Residence.

HI-STANDARD

House of Five Dreams
Paradise Valley, Arizona, 2004

After Eddie left his full-time job in 1979, he jumped at the chance to teach architecture at ASU for a regular paycheck. He bonded with one of his colleagues, designer Mitzi Vernon, the two dissecting the machinations of the University together. One day, decades after he taught with Mitzi, Eddie got a call from Maxine Linde who said her friend Mitzi had recommended Eddie for a new home—would he be interested in chatting? Maxine and Ron Linde, originally from Chicago, assembled their major art collection primarily with objects found underground; they purchased their first Pre-Columbian object in 1966. The Lindes wanted a home that would showcase and honor their collection, relate to the Sonoran Desert and inspire their living in a climate radically different from their mid-west roots.

As with every project, Eddie got to know the Lindes and their desert parcel with its mix of spindly forms emerging from rock and dirt. An Army Corps of Engineers flood control drainage canal angled across the north side of the property. This slice of modern water management led Eddie to design a parallelogram shaped home, its water harvesting strategies feeding the gridded desert garden layout interspersed with art works by Ron.

Given the origins of the collection, Eddie looked for a poetic interpretation that would link past to present. Many cultures describe three realms in their ancient origin stories that acknowledge the land, the sky and the Earth below. These realms ground us and inspire our ancient impulse for myth-making and art making to interpret these worlds. Eddie used this framework to organize the spaces of the House of Five Dreams.

The first floor is anchored to the ground using rusted steel, soil and glass, all materials pulled from the Earth. The fragile glass is countered by the muscularity of giant steel trusses marching across the site like mining equipment, organizing and segregating the public and private activities of the

Above Elevation study - Brian Farling. **Opposite page** Upper level "sky" residence over rammed earth walls.

Above Upper level shade screen with operable "petals". **Opposite page** Concept and plan sketches - Eddie Jones. **Following spread** Stacked glass wall at upper level and at entry.

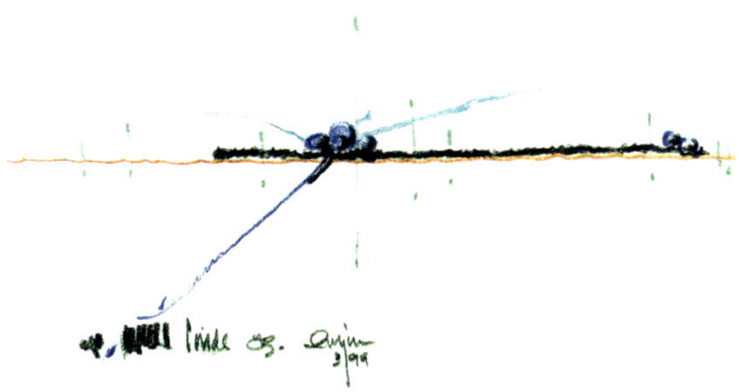

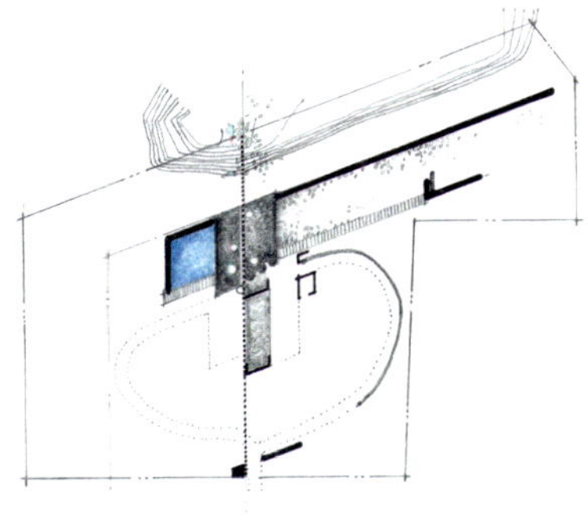

family. The desert's heartbeat can be traced in the banding of the rammed earth walls, created from excavations on site and colored by the region's geological history.

Hovering above the mineral rich ground floor is the residence of terrazzo, stainless steel and other transparent or reflective materials. Glass walls open to views of mountains, the city and sky. There are few interior walls; gauzy curtains create or make spaces disappear. Portions of the residence floor are glass, letting light seep back to the ground. Connecting the land to the upper-level residence is a unique sculptural wall composed of one-quarter-inch thick pieces of stacked plate glass, each individually cut to a curve and hand placed. To achieve this unprecedented element, the team turned to Andy Byrnes of Construction Zone, general contractor and partner for the project. Andy suggested hiring two bicycle mechanic friends, patient, detail-oriented craftspeople and experts at precision assembly and alignment of unique parts. The mechanics were willing to experiment with the unorthodox construction of a 72-foot-long, 25-foot-tall, stacked glass wall. A glass fabrication shop (see page 204) was set up in the single car garage, and over the course of nearly a year, the tall and precious wall took shape, refracting light into the home.

Below-ground is the 300-foot-long by 65-foot-wide, 20,000-square-foot rammed earth gallery. Four-foot-thick dirt walls mirror those above-ground, connecting again the ancient realms of above and below. A skylight runs east-west for the length of the space, making the cool space glow. Precious objects are encased in softly lit vitrines that shine in the low light levels. This underground sanctuary returns the excavated objects back to their original location below the horizon.

The Linde residence is a soaring spiritual space, a dream pillow that rests on negative spaces of the first floor, a cloud that hesitates to touch the ground. The home's floating residence is anchored by its ancient treasures. Eddie created a portal connecting the rich human creations of the past to human lives of the present. The House of Five Dreams—the reference for this name is a secret kept by the Lindes—changed the trajectory of Jones Studio. It exemplified a sensitive synthesis of the material world and the ideals of human life, combining the refinement and restraint of Modernism's most precious spaces with the *sui generis* originality of place.

Family Table #1

Family Table #1

Opposite page Glass cutting and stacking workshop on site. **Above** Upper level residence.

Top left 70' long steel beam installation. **Top right** Lower level conference space with Albert Paley gate sculpture. **Above left** Lower level library. **Above right** Lower level gallery. **Opposite page** Lower level sculpture pedestal at gallery termination with glowing red exit stair. **Following spread** Main entry and single car garage at dusk.

Logan House

Scottsdale, Arizona, 2008

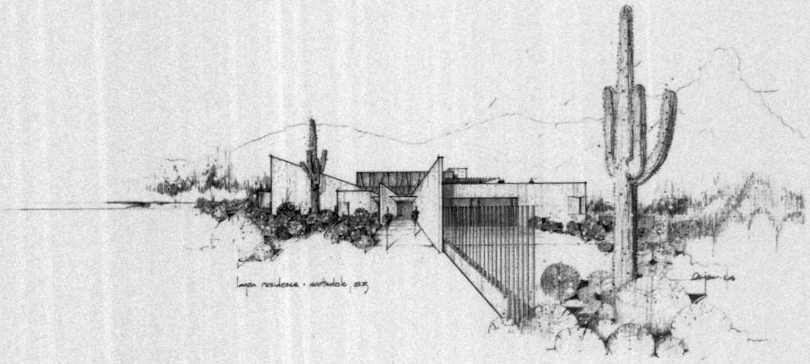

Jones Studio's second private "museum" was for two of America's most significant collectors of contemporary global art whose collected treasures have been celebrated in dozens of museum exhibitions over the past 20 years. The Logans are very public in their support for artists; their Scottsdale home would be a private retreat for reflection and enjoyment of their art.

Jones Studio's close working relationship with Construction Zone assured the Logans that there would be cohesion between the designers and the construction team. The Logans' home would be a beautiful sculpture providing all the environmentally sound conditions needed for the protection of the works. The collector's sophisticated appreciation of the arts matched Jones Studio's culturally and intellectually expansive practice, allowing the building to shine.

The Logan house is screened from the street, long and low like the desert, spilling across the landscape like an ancient structure. The pebbly mountain above echoes the dense tumble of textures and shades in the landscaping. Every saguaro was saved, every boulder and contour preserved. Native plants and the creatures that live in and around them are fed by hidden water retention systems. Nestled amongst the diverse life-forms of the Sonoran Desert are works from the collection, highlighting the questions and assertions posed by the best art of our time.

The building's materials pick out and enhance the grain of the land and include natural cast-in-place concrete, rusted steel, copper and glass. Two stylized sets of eyes etched into the concrete walls, suggesting Vicki and Kent's different ways of looking at art, identify where the art resides. Controlling light and providing flexibility in how the works could hang drove the design, with living spaces radiating out from the galleries so that the connection between art and life is constant.

Above Early concept perspective drawing - Eddie Jones. **Opposite page** Cast concrete wall with custom sandblasted "eye" patterns and perforations.

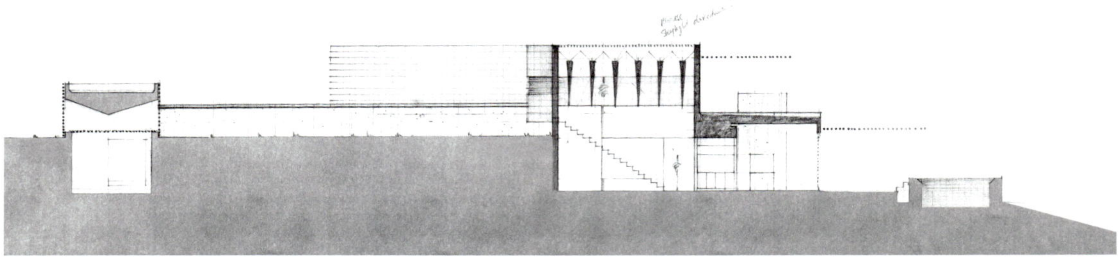

Opposite top Daylit entry gallery. **Opposite bottom** Section drawing - Eddie Jones. **Above left** Vicki's eye pattern drawing. **Above right** Sandblasted and copper lined perforation. **Below** Interior galleries.

In each art space Eddie used a unique strategy to address light, with galleries that bounce, concentrate, diffuse or disperse light. One large gallery space was designed specifically for an enormous painting by internationally renowned Japanese artist Takashi Murakami; other gallery spaces allowed diverse works from around the globe to commingle in aesthetic conversation. In every pocket of light and square of concrete the Logan home is alive with opportunities for intellectual stimulation.

Eddie wanted to transport to the desert the iconic natural phenomenon of quaking leaves experienced in his trips to Aspen, Colorado to visit the Logans. Jones Studio's team cut and hung thousands of brass plates from the Logans' outdoor shade structures. Golfers on the golf course below the home found the gentle hush distracting; half of the installation now hides the HVAC systems in Jones Studio's conference room, an elegant memory from an arts-focused project.

Above Daylit entry gallery. **Opposite page** Skylights above gallery. **Following spread** Logan house with Pinnacle Peak Park in background.

Opposite page & above Shade trellis of brass 'leaves" at entry. **Below** Copper cladding at south elevation. **Following spread** At dusk, architecture unified with topography and landscape.

Art as a Challenge to Public Space

Mid-century America saw a rush of interest in public art, spurred by a flush post-war economy and creative leadership in the White House that launched public art programs through the National Endowment for the Arts. The non-profit impulse to bring art to the streets, and artists' interest in moving out of the white cube of museums and galleries to bring their art to the public, inspired public art programs in municipalities across the country. These programs generally specified that 1% of any capital project was to be set aside for art, so that between the 1960s and 1980s, large sculptures, much of it minimal geometric abstraction, were placed (or plopped) outside. But the problem with much public art of this genre was, at its most basic, its job was to distinguish one generic International Style building from another, not to provoke any aesthetic, intellectual or emotional response to our place and time.

Today, most public art programs require some response to place, particularly in an era when a new generation of socially active artists, and within a more diverse and changing America, are demanding a reexamination of what goes into the public realm. Our contemporary critique of monuments has forced residents, politicians and self-interest groups to understand the impacts of their most-cherished monuments. New forms of monumentation honoring those not celebrated in history books become a flashpoint for memories erased, forcing an evaluation and, possibly, reconciliation to the histories embodied in public art. Americans are evaluating who we memorialize in our landscapes, and why, yielding great new opportunities for public connection and communication.

Public art has become a battlefield for conflicting social intentions and the narrative of place. Citizen disenfranchisement is often acted out on public art since there are so few mechanisms for citizen input on the life-altering and mostly opaque decisions made for us daily. Public art's public is everyone and no one, which challenges artists and designers to consider the longer timeframe of the human condition. Jones Studio has stepped into this fray to expand the ways in which they engage with our changing social landscape.

Opposite page Bus stop shelter as public art - *Sew-cial.*

Moving Memories, Arizona 9/11 Memorial

Phoenix, Arizona, 2006

9:58
WTC SOUTH TOWER
COLLAPSED

PEOPLE STOOD
IN LINE FOR HOURS
TO GIVE BLOOD

HAD TO BE WITH ANOTHER,
NEVER ALONE

FEELING OF
INVINCIBILITY LOST

THOUSANDS EVACUATED
FROM PENTAGON

MUST BOMB BACK

PEOPLE OF YUMA PLANTED TREES

10 28 01
WTC SITE DIGGING STOPPED
FIRST TIME FOR MEMORIAL SERVICE

Jones Studio worked with coLAB, the public art collaborative founded by Maria and Matt Salenger, on a proposal for the Arizona 9/11 memorial because of their overlapping questions about the United States' foreign policy. The team was eager to site a work at the State Capitol grounds, the heart of Arizona's political and financial power, where the memorial would have lasting allegorical significance.

The 9/11 attacks meant different things to different communities, but like the Kennedy assassination, anyone alive on September 11, 2001, remembers where they were when airplanes struck. As the attacks unfolded in Shanksville, Pennsylvania, the Pentagon in Washington, D.C., and the World Trade Center, New York, the reality of the country's geopolitical policies came home. Finding the right expression and scale to represent the era-defining moment would be fraught with many pitfalls. Jones Studio and coLAB's goals would be to hold close the memories of those killed outside of a war zone while finding a way to speak to the cultural clash that triggered it, and to honor those Arizonans, near and far, whose lives were changed as a result.

In preparation for the call-for-artists, the 9/11 Memorial Commission and historian Nancy Dallett collected hundreds of pages of research documents along with interviews with citizens from Arizona affected by the 9/11 tragedies. After the team received the commission, and upon reviewing the research documents, they knew this material would be at the heart of the memorial.

> ...monuments are "material representations of idealized history", memorials are "expression of local, more complicated histories..."
>
> Patricia E. Rubertone[11]

Above Early layout of collected phrases. **Opposite page** Concrete, steel, stainless steel and sunlight.

Above & opposite page Memorial in the park.

With prohibitions against moving parts that would require maintenance, the team immediately hit on the idea of utilizing the sun because of its dependability. After a weekend experimenting with cardboard stencils, Eddie proposed using the sun to illuminate 54 quotes and two timelines cut into a giant flat metal circle. A strategically placed opening illuminates a salvaged piece of the World Trade Center at noon every September 11. The giant sun dial was then bermed to create a contemplative space. The memorial would have no beginning or end, suggesting the circle of life that binds us.

The designers engaged poet Ron Phares to write the dedication "Memory is the sun that lights the material of history," which suggests how 9/11 will fade in and out of our memory over time. A steel plate with bent bolts from the World Trade Center, rubble from the Pentagon and dirt from Shanksville tie together the three sites of tragedy. The combination would communicate the spectrum of emotions in response to the empire-shaking tragedies.

Just as the memorial was completed, it was caught up in the brittle politics of an Arizona election cycle. Jones Studio and coLAB posed questions about America's connection to its citizens and the rest of the world while some of Arizona's politicians exploited this collective, mournful memorial to further their own agendas. The design team was raked over the coals by the *Arizona Republic* newspaper for about a year, facing challenges over which phrases they used, how they named political leaders and questions about whose side were they on anyway. Their final fee payment was held until the designers replaced one stainless steel panel with new text cut into it.

Because of the political flak, the team designed and installed a plaque that explained how they developed the ideas and what the timelines represent. This helped guide the folks wanting a more literal expression of the 9/11 events while supplementing the monument's elegiac consideration of trauma and loss. The flying circle metaphorically looks up towards a better future—leaving which version of history would be better up to the visitor to define.

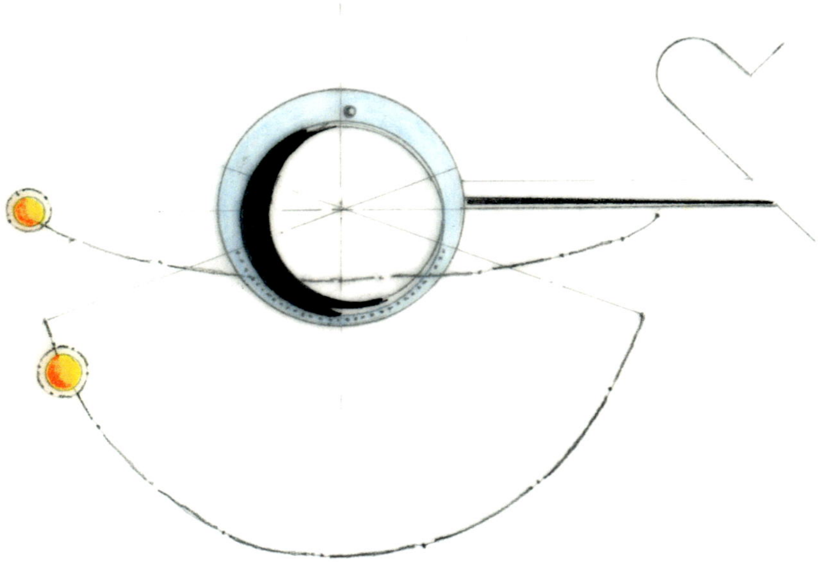

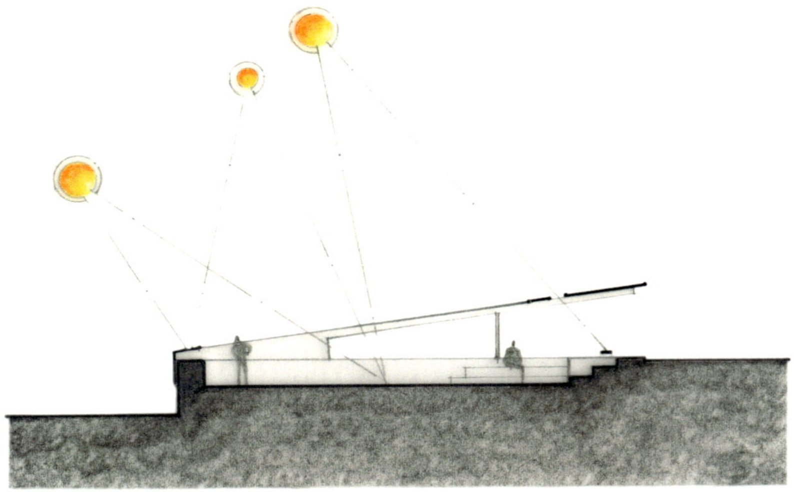

Above Plan and section drawing - Eddie Jones. **Opposite page** Quotes of light set in motion by the sun.

8:30PM
PSYCHOLOGIST
NYC NORTH TOWER
COLLAPSES
COUNSELED NYC
WORKERS

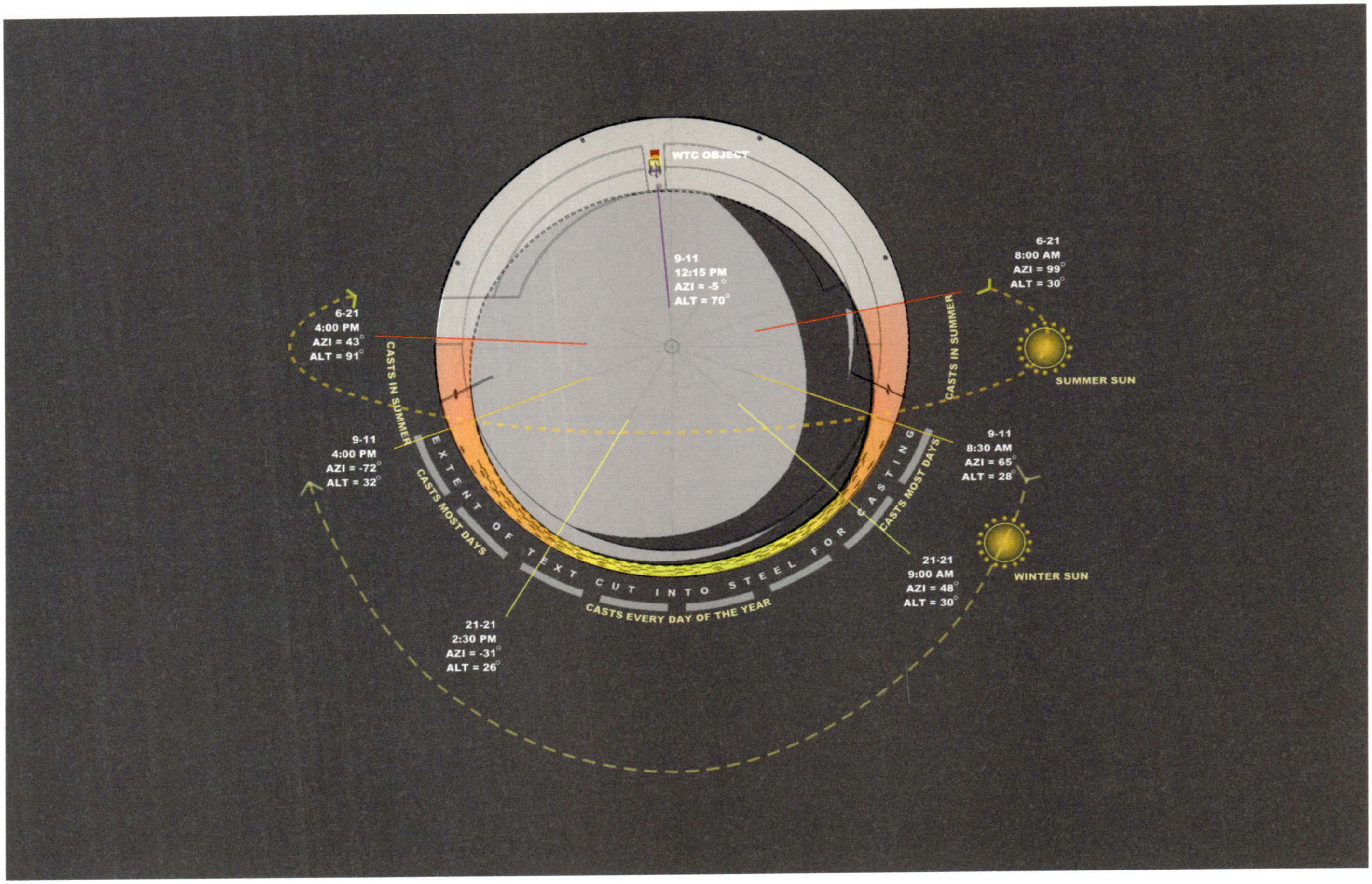
WTC OBJECT
9-11
12:15 PM
AZI = -5°
ALT = 70°
6-21
8:00 AM
AZI = 99°
ALT = 30°
6-21
4:00 PM
AZI = 43°
ALT = 91°
CASTS IN SUMMER
CASTS IN SUMMER
SUMMER SUN
9-11
4:00 PM
AZI = -72°
ALT = 32°
9-11
8:30 AM
AZI = 65°
ALT = 28°
EXTENT OF TEXT CUT INTO STEEL FOR CASTING
CASTS MOST DAYS
CASTS MOST DAYS
WINTER SUN
21-21
9:00 AM
AZI = 48°
ALT = 30°
CASTS EVERY DAY OF THE YEAR
21-21
2:30 PM
AZI = -31°
ALT = 26°

BATTLES OF TERRORISM
WITH MORE BATTLES"

Opposite top Sunlight study drawing. **Opposite bottom** Shadow and light drifting with the sun. **Above** Layers of solid material anc light. **Following spread** A circle of light every September 11th at noon.

Sew-cial, Public Bus Shelters
Phoenix, Arizona, 2019

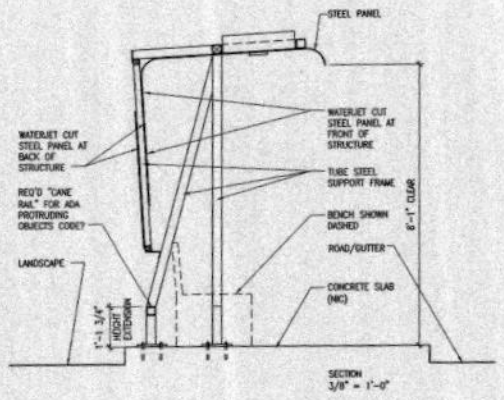
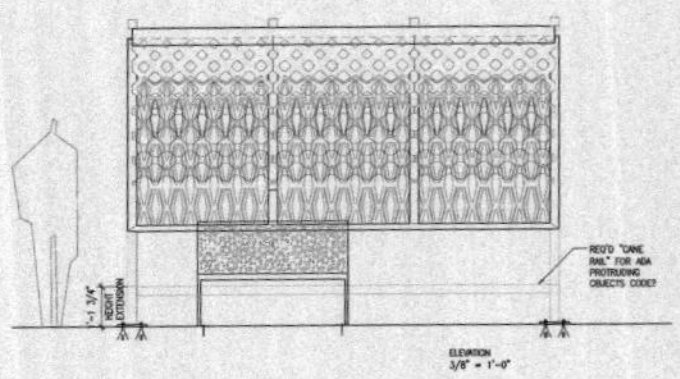
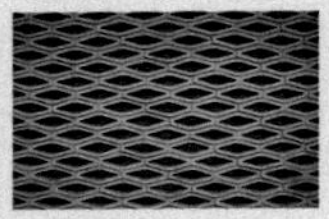
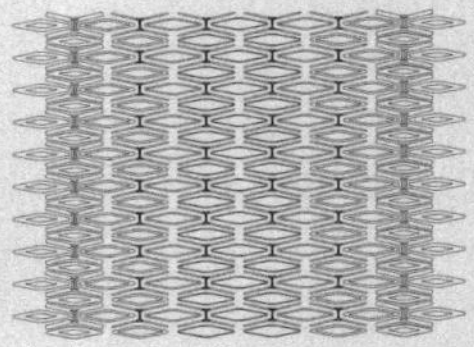

Many cities around the globe embrace how public art creates identity and thus pride of place. Several departments in the City of Phoenix collaborated to use public art in the "Fight Back" grant program to help local businesses mitigate the rising street violence at 16th Street and Bethany Home Road, a largely suburban, residential area north of the City's central core. Like many suburban areas, the streets are so wide that drivers move too fast, destroying any sense of neighborhood and with that, a sense of ownership and belonging.

The idea that suburbs are safer than cities is untrue in many ways—public space is often structured by conflict.[12] Jane Jacobs talked about how active sidewalks along slower streets are safer because of eyes—the eyes of shopkeepers, residents, shoppers, visitors—that provide passive security for everyone whether friends or not.[13] America's suburbs were touted as superior to the "dirty" city, although with 70 years of suburban sprawl under our belt, many planners and historians have understood that the reality of the suburbs is more complicated than a homebuilder's aspirational brochure. Maria shaped Jones Studio's public art proposal—two eye-catching public transit bus shelters—with the goals of providing shade for bus riders, putting eyes on the street and creating a visual identity for the area by honoring its design pioneers.

Maria looked to the mid-century experimentation of architects like Ralph Haver, whose nearby subdivision features decorative use of workaday masonry block, as well as fashion and graphic designs of the era, for the shelter's aesthetic.[14] She developed overlapping and contrasting shapes and forms as calm bookends for the frenetic intersection. On the northwest corner, an elegant gold colored powder-coated bench with cutouts evokes mid-century modern forms inspired by global designs. Two bright blue screens layer behind the benches, their circles and lozenges overlapping to highlight the decorative masonry wall in the parking lot behind them. The southeast corner's blue canopy screen has quatrefoils and elongated pastilles. The varied thickness of lines create shifting

Above Detail drawings and pattern studies - Maria Salenger. **Opposite page** Layers of laser cut steel patterns.

Family Table #1

Opposite page Steel benches and shade. **Above** In context along street. **Below** Cast shadows **Following spread** Bus pick up.

patterns that screen another lurking parking lot. Like the 9/11 Memorial, the sun's movement pushes the designs across the concrete and asphalt lips of the shelters, changing how residents and passersby see the glittering street furniture left outside for everyone to enjoy.

Despite the modest scale of this intimate gift to residents, the project won several design awards for pushing the streetscape beyond its boring blanket of beige. The shelters are a reminder that art can be created on any budget, not just for high end clients. The benches stitch together hidden and overwhelming forces at work at this public corner.

lash
Acne Laser
Laser Skin Tighten
Gift

Family Table #2

Before and After Mariposa

Jones Studio's inventive risk-taking is plaited through each public, private and corporate space, which often means the actual risks are buried inside bricks and concrete. Exposing their risk-taking in a museum exhibition, or through the audacity of applying for a huge project that would explode the firm's knowledge-base and force them to scramble to reconstruct their team, demonstrates the firm's willingness to play in public. Any architecture firm's play in fact requires very difficult work. Why would a thirty-year-old firm risk up-front failure in a gallery space, or waste time applying for a project that is so out-of-scale for their experience but follows their mantra of "we've never done that before" that has brought Jones Studio success?

As the firm chased unpredictable opportunities for new building typologies and braved the chance to promote their field inside a museum, their intuitive risk also gave them a buffer that saved them from the fate of many firms crushed by the global 2008 economic collapse. The designers continued their mindful work solving problems but also throwing lifelines to colleagues so that they all might survive to compete another day.

For many, this period of growth could have rendered the firm more conservative and less willing to let risk reign. Jones Studio, by contrast, continued to push forth into new territories, finding clients on their own path of discovery. This era in Jones Studio's life is almost as dramatic as Eddie putting out his shingle and proved that Jones Studio's intellectual curiosity and flexibility was central to their enduring success.

Opposite page View from Mexico of the completed Mariposa Land Port of Entry.

CNS
POLICÍA
FEDERAL
FEDERAL

Scottsdale Museum of Contemporary Art, *southwestNET: Jones Studio, Inc.*

May 27-September 24, Scottsdale, Arizona, 2006

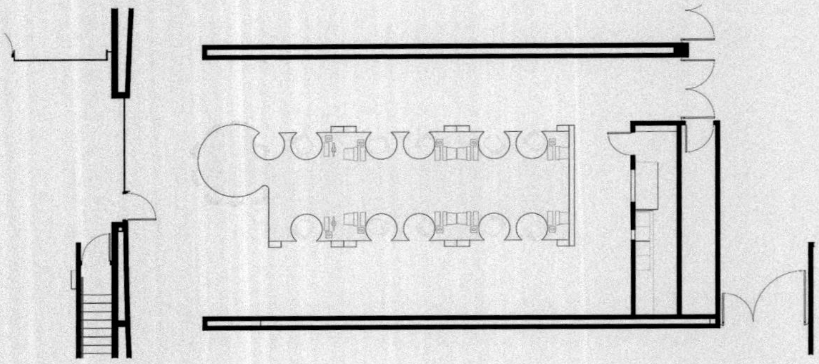

In *PHX: Phoenix 21st Century City*, it was clear that the most mature cultural community in the area was its architects.[1] Hosting architecture in a contemporary museum was important in a city like Phoenix where architecture and urban development are central to "social life and cultural policy," and including architects in a larger cultural mix was an opportunity to promote how creativity suffuses every aspect of our daily lives.[2] Under the leadership of Susan Krane, the Scottsdale Museum of Contemporary Art [SMoCA] added a focus on architecture to its diverse and international programming. This included hosting the traveling Samuel Mockbee exhibition from the Birmingham Museum of Art as well as the touring exhibition *Strangely Familiar: Design and Everyday Life* from the Walker Art Center in Minneapolis. The curatorial and education teams commissioned architects Teresa Rosano and Luis Ibarra to provide a frame for an exhibition featuring photographs taken by immigrants crossing from Mexico into the United States alongside pictures taken by members of the Minute Men, a group of volunteers aligned along the border to report illegal crossings to the U.S. Border Patrol. Cameras were distributed by the activist group who gave gas cards to whomever returned the cameras with images. SMoCA provided a public outlet for some of the most contentious relationships in the region, and a platform for opposing sides to understand the humanity of one another. The architecture community showed up for these programs, creating a dynamic circle of action and interaction that benefitted both museum and the cultural community.

Above Family Table #2 plan drawing. **Opposite page** SMOCA gallery studio.

INNER LIGHT

Family Table #2

When Susan Krane and I approached Jones Studio to feature their work in an exhibition it was because of the firm's beautiful body of public and private buildings, their growing national and international reputation and a rock-solid commitment to experimentation. At the end of our discussion and invitation I told Eddie and Matt that I thought most architecture shows were rather staid: how were they going to create a show that evoked the physical and emotional spaces of real buildings while matching the dynamism of the exhibitions the museum typically organized? We all left the meeting excited about what this group of thinkers might come up with.

In the late 1990s Jones Studio had come in second to Will Bruder to carve SMoCA from a former movie theater, so Eddie was thrilled with the invitation—but he was cautious. Exhibitions take a lot of time to put together, with little ability to measure results relative to effort. He was reluctant to commit to a process only to dismantle the project after four months. At a regular Jones Studio happy hour, Eddie told the family about the opportunity. He expressed his doubts, but after some excited conversation and a bit of beer to lubricate the discussion, Jacob suggested that they, the entire family, *be* the exhibit. Laughter erupted, but as the late afternoon turned to evening, they found themselves still thinking about how innovative a working architecture firm would be inside a museum. The chance to communicate with visitors, see reactions and receive real-time feedback was seductive. The possibilities outweighed the risk. Eddie assumed SMoCA would never go for it, but the Director and I loved the boldness of the Jones Studio proposal. Now for the hard part: making it work.

Jones Studio had a lot to consider. They would need a redesigned and compacted Family Table #2 to fit into the gallery, upgraded computers to protect client data and to sublet their office space while keeping clients happy and projects on schedule. Alongside the living exhibit of architects, the walls were covered with a select number of milestone projects, while suspended above were recycled construction drawings fluttering below the ceiling. SMoCA had to modify its security arrangements to give the team access for their normal irregular working hours.

The air in the gallery during the Jones Studio show was electric with purposeful activity that included several Jones Studio and SMoCA staff couplings. Introverts transformed into extroverts. Client and construction team meetings put the firm's business in full frontal view. Jones Studio's productivity suffered due to constant interruptions, so temporary "Do Not Disturb" (see page 248) signs were installed. Neal's least favorite part of the project was the weekend hours—at one point he was in the gallery 22 days in a row. Eddie and Neal's favorite part was inspiring children with a nascent interest in architecture. Jacob still runs into people fifteen years later who saw him in the exhibition. Brian was deep into the CAPLA project and largely in Tucson

Opposite page Jones Studio in SMoCA gallery.

southwestNET: Jones Studio, Inc.

southwestNET: Jones Studio, Inc.
Jones Studio
staff has
temporarily
stepped out
of their minds

ARTS & ENTERTAINMENT

BEST BETS

MUSIC

Raun Alosi Band concert Sunday at Railroad Park

The Raun Alosi Band performs from 7:30 to 9 p.m. Sunday at McCormick-Stillman Railroad Park, Indian Bend and Scottsdale roads.

Train and carousel rides are available for $1 each.

Concerts continue Sundays through July 16.

THEATER

'Ruthless!' run extended at Desert Stages Theatre

Scottsdale Desert Stages Actor's Cafe has extended *Ruthless! the Musical!* at Scottsdale Desert Stages Theatre, 4720 N. Scottsdale Road.

The musical spoof is about an 8-year-old girl whose parents murder the leading lady in the school production of *Pippi Longstocking* so their daughter can get the role.

The show runs through June 24.

Information: (480) 483-1664.

'George M!' continues at Fountain Hills Theater

George M! continues at Fountain Hills Community Theater, 11445 N. Saguaro Boulevard, Fountain Hills.

The tap-dancing musical extravaganza celebrates the life and loves of America's first musical-comedy man, George M. Cohan, the Yankee Doodle Dandy.

Songs performed include *Over There, You're a Grand Old Flag* and *Give My Regards to*

Architects move office into SMoCA

Business becomes part of art exhibit

DOLORES TROPIANO

SCOTTSDALE

The Scottsdale Museum of Contemporary Art has had its share of architecture and design exhibitions.

But for the first time in the history of the museum, an actual architectural firm has become an exhibition.

Last week, Jones Studio Inc. moved its entire Phoenix office into a gallery at the museum where it will remain for three months. The exhibition, *southwestNET: Jones Studio Inc.*, opened Saturday.

"We love it. We're having a ball," said Neal Jones, who with his brother, Eddie, run the award-winning architecture firm. "It's new and exciting and great to be around all of this art and creativity."

The idea behind the exhibition is to demystify the architect and make him more accessible to the general public.

The exhibition has three main components: the day-to-day operation of the studio, a changing display of working drawings for projects and a mini-survey of pivotal projects.

Jones, a disarming Oklahoma-native with a quick laugh, is the perfect person to facilitate this goal.

"People should not be shy," said Susan Krane, director of the museum. "We are all counting on the public to speak up and ask questions. It's not just architecture on view at the zoo. We re-

southwestNET: Jones Studio Inc.

Where: Scottsdale Museum of Contemporary Art, Second Street and Drinkwater Boulevard.

When: Through Sept. 24.

Architect Neal Jones of Jones Studio Inc. works at the Scottsdale Museum of Contemporary Art.

The small Phoenix firm is internationally known for creating everything from sports stadiums to performing arts centers to Arizona State University buildings and residences in Tempe. It has work everywhere from Phoenix to Texas, Minnesota, Rhode Island

lct of people."

While on view, the firm will be working on three projects: the Arizona 9/11 Memorial in downtown Phoenix, a police station and a private residence that will incorporate an art gallery for prominent Scottsdale private collec-

adise Valley.

It is not uncommon for Jones Studio Inc. to design a door in the shape of a square.

The museum exhibition will present some challenges for the Jones Studio staff, who will work seven days a week,

Kimberly Linderman, 13 (left), and Elizabeth Bracamontes, 14, watch Brian Farling carry on with the day-to-day workings of an architectural firm. Jones Studio moved its business into SmoCA for the summer. It's an interactive exhibition.

Photos by Deanna Dent/The Republic

Opposite page Life in the SMoCA gallery. **Above** Newspaper article. **Following spread** Jones Studio and Family Table #2.

overseeing one of the firm's signature projects, but together, they all agree that SMoCA helped Jones Studio proselytize about their stimulating and city-shaping field. Neal and Jacob don't think they got any new work because of the show, but they agree they would do it again.

The show's impact on SMoCA? When contacted a few years ago, SMoCA staff reported that *southwestNET: Jones Studio Inc.* recorded one of SMoCA's highest attendance records to date. While smaller alternative spaces or galleries host durational projects by performance artists, no museum had hosted a professional firm inside their galleries. The exhibition was not an abstract gesture; it was a real-world opportunity to expose the work of architects to the public, and to support one of the region's most original team of designers.

STAPLES
multiuse

Landing on the Border

While Jones Studio was living at SMoCA, Eddie asked Maria to track government infrastructure RFQs based on a suggestion from John Meunier, former Dean of Architecture at ASU. Arriving as if on cue, the Mariposa Land Port of Entry [MLPOE] project description came in the mail. Maria approached the team about chasing it during an afternoon team meeting at Family Table #2. Neal responded they didn't have any experience in that type of huge government project and assumed they would not have a chance. But they *did* have some experience and thus a chance.

In 2004, Eddie was invited to be a national peer reviewer for the Design Excellence program to help the U.S. General Services Administration [GSA] evaluate government building projects across the country. The GSA's "Guiding Principles for Federal Architecture" were written by Daniel Patrick Moynihan, then assistant to the Secretary of Labor, in 1962 during the Kennedy Administration, to put arts production on equal footing with economic development.[3] These guidelines emphasize both the inspirational—"visual testimony to the dignity, enterprise, vigor and stability of the American Government"—and the functional—"commissioning the finest contemporary architectural work in the country." Other elements to be considered included regional architectural traditions, sound construction values, dependable materials and building methods, economical construction, accessibility for the handicapped, sustainability and efficient energy performance, efficient and functional operations and effective building maintenance.

The Design Excellence program, launched in 1994, signaled the government's renewed interest in expressing "positive perceptions Americans have of their government" and "superior workplaces that enhance the nation's communities" that result from good design. These guiding principles highlight the best values of contemporary architecture. Eddie observed first-hand how the GSA held high standards for buildings while allowing professionals to design for place, values held by Jones Studio. With Eddie's experience as a Design Excellence peer reviewer, the studio thought the risk of submitting qualifications would be low, so they took the time to put together a proposal and submitted for this colossal, firm-altering undertaking.

Opposite page "Welcome to America" collage image at border wall - Brian and Melissa Farling.

Mariposa Land Port of Entry
Nogales, Arizona, 2014

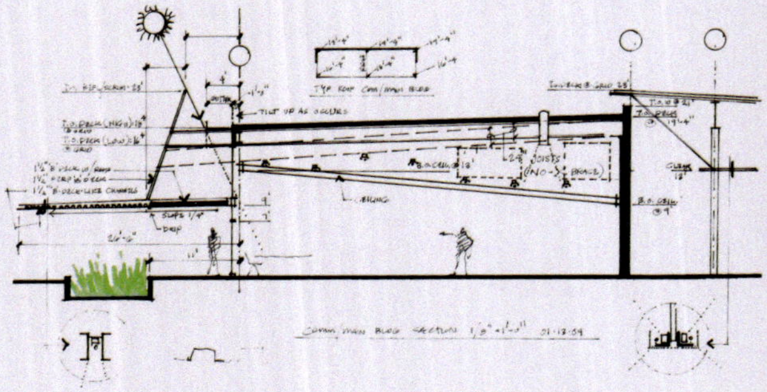

Eddie's first GSA peer review project was not for just any government building, it was for the Anzalduas International Bridge Crossing in McAllen, Texas, which gave him insight into the building demands required to regulate global trade and travel. Recognizing the substantial civil engineering component for the Mariposa application Jones Studio teamed with engineering firm Stantec to bring additional "bench depth" needed to take on such a large job.

As important as engaging with Stantec was Eddie's decision to reach out to poet Alberto Ríos for permission to quote from his book reflecting on growing up in Nogales, Arizona, and Nogales, Sonora, Mexico, formerly one city now split by the Border Wall, to frame Jones Studio's approach to the project. Ríos's emotionally rich poem, "Border Lines/*Líneas Fronterizas,*" allowed Jones Studio to express their personal experiences living with the histories of the desert southwest and how their hopes for Mariposa would drive them to live up to those expressed in Ríos's poem. Jones Studio would use design to address both the conflicts and joys of human connection and exchange at the border.

With Jones Studio's record of accomplishments and the strategic thinking in their submission, they were one of five firms shortlisted for interviews. They were the smallest firm on the list and the only firm from Arizona, which gave them a leg up on their competitors. But they were also the only firm with no direct GSA experience, which was their biggest disadvantage.

Just over a month after the interview, Neal was at the office when the fax machine jerked to life at the end of the day on January 31, 2007. Jones Studio got the job! It would be their biggest design challenge, allowing (or forcing) them to find ways for their core team to grow. They would have to sift through the dense demands of the political structure while meeting their high ethical standards of finding balance and equity through the design. Each family member would juggle

Above Section study drawing - Brian Farling. **Opposite page** Glazing at pedestrian processing lobby under larger vehicle canopy. **Following spread** Vehicle canopy stretching from west end of site (red) to east end (blue).

OPEN ABIERTO
OPEN ABIERTO
OPEN ABIERTO
OPEN ABIERTO
OPEN ABIERTO

Opposite left Mariposa aerials - "before". **Opposite right** Mariposa aerial - "after". **Above** Central oasis garden courtyard.

interlocking sets of relationships and expand their oversight capacity to achieve consistency at every step of the process while suffusing each detail with an elegant harmony. Mariposa would provide unforeseen challenges and unbidden successes as the close-knit team walked into the firm's future together.

Neal and Jacob dug into the intense fee and contract negotiations. The number of lists, matrices, graphs and cross-referenced workload hours required by the GSA reflected the stringent guidelines applied when spending public funds. After much back-and-forth and a 600-page spreadsheet on expenses, Neal made a concrete proposal on the fee range and was able to wrap up negotiations, allowing the seven-year project to get underway.

The first phase of what would be a four-phase project was funded by the Obama Administration's American Recovery and Reinvestment Act [ARRA] for shovel-ready projects (in this case, the site preparation), with additional funds to follow as the project progressed. At a time when the Great Recession was devastating so many industries and livelihoods in the United States and around the world, Jones Studio was fortunate to be gearing up for what would be an unparalleled opportunity to make a difference in the global marketplace and to reset our connections with our neighbors.

Ambos Nogales: Culture and Politics of the United States-Mexico Border

> Landscape is not neutral; histories of violence, theft and displacement are written on it in invisible ink.
>
> W. J. T. Mitchell[4]

Ambos Nogales—Both Nogales—sits astride the U.S.–Mexico border in a narrow canyon that funnels people, goods, animals, water and pollution from one side to the other. Arizona's vibrant landscape holds many stories of loss and division at the increasingly militarized border. The Tohono O'odham, successors of the Hohokam, saw their ancestral lands split in half when Mexico lost nearly 55% of its territory to the U.S. at the Treaty of Guadalupe Hidalgo, signed February 2, 1848. Today the Tonoho O'odham have the second-largest Indigenous homeland in the U.S., 2.7 million acres, still a fraction of the land they had used to sustain themselves.[5] The very notion of nationhood and land ownership was changed as America continued its march westward to assert ownership over real estate and minerals to fuel its booming industrial economy.

The first border marker at *Ambos Nogales*, designed to prevent cross-border raids that erupted after the Mexican revolution in 1910 and later during the First World War, was ordered by the Nogales, Mexico, Mayor in 1918. The early fences were designed to halt the loss of livestock and the infiltration of spies. The *Ambos Nogales* fence became the model for the fences that sprung up between twin border towns across the southern border, erecting ever-more rigid barriers to exchange. As migrants found ways to evade each generation's iteration of the border wall by pushing into more rugged territory, the death toll for crossing laid a humanitarian crisis atop the divide.[6]

Today, *Ambos Nogales* residents live with the spiked dragon back of the border wall, begun in 2006 with the ratification of the Secure Fence Act.[7] It snakes east and west into the distance, a constant reminder that neighbors do not always share the same ideas about mutual benefit and support. Nogales, Sonora, is often unfairly characterized by its lack of water and ineffective wastewater treatment, inadequate roads and numerous *maquiladoras* (factories) (see page 263) that produce cheap items for low wages. Added to the cyclical natural disasters endemic to the region—flood and drought—are the human disasters of a drug war and social stresses caused by the North American Free Trade Agreement [NAFTA] signed in 1993, and the 2008 economic pandemic that swept the globe. Finding balance as trade moved north and south was complicated by these issues.

Nogales, Arizona, is one of the top six busiest economic gateways to Mexico.[8] While approximately a tenth the size of its Mexican sister, Nogales makes much of its revenue from goods, services and sales to Mexican residents. NAFTA was primarily about facilitating the flow of money and products, not about the day-to-day human exchange that shaped these border towns. Jones Studio would have to consider how to cradle humans crossing the border for work, shopping or play while guiding trucks carting billions of factory items flowing through the LPOE. The demands for importation, customs and security were articulated clearly in the Mariposa guidelines; Jones Studio would adapt their human and nature-centric design skills to ensure Port staff and visitors would be equal users.[9]

Above International border at Nogales, Arizona - early 1900s. **Below left** International border at Nogales, Arizona - 1899. **Below right** International border at Nogales, Arizona - 2007.

Border Lines

A weight carried by two
Weighs only half as much

The world on a map looks like the drawing of a cow
In a butcher's shop, all those lines showing
Where to cut.

That drawing of the cow is also a jigsaw puzzle,
Showing just as much how very well
All the strange parts fit together.

Which way we look at the drawing
Makes all the difference.

We seem to live in a world of maps:
But in truth we live in a world made
Not of paper and ink but of people.
Those lines are our lives. Together,

Let us turn the map until we see clearly:
The border is what joins us,
Not what separates us.

Alberto Ríos, 2003 [10]

Líneas Fronterizas

Un peso cargado por dos
No pesa más que la mitad.

El mundo en un mapa parece el dibujo de una vaca
En la carnicería, todas esas líneas mostrando
Dónde cortar.

Ese dibujo de la vaca es también un rompecabezas,
Mostrando cómo caben muy bien juntas
Todas las piezas extrañas.

La manera en que miramos el dibujo
Nos hace ver la diferencia.

Parecemos vivir en un mundo de mapas:
Pero en verdad vivimos en un mundo hecho
No de papel ni de tinta sino de gente.
Esas líneas son nuestras vidas. Juntos,

Demos vuelta al mapa hasta que veamos claramente:
La frontera es lo que nos une,
No lo que nos separa.

Alberto Ríos, 2003 [10]

Opposite page An example of a Mexican *maquiladora* (factory).

Above left International border at Nogales, Arizona - 2019. **Above right** Narcotics in watermelon crates. **Below** Banner sign - *No Mas Muertes* (No More Deaths).

"Border Lines/*Líneas Fronterizas*" (see page 262) was commissioned in 2003 by Arizona's then-Governor Janet Napolitano in honor of Vicente Fox, the first Mexican President to ever visit Arizona. In the poem Ríos reminds us of our responsibility to one another, despite or because of the borders we draw around ourselves. The irony of borders is that they are all but invisible to the land while exerting an overwhelming force on the people bound by it. Borders filter, protect, confine and embrace. Animals, adapted to the land, adhere to a different set of boundaries that help them survive. Oddly, humans seem to seek out boundaries that threaten their ability to thrive.

Nearly 90% of reporting on the border is negative; Jones Studio was determined to find ways to filter out the overwhelming critical aspersions tossed at those living at the border through a design of grace. In preparing for their work, they conducted extensive research on the current conditions and history of *Ambos Nogales*. The studio toured with the international aid group BorderLinks, whose programs focus on "immigration, community formation, sustainable development, and social justice" in the face of trans-global trade. BorderLinks was connected to other migrant aid organizations to help protect, prepare and defend individuals as they deal with the border.[11]

The line drawn in the sand between the two countries does not delete millennia of cultural interactions and exchange. By witnessing the impact of official policies on two unequal partners, Jones Studio drove many of their design decisions to redress the imbalance, even if just for the pivotal moments of interchange. How could they make the Port functional at a scale of its human users? How could architecture represent and celebrate the ancient and never-ending flow of people and ideas between the two countries? While the idea of allowing the desert's own rationale to dictate how we live gently upon it has been a central tenant for Jones Studio, how could the team upscale this ethos while maintaining a high level of adherence to the client's program? How long can degradation and segregation displace the American ideals of equality and liberty for all? Each administration grapples with the incontrovertible issues of trade and migration, but new ways of thinking about our permeable border must be found. Mariposa needed to keep up with this flow while creating humane spaces for the people who make the flow happen.

Ríos reorients how we look at the puzzle pieces of a map to find connection. The Mariposa Land Port of Entry would allow Jones Studio to confirm that, by reorienting the Port's puzzle pieces, they could foreground the people who make our ancient connections come alive, and dull, just a bit, the knife edge that keeps us apart.

Out of respect and gratitude for Ríos's stirring words, Jones Studio included the poem's text, in both English and Spanish, in the public processing lobby of the Mariposa LPOE, a sign of Jones Studio's goals and aspirations for the facility. The poem reflects a commitment to creating a new way of working together based on respect for each side's hard work, not based on extractive or colonial relationships that would not be repaired by one single building.

Designing for Public Purpose

While researching historical forms that speak to "public purpose," Jones Studio looked at traditions in urban planning, architecture, landscape architecture, industrial design, craft and art for inspiration. Significant public gathering spaces, such as Mexico City's central Zócalo or the National Mall in Washington, D.C., served as examples that speak to the permanence of a stable government. Many celebratory spaces use perfect geometries, such as the dome at the Pantheon, Rome, or virtually every aspirational state capitol building in the United States, to mediate the conflicting forces of place. Being realistic about the Mariposa site but inspired by history, Jones Studio would balance might and humility, partnership and conflict, commerce and connection.

The Mariposa project, a 55-acre campus with 216,000 square feet of building and canopy space, should express culture with a sense of dignity, elegance and strength. Jones Studio was acutely aware of the ongoing struggle between safety from harm and freedom from tyranny expressed in other public spaces and in America's own founding documents, and worked to find a truthful balance between the public and private spheres at Mariposa.

Mariposa broke the two times formula for Jones Studio's growth: it was nearly four times their previous large project and thus required new modes of organization and design. After reviewing the hundreds of documents generated by numerous governmental agencies and stakeholders involved in the project—from guidelines set out by the GSA to the meshing of transportation systems governed by the Arizona Department of Transportation, from the new technologies employed by Customs and Border Protection [CBP] to the standards required by the National Environmental Policy Act, from laws that govern design to accommodate Americans with Disabilities to Animal and Plant Inspection—Jones Studio developed three different master plans that would replace, enhance and extend the functions of the original 1970s facility and its cobbled together additions. Each master plan concept created a concise relationship between functioning parts which in turn would generate forms of elegance and balance. Flexibility was built into the project, knowing that technologies, personnel, government policy and local conditions would change demands on the Port over time.

In a crucial meeting with the client in January 2008, after one year of hard work, the Director of Field Operations for CPB—new to the project but a skilled hand at managing this type of complex building—respectfully rejected all three proposals, suggesting instead a facility that functions like an old-fashioned rail yard (see page 269). In this model, traffic would flow in a linear direction, branching off on parallel runs for different inspection types, then rejoining the uninterrupted march out of the facility.

That a 19th century model for a transportation hub should yield an effective form for a 21st century facility is surprising. What at first appeared to be a significant disruption became an opportunity to re-think the campus, streamline paths for in-bound and out-bound passengers and freight, add connective, life-affirming public spaces for visitors and staff, integrate new technologies

Above Mexico City's central Zócalo.

both for security and tracking and to create a sustainable, adaptable campus of buildings. The existing Port had been configured in a radial "pinwheel" pattern, with trucks circulating around, moving in and out, crossing paths, not very efficient or safe. Blowing up the traditional pinwheel design of Land Ports of Entry was a breakthrough, with a planning paradigm that separated human movement from vehicular circulation. All the buildings with the highest intensity of officer and staff use were pulled to the center of the campus so vehicular traffic could circulate around this more human scaled zone.

From a distance the Port looks lacy, fluid, as if air circulation drove design decisions. Yet make no mistake: Mariposa is a rugged response to a rugged set of demands. Tough, durable and low maintenance materials were used in ways that would still fulfill the commitment to emphasizing human dignity and experience. There had to be a balance between a message of welcome and the laws that regulate commerce. One interesting wild card was that the existing facility had to stay functional while its replacement was built and brought on-line. The high-security, highly trafficked Port would require multiple layers of overlapping activities to keep humans and products humming along.

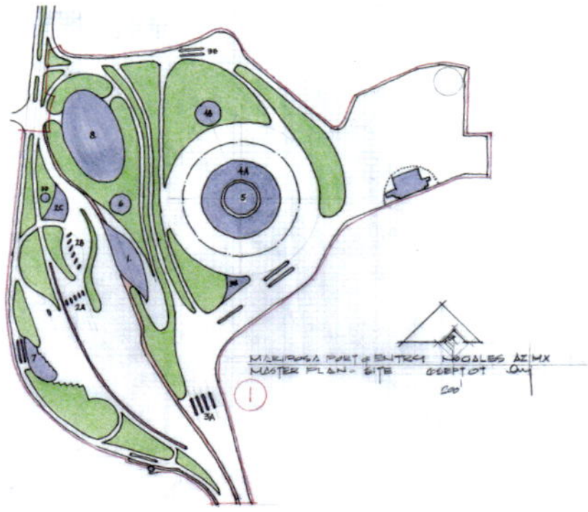

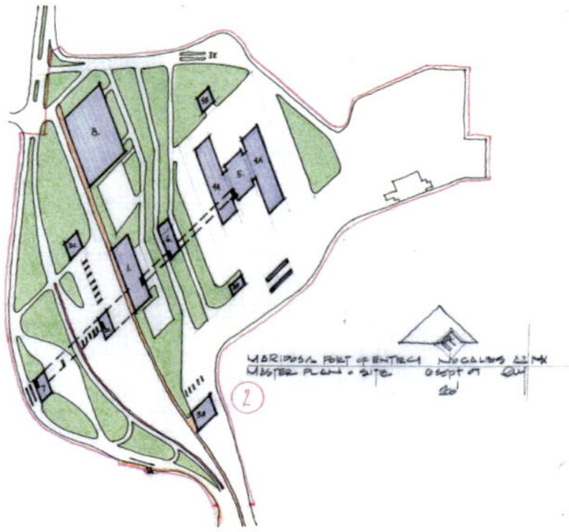

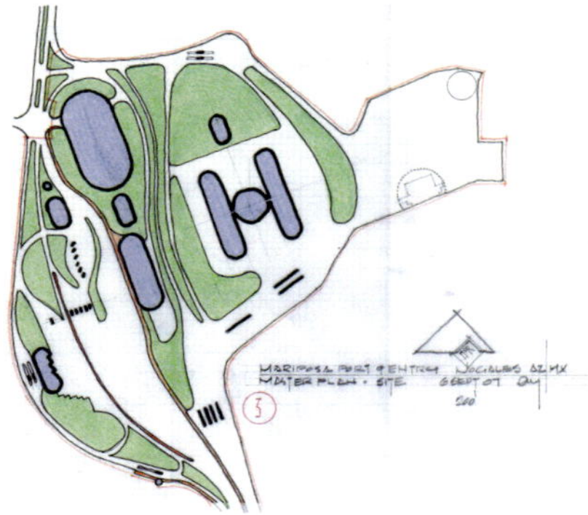

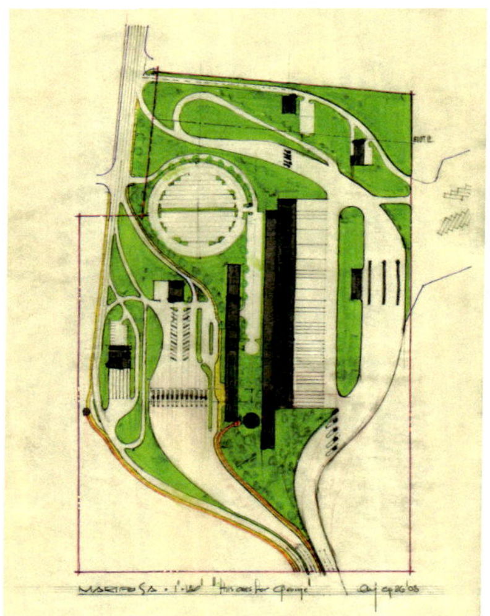

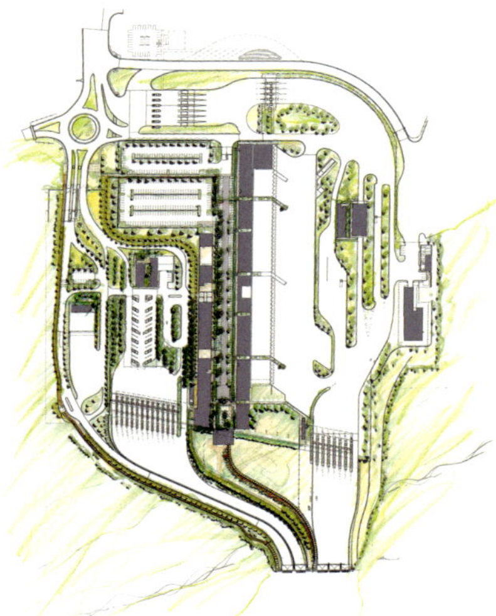

Opposite above Three early site plan study options - Eddie Jones. **Opposite below** Three site plan iterations that arrive at the final design from left to right - Eddie Jones, Brian Farling and Chris Winters. **Above** Aerial - Union Pacific Bailey Yards railroad yard, Nebraska.

Oasis: Returning the Desert to Itself

Humans created the break between the U.S. and Mexico; Jones Studio would use the desert's most precious natural resources to reconnect them. The puzzle piece that fulfilled Ríos's dream was the garden at the heart of the Mariposa facility. Jones Studio worked again with landscape architect Chris Winters to create an oasis that would welcome visitors and nurture the daily experience of officers and staff. The oasis allows officers to let their guard down and relax, where work, conversation and collaboration can happen casually and comfortably. Melissa Farling, who joined Jones Studio just after the team won Mariposa, offered the team her research experience focused on the benefits of a connection to nature through vistas and proximity to gardens. A central "safe" zone, and the restorative properties of the oasis, offered the potential to reduce cognitive fatigue and improve attentiveness. The goal was to pass these benefits along to visitors too as they navigate the Port.

Jones Studio used living elements of the desert to repair the gaps between north and south. Streams of green plant life reach beyond the border's hardware, seeping across the boundaries invisible to nature. The public and "safe zone" oasis areas would tie the campus together and provide a welcome mat to visitors while exalting the landscape where we perform our rituals of

Opposite page Inspiration - Oasis de Huacachina, Ica, Peru. **Above** Mariposa wood site model.

life. Every trucker, worker, shopper and shipper is welcomed by the desert gardens. Pedestrians are separated from private vehicles and the huge rigs hauling goods to market, sheltered by the singular forms of the Sonoran Desert. By creating these landscaped cocoons, nature has been restored to her role supporting, sustaining and protecting life. The desert garden was used not only to blur buildings and landscape but to blur nature and city as visitors pick their way through the twin cities that anchor the Port.

Buildings and hardscape were also enlisted to support the oasis. Permeable ground pavers were strategically placed to allow rainwater to filter to the aquifer rather than run onto public walkways. Building roofs slope to various gathering scuppers, conveying water that does a little dance as it soaks into gardens then into a one-million-gallon tank used to irrigate the landscape across the 55 acres. Additionally, barriers—both physical and aural—were designed to protect the green oasis from traffic noise. Trellises, screens and light reflectors create shade. Native plants soften building edges and transitions while generating air-cleansing oxygen. Storefront offices, shaded by the deep canopies, and ample glazing allows staff to stay connected to the environment around them. By orchestrating water's pathways, nature has been given back her stage. Jones Studio has reinforced the value of water consciousness by making it visible to visitors and operators of this desert portal. Ríos's puzzle lines are drawn in green at the Mariposa Land Port of Entry.

Family Table #2

Opposite page Central oasis garden. **Above** Construction of 1 million gallon water harvesting reservoir. **Below** Section drawing of water harvesting concept - Brian Farling. **Bottom** Central oasis garden courtyard with bio-remediation fountain.

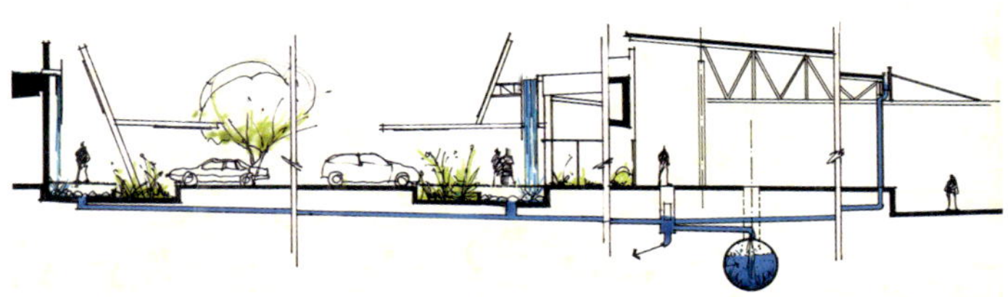

Above Central oasis garden courtyard with bio-remediation fountain. **Below** Pedestrian and vehicle arrival - "before" conditions. **Opposite page** Layers of powder-coated, perforated metal at canopy. **Following page** Pedestrian arrival in a garden - "after".

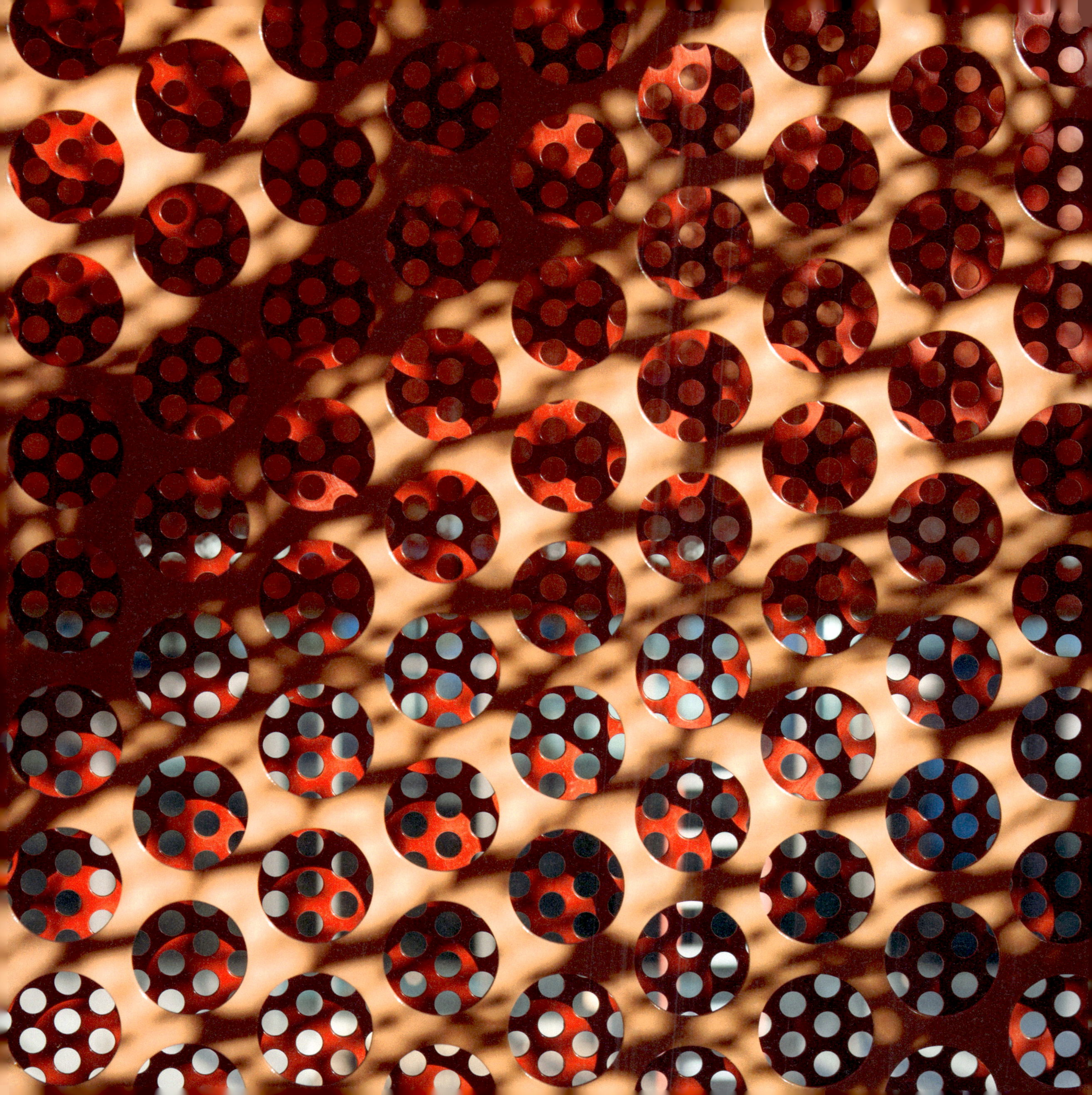

Open
Open
Open
Abierto
Open

Who's Afraid of Red, White and Blue

Just as the forms of buildings are symbolic, so are the less tangible visual elements that define a place. Jones Studio wanted to use colors drawn from the Sonoran Desert in their wayfinding, especially at the giant steel canopy threshold that runs the width of the facility. Their original wayfinding color scheme—greens, ochres, reds and oranges found in desert washes and sunsets—was rejected because it did not have a clear "Welcome to America" sensibility. Jones Studio pivoted and designed a stylized, graduated array of red, white and blue shades abstracted from an American flag fluttering in the wind.

Stretching 1000 feet from one side of the Port to the other, the entry canopy provides welcoming shade and a colorful greeting for visitors. The west end of the canopy, over the booths intended for public use, is the hot red of movement. This red gently fades to white at the central oasis zone for staff and pedestrians, signaling respite. The canopy shifts again to a cool blue surmounting the commercial booths and the trucks moving below. This subtle color coding helps visitors navigate the facility, a friendly guide rather than a wall of rules typically associated with government.

Above Abstracted American flag entry canopy conceptual rendering and color influences - Brian Farling. **Opposite page** Canopy and catwalk connecting west and east ends with Mexico beyond. **Following spread** Recycled concrete filled gabion wall with shifting blue tones of the canopy beyond.

Abierto
Open

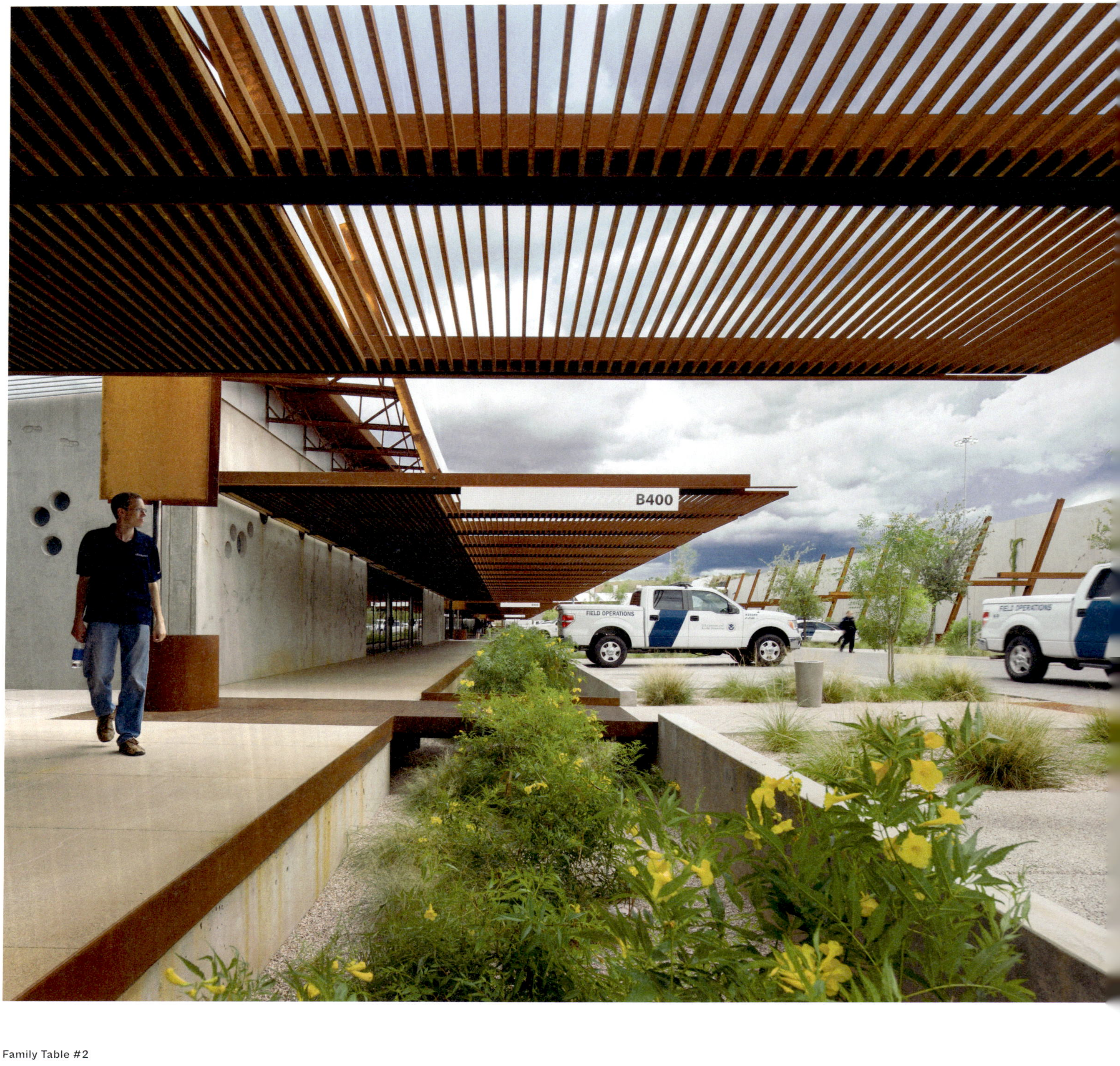
B400
FIELD OPERATIONS
FIELD OPERATIONS

Opposite page Central oasis garden. **Above** Pedestrian path through Mariposa. **Below** Commercial trucks approaching inspection.

Art of the Border

Tilt-up, site-cast concrete walls are efficient and effective and were chosen for durability, constructability, low maintenance and natural beauty while providing CBP the bulletproof protection they needed. The casting process afforded the team an opportunity to build on their collective interest in the emotional and intellectual importance of art. After many studies inspired by the complexities and intricacies of place—such as a thatch pattern of truck tires—the team settled on telling a story of a family's travels on the concrete walls themselves. Brian designed the footprints of a man, woman and child whose journey is "stamped" into the face of the concrete. Jones Studio has enshrined a recognition of the Tohono O'odham's ancient migratory patterns back onto the site, patterns replicated by the modern-day migrants, businesspeople and shoppers moving across the border.

The visual heaviness of the walls was solved with the footprints, but their physical heaviness needed to be addressed as well. The circle is one of nature's most frequent geometries although infrequently used by architects. Jones Studio designed bubble window forms that were cast into the concrete, reducing concrete cracking. (This strategy recalls the custom inserts of ISTB3.) The playful distribution across the campus of these two conceptual and practical elements, footprints and bubbles, meant that everyone—the staff, drivers, day laborers and visitors—shared in the lighthearted relief.

In addition to these custom architectural details, for each project the GSA commissions public art—there are an estimated 75,000 works in their collection—and at Mariposa, two projects augment the overall design. Matthew Moore chose to amplify issues of migration, land and belonging.[12] For Mariposa, Moore created an upside-down topographical map of the sacred Baboquivari Mountains that run north-south across the border. Baboquivari Peak, center of the Tohono O'odham universe, is home to I'itoli, their Rock God and creator.[13] *Passage*, 2014, (see page 286, 287) was inspired by the artist's connection to the landscape that has provided shelter and inspiration for thousands of years. Normally we see inverted topography maps to describe the cliffs and valleys of the ocean floor. Moore upends the Baboquivari Mountains just as changed borders have upended the Tohono O'odham's stewardship of the Peak. The sculpture shades citizens moving along a path used by the ancients on their migratory paths to find food, water and trade, just as today's travelers do.

The people filmed for South Korean conceptual artist Kimsooja's *An Album: Sewing into Borderlines*, 2013, were residents who live with the daily reality of commuting across the Nogales border. The diverse subjects are in three different positions: facing the viewer, facing away and turning towards the viewer. The figures facing the camera suggest arrival/encounter, whereas those same figures facing away from the camera evoke departure/separation. The new-media work of art and its position at the border crossing asks the viewers who pass beneath it to do the same—to look back and reflect on their own personal, interior journeys.[14] *An Album: Sewing into Borderlines* asserts it is the movement and humanity of the citizens of *Ambos Nogales* that stitch Ríos's puzzle parts together.

Above GSA's Art in Architecture - Kimsooja's *An Album: Sewing into Borderlines.* **Following spread** GSA's Art in Architecture - Matthew Moore's *Passage.*

Our greatest buildings embody, and on occasion, reconcile the conflicts that create them. Some of our most significant monuments and works of art have questioned the application and use of power. While many governmental buildings hide behind dense bureaucratic processes and an urban context while conducting their business, the Mariposa Land Port of Entry is in full view. Jones Studio made the muscular, high-volume facility sit lightly on the desert. They created a building of grace and dignity that is of the two Nogales, giving the GSA a new model for creating a highly functional, high design federal building that fulfills the goals for the Design Excellence program. In addition to exceeding the performance goals for the campus, Jones Studio used sustainable strategies to make the building a leader in the Land Port of Entry typology facilitating equitable cross-border travel with a unique aesthetic to match. Mariposa received LEED gold certification and in 2016 won both the GSA's Design Excellence Honor Award and the AIA National Institute Honor Award. In fact, Jones Studio's design solution has become a standard for GSA Land Ports of Entry across the United States and has led to subsequent Land Port of Entry commissions for the studio.

Eddie once asked Melissa how they pulled off the Mariposa project. She replied: "It was the Family Table." Each iteration of the Family Table personifies the spirit and culture of Jones Studio: its open, non-hierarchical tradition of distributed leadership and collaboration; its focus on design freedom, with a safety net to catch anyone before they fall or fail; a transparency of purpose and process; and a potent learning environment. Jones Studio "grew up" with Mariposa. It changed their perception of what they were able to accomplish and manage. The studio swelled to 22 designers requiring more space, but they benefited from the rich experience brought to them by the unfortunate circumstance of a global recession, when parts of the business world ground to a halt and experienced colleagues were available to join them.

Jacob reflects that if they ever got a similarly large project, they would approach decision-making differently simply because they now have experience on what worked and what didn't. Things can and do pivot multiple directions, underscoring that nothing is ever a given. Relationships must be nurtured and constantly rekindled. They must always confirm a common alignment of goals and consensus on the pathway to completion to ensure a successful outcome.

Brian and Jacob had worked in the same office since 2002, but Mariposa was their first time working together in such an intense and sustained way. They shared in the Jones Studio "initiation" when both were tossed into the deep end of the firm's work when they first joined, but their friendship was forged in the furnace of Mariposa during years of three-hour drives to Nogales to tend to Mariposa's eruptions and achievements. Their complementary and overlapping skills, matching work ethic and ability to manage teams prompted them to begin conversations about joining the firm as partners. Defining their new roles would take time. Neal and Eddie recognized that protecting Jones Studio's legacy is one thing; keeping the flame of discovery and invention alive would be their most important legacy for future generations of associates, family and clients. Brian and Jacob became partners at Jones Studio in 2014, another part of Jones Studio's "growing up."

While the lessons of Mariposa continue to resonate through Jones Studio's work, the grounded dreams of Alberto Ríos's poem do as well. Ríos suggests that every place and its peoples can, or should, be healed across borders. The Earth naturally skins over the scars border create; Ríos would like to see humans work on repairing those scars too. Jones Studio understands Ríos's meaningful call by using their skills to create buildings that address conflict and supporting nature that provides calm and connection for their shared dreams.

Opposite page Custom cast-in-place punch windows and footprints. **Following spread** Custom cast-in-place footprints in geometric pattern.

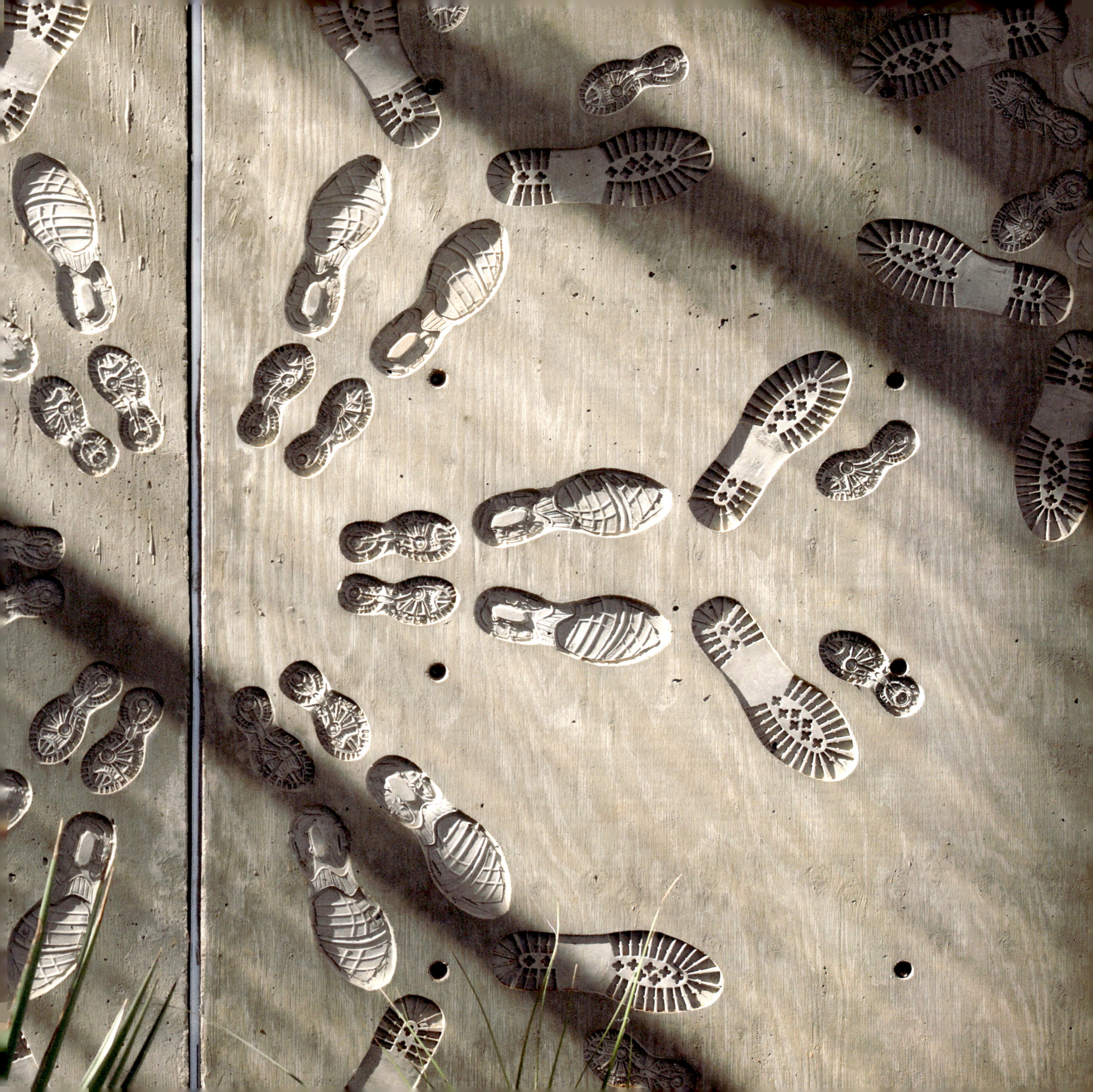

Above Celebrating the rain with sculptural scuppers. **Below** Interior open office. **Opposite page** Pedestrian lobby. **Following spread** View of Mariposa from Mexico at dusk.

CBP
EXAM
PERM
EXIT

Devoted Generalists

Modernist architecture devotees criticized Frank Lloyd Wright because he experimented too much, began "again and again" to arrive at a new manner.[15] The idea of being a specialist with a typology or using the same stylistic approach across types of buildings was anathema to Wright who believed each opportunity was full of possibility for something new and original.

Jones Studio too believes in beginning "again and again," cherishing each opportunity to respond to a new challenge by researching, asking questions, collaborating and listening. Specialization be damned if the results are formulaic; falling back on conventional solutions or forms is the easy answer. Rather perversely, if the process of design is not arduous and difficult, it is probably not worth doing, which is why Jones Studio perseveres, making them proud and devoted generalists.

Opposite page Valley Presbyterian Church, Paradise Valley, Arizona.

Mesa Community College Performing Arts Center

Mesa, Arizona, 2014

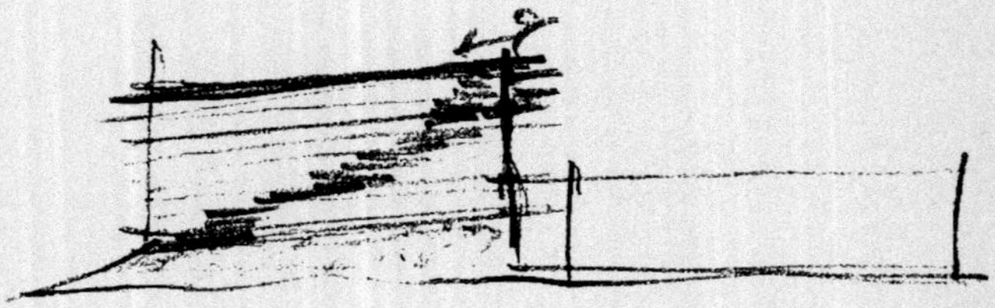

With the lengthy Mariposa project coming to a close, Jones Studio began to seek new project opportunities. They found themselves among an usually large "short list" of seven firms for the Mesa Community College Performing Arts Center [MCC PAC] job. Following a strong interview, they were sitting down for breakfast at Garland's in Oak Creek Canyon, outside Sedona, Arizona, for the firm's annual retreat. Garland's is an historic place where modern architects go to remember the woods. Neal was notified of an important call which he took on a wall phone in the office, the only phone on the property in the otherwise "disconnected" realm. After a brief time away, Neal returned to announce that Jones Studio was selected for the job. A good breakfast turned into a great celebration.

Winning the MCC PAC project allowed the team to build on and extend their skills developed at South Mountain because of MCC's addition focus on dance and musical theater. It allowed a great reduction in carbon footprint because it was a remodel, the repurposing of a 1970s fiveplex movie theater the College had recently purchased. Jones Studio was excited about engaging with another public space outside of Phoenix's cultural core, one dedicated to training generations of musicians, dancers and actors from diverse backgrounds. Over 50% of Mesa Community College's 20,000 students are people of color, largely Latino, who will lead the cultural field's commitment to broadening its demographic representation.[16] The school includes many technical training programs, and was committed to bringing the arts—performing and visual—to the diverse community.

Primary conceptual design drivers came together after many meetings with the MCC faculty who nurture the long-celebrated music program. Inspired by a survey of the faculty's favorite music, at one of the key design presentations the team showed up with a boom-box to complement their usual computer and digital projector presentation. Jones Studio played faculty favorite "Rhapsody in Blue," 1924, by George Gershwin, and explained how it would inspire the architecture. "Rhapsody

Above Elevation sketch - Brian Farling. **Opposite page** Marquee sign at courtyard entry with repurposed chair stanchions at right.

MCC PERFORMING ARTS

Above Waterfall roof drain opening. **Below** Folded masonry composition. **Opposite left** Repurposed chair stanchions. **Opposite right** Courtyard entry. **Following spread** Entry courtyard repurposed from previously enclosed movie theater space.

in Blue" combines an orchestral sweep with the jittery jazz syncopations of a modernizing and changing America, an interesting mirror for Mesa's own evolution.

The dramatic opening sequence of "Rhapsody's" clarinet is captured in the irregular upward sweep of standard gray and dark charcoal masonry blocks on the exterior. The main entrance masonry wall folds forward, like sheet music waving on a stand. An updated movie "marquee" entry is anchored by red powder coated, repurposed chair stanchions, part of the old movie theater's seating. Fragments of red stanchions flutter up along the adjacent wall, like notes floating to the sky. The entire 16,000-square-foot roof slopes to the corner of the building opposite the main entry, where the walls split apart and open to the sky. During rain events, a trickle or a torrent of rain pours down creating a waterfall in the desert. This water is then passively harvested, pooled and directed to the trees and plants punctuating the garden. Even water would perform for the audiences of the MCC PAC.

Maria had suggested a welcoming outdoor courtyard replace one of the movie bays, borrowing light for a new lobby amphitheater. This new lobby was draped in rows of red and gray carpet and lit from above by a deconstructed chandelier built of mirrors from the original Harkins theater. The shaded inner courtyard provides a break from the sun while audience members linger or purchase tickets. Inside the team connected the first floor to the upper mezzanine which is lined with faculty offices, making them immediately visible to students, many of whom are the first in their families to attend college. In the main 455-seat performance hall, the charcoal masonry takes on a more refined finish, used as an enveloping inner shell that modulates sound reflection for optimum acoustics. Because the arts, and artists, are constantly starting over, again and again, this transformation supports the very notion of artistic production and discovery at the heart of the school.

The MCC PAC demonstrates that existing building stock can be brought back to life. This was not the first time Jones Studio had reimagined an existing building. More important is the studio's moral imperative to reduce the extractive damage and material waste inherent in their field. While new-build is sexy, there are a million more opportunities to reshape the building stock in Phoenix with more high-functioning, elegant and beautiful buildings. While the MCC PAC was small relative to Mariposa, its lessons are outsized for how client and architect can work together for a better Earth-centric outcome.

TICKETS

Opposite page & above Performance hall. **Below** Lobby and flex performance space.

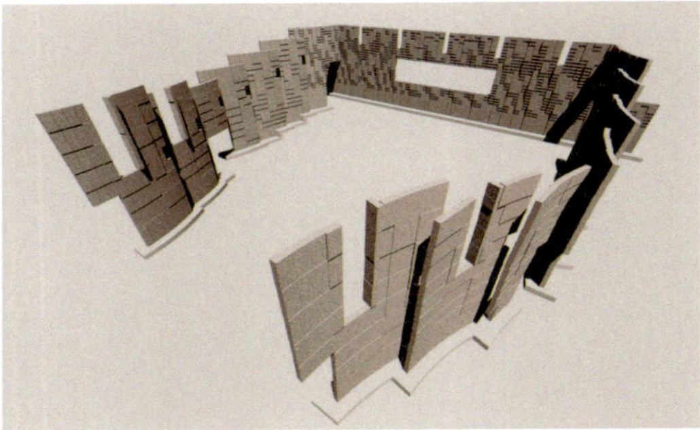

306 **Above left** Performance hall sound reflecting side wall. **Top right** Performance hall digital study model. **Above right** Scene shop with original Fiesta 5 movie theater sign. **Below** Performance hall perspective section rendering. **Opposite page** Offset masonry sound reflecting walls. **Following spread** Performance hall expansion in foreground with reimagined former movie theater at right.

PERFORMING ARTS

Cornell Iron Works Enterprises
Cornell/Cookson Door Manufacturing Facility
Goodyear, Arizona, 2015

Developer Scott O'Connor recommended Jones Studio to Bob Cookson for his new door manufacturing facility in Goodyear, a western suburb of Phoenix. Modern architecture found some of its earliest expression in factories, the streamlined aesthetic matching the functional demands of industry. Although the company did not expect more than a building, this was a chance for Jones Studio to create new connections between parts so the building would be sustainable and efficient for the owner as well as comfortable for the employees.

The building was organized around some core ideas: implanting desert gardens to anchor staff to place with the positive bump that views of nature provide; providing lots of natural light that reduces electrical needs and allows staff to track their day; collecting rainwater to nurture a protective garden envelope that shades the building; and create a shaded parking lot and optimize traffic patterns (after Mariposa, creating better traffic flow would be a piece of cake). The manufacturing and office zones are connected by three internal courtyard gardens, an equalizing gesture that recognizes and rewards both blue and white-collar workers. The building would collect rainwater into 11 tanks with a total 140,000-gallon capacity for irrigation of the facilities' gardens and courtyards.

As with virtually every Jones Studio building, natural light is prioritized and finds its way into every occupied space. For the manufacturing zone, they designed a 370-foot-long, nine-foot-tall north-facing clerestory that floods the spaces with indirect light, allowing the natural clock of the sun to anchor employees in the world outside, and LED lights make the building glow in the night. Jones Studio prepared for the future installation of a photovoltaic power array for further reduction in energy costs.

Working closely with the City of Goodyear proved fruitful in two distinct ways. First, by providing an extensive rainwater harvesting system, Jones Studio was able to argue that the normal drainage requirements could be reduced. This allowed the owners to use the money normally required for on-site

Above Perspective rendering - Brian Farling. **Opposite page** Garden courtyard. **Following spread** Perforated enclosure at north courtyard and office wing with high-bay manufacturing in background to the left.

1901

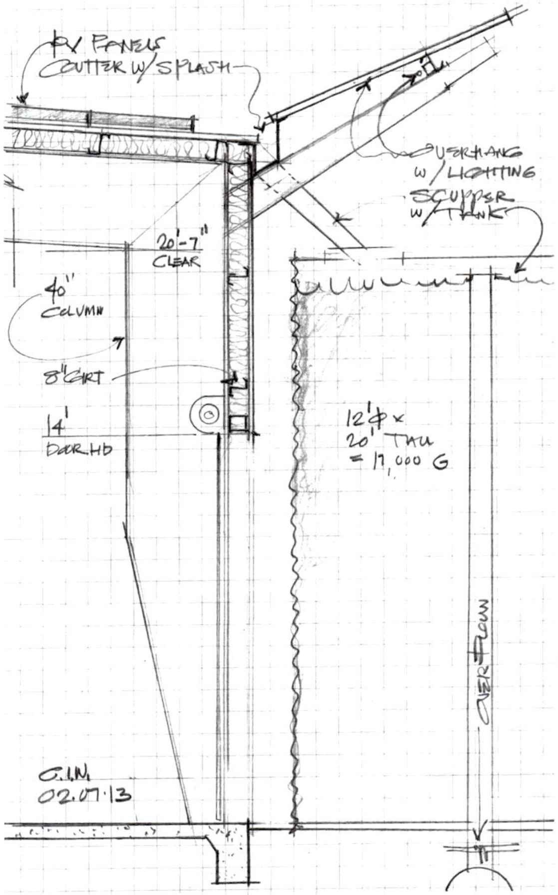
PV PANELS
GUTTER W/ SPLASH
OVERHANG W/ LIGHTING
SCUPPER W/ TANK
20'-7" CLEAR
40" COLUMN
8" GIRT
14' DOOR HD
12' ⌀ x 20' TALL = 17,000 G
OVERFLOW
G.I.M. 02.07.13

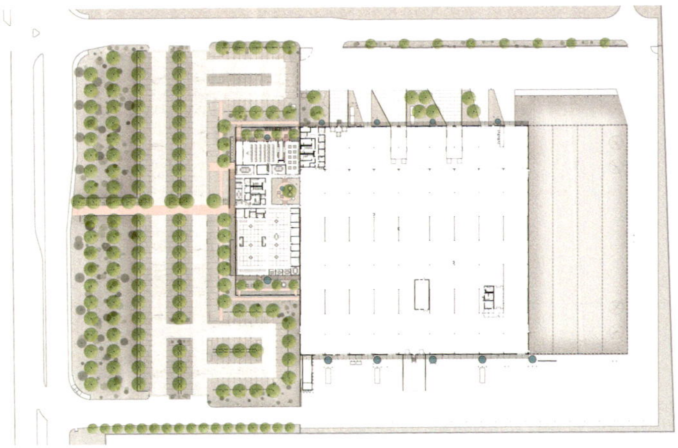

Opposite page above far right One of eleven galvanized water harvesting tanks. **Opposite page above right** Water harvesting detail sketch - Brian Farling. **Opposite page below** Site plan drawing. **Above** North courtyard adjacent to interior dining.

water retention to pay for the rainwater harvesting system that feeds trees and other native plantings that give life, shade and a water conscious win in this suburban enclave. Goodyear at the time also mandated that warehouses must be concrete tilt-ups with (an apparently) preferred palette of beige with horizontal blue stripes. Since prefabricated steel buildings are more economical for large open spaces, Jones Studio built a scale model and detailed renderings that won everyone over; this would be the first metal building in Goodyear.

In one of the simplest buildings the firm has designed, the manufacturing facility showed how companies can commission forward-thinking architecture that is business friendly and cost-effective while providing a sympathetic work environment for the staff. Humans blossom in gardens too.[17] The designers again blurred the boundaries of nature and culture, setting an anchor for their righteous design ethos into the far reaches of Phoenix's suburban spread.

Above & below Daylighting in manufacturing space by continuous 9' tall x 300' long clerestory. **Opposite page** Perforated enclosure at south office courtyard with main entry at left. **Following spread** West elevation from street.

1901

Mohave Community College Student Services Center

Kingman, Arizona, 2016

The Mohave Community College system was founded in the early 1970s to expand the educational opportunities in an underserved, less populated portion of the state. The Mohave campus consisted of few permanent buildings but mostly portable building structures added on an ad hoc basis without a master plan in mind. As a result, the campus lacked a central hub for student life. Mohave's graduation rate was lower than the state average, and a campuswide campaign to support student graduation was doing nothing to help. Campus leadership felt building a strong sense of pride for their campus could make a difference. The School's President Dr. Michael Kerns recognized the importance of providing a safe and beautiful space for student life, determining that a new Student Services Center would make a difference for student satisfaction and success. While seeking an architect for the project, Dr. Kerns appreciated Jones Studio's unique approach, led by Aaron Forbes, and hired the firm to help transform the campus.

Jones Studio recognized the importance of putting the Student Center's computer commons, library, student enrollment center and a tutoring hub on display to the students, faculty and parents passing by. The building would take advantage of the sweeping views across the Mohave Desert.

Every design element was enlisted to blur the lines indoors and out, from the large transparent northern walls to the materials, finishes and the campus's various lighting strategies. All outdoor elements—sidewalks, paths, landscaping and vistas—were shaped and designed to draw people in to this hub of student life. The Student Center's transparent student study lounge and its contiguous outdoor shaded patio were oriented to face the well-landscaped college quad. The bustle of the campus would expand the student experience, and the new academic and commons spaces would encourage greater social and cultural cohesion.

The Student Services Building was the start of a campus-wide renewal program and set the architectural tone and expectations for all future campus development. Since its completion, student activity on campus has drastically increased as has enrollment, proving that great design can shape and elevate user experience and the institution's public service.

Above Section drawing. **Opposite page** Shade ramada at student commons.

LIBRARY

Opposite page Collaboration and study space in library. **Above** Daylighting and exterior connections. **Below** Entry and shade canopy study sketch - Eddie Jones.

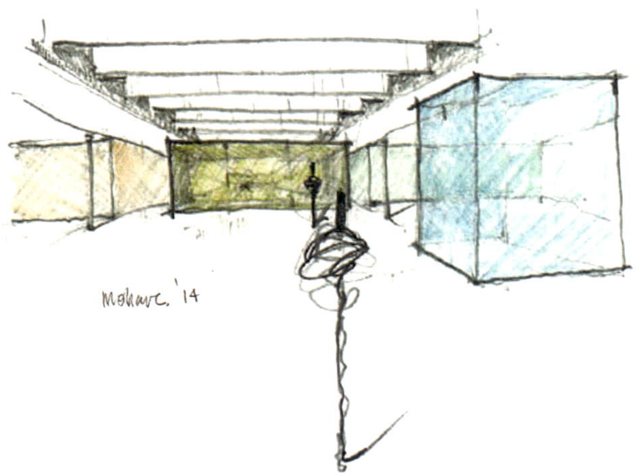

324

Above Private study rooms. **Below** Roof framing plan study - Eddie Jones. **Opposite page** Student commons. **Following spread** Shade ramada at student commons.

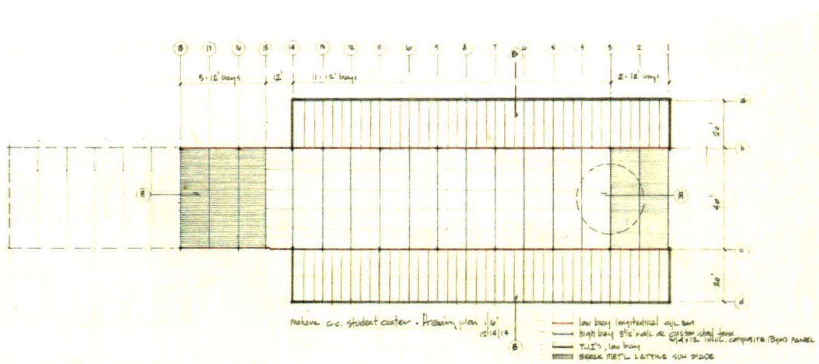

Valley Presbyterian Church
Paradise Valley, Arizona, 2020

When Valley Presbyterian Church's Pastor David Joynt approached Eddie about their "New Heart" program—to transform the Church for the future while engaging the pressing needs of today—there was an alignment between Jones Studio and the client. This would be the designer's first opportunity to apply their critical design thinking to enhance the expression of beliefs and creation of community through ritual spaces for the 21st century by reanimating an existing campus.

Valley Presbyterian Church [VPC] was designed in 1963 by Philadelphia architect Harold E. Wagoner, who chose this church, out of the over 500 he designed, for his final internment. The complex, in the wealthy Phoenix suburb of Paradise Valley, is surrounded by asphalt parking lots and single-family stucco homes, neither of which celebrate the desert-inspired mid-century modern building. Jones Studio was tasked with re-orienting the full campus experience to create a connection across the Church's diverse activities and membership, and to restore natural life to the site.

Historically, VPC only offered traditional services, but with the area's changing demographics, a contemporary service had been added. As a result, the campus was effectively split into two congregations, worshiping in different buildings and at different times. A critical driver of the "New Heart" project was to gather these disparate groups in a single location, providing space in which all members could offer and receive fellowship on the campus.

Rob Huff, who originally learned of Jones Studio while working for the company that installed glass film at the House of Five Dreams, led the Jones Studio design team. Reimagining a new and refreshed master plan was dependent on working again with landscape architect Chris Winters, who introduced habitable gardens with native plantings and large shade trees. They linked the north and south halves of the campus by elevating an existing hardscape patio space with a large circle of grass (there *would* be gamboling here), creating the Fellowship Plaza, a buoyant outdoor space

Above Perspective sketch - Eddie Jones. **Opposite page** Reimagined sanctuary.

Above & opposite page Awaken Café.

that expresses the spirit of the New Heart program while symbolizing unity and fellowship. The Plaza is the Church's commons, where congregants share space. The circle gathers the scattered geometric forces of the surrounding buildings and pools them in a space for rest and reflection. Outdoor chairs and tables ranging in size and style ring a children's grassy play area, kept safe by the surrounding ivy-draped retaining walls. The adjacent classroom building received various forms of upgrade, including new ministry spaces for children, youth and adults, reinforcing the intergenerational feel of the Church.

The center of the "New Heart" renovation is the "Awaken Café." By breathing life into the formerly closed-off meeting room facing the Fellowship Plaza, a transformed, transparent glass box became a full-service coffee hub used for formal and informal meetings. The design goal was to blur the lines between indoor and outdoor space, putting visitors on stage and metaphorically asking if our inner worlds are reflected in our outer behaviors.

In meetings with the VPC congregation, respondents stressed the desire to respect the traditions of old while embracing the future. The Sanctuary's original solid mahogany pews were salvaged and re-worked to become the Awaken Café's tables. A solid concrete baptismal font was relocated to the Fellowship Plaza as a water feature, and a 16-foot fluted concrete alter was relocated to the Sanctuary Garden, becoming a bench nestled into a lush hidden garden at the southern

entry point, preserving the structure's history.

Multiple layers of meaningful change improved the practical performance of the lyrical Sanctuary space that now holds 600 worshipers. A shift in the original orientation of seating into a radial pattern increased intimacy and improved sight lines. With its selection of natural materials, celestial blue fabric seats bathed in the desert's sun and white flowing fabric treatments at the ceiling, the Sanctuary evokes a clear connection between Heaven and Earth. Vertical wood lattice unifies the asymmetrical hall and frames the stage's pulpit, piano and seating. Jones Studio's experience with performing art centers allowed them to improve the acoustic environment to support all manner of services. A state-of-the-art immersive visual projection system was installed to augment and enliven the Church's spiritual experiences. Flanking the front and rear of the space are the original brightly pigmented stained-glass windows of organic shapes that pour color onto the walls. The windows were designed by Phoenix-based artist Maureen McGuire, who specializes in liturgical glass. McGuire's abstract forms express a boundless emotional and spiritual life.

At every level, Valley Presbyterian beams joy and welcome, place and community: there is indeed a "New Heart" to the campus. Jones Studio's success at Valley Presbyterian has prompted other faith communities to approach them to invigorate their spaces. Valley Presbyterian exemplifies Jones Studio's ability to preserve the past while reimagining a mission-driven future.

Above New custom bench at existing stone wall. **Below** Master plan drawing - Chris Winters. **Bottom** Section perspective rendering - Rob Huff. **Opposite page** Sanctuary with existing stained glass and new digital projection system.

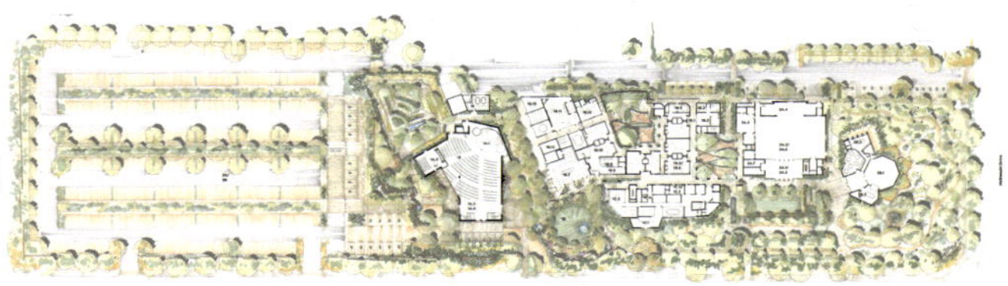

Opposite page Reimagined sanctuary with existing stained glass windows. **Above** Maureen McGuire stained glass. **Below** New custom woodwork at alter. **Following spread** New shade ramada opening into sanctuary.

Family Table #3

Home and Garden

Architects often get their first work designing their own home, or one for family or friends. These become critical calling cards and allow clients insight into an artist's visual thinking. After 33 years in the Al Beadle building, Neal and Eddie determined it was time for them to build *their* own home.

There were many lessons the studio took from living in the Beadle, particularly the role of the shaded sunken garden to protect against the lengthening summers of Phoenix. Just as important was their experience at SMoCA with Family Table #2; Jacob observed that their time in the museum taught them that they needed more storage to contain the growing archives and support materials that spread like weeds in and amongst Family Table #1. Family Table #3 would start a new chapter in the firm's life and create a living model for the team's accomplishments and aspirations for future family generations to come.

Opposite page Entry gate at Jones Studio office.

Jones Studio Office
Tempe, Arizona, 2016

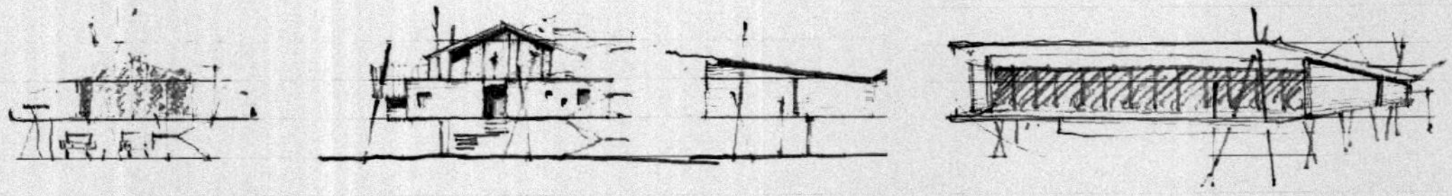

In 2009 Eddie and Neal took advantage of reduced land prices after the 2008 economic collapse, when the firm was buoyed by Mariposa, and purchased land close to ASU, light rail and restaurants in downtown Tempe. While this was late in the firm's history to be building their own showcase, it would still serve as a nest egg and sales tool but most important, it was a well-deserved bespoke space for the Jones Studio family. Given the lessons from their previous Family Table sites, and the acute sensitivity they have to clients' needs through observation and research, an appreciation of budget constraints and site capacity, the goals for Family Table #3 were obvious. They must surround themselves with the variegated tones and textures of the desert, sit unobtrusively on their site and provide space for collaboration, community engagement, storage and team growth. They must also surprise themselves—even small details become opportunities to delight and challenge how the designers think about the various physical, psychological and spatial facets of home.

Family Table #3 is wrapped by a shifting and changing masonry wall, barely visible from the street, shielded behind the exuberantly planted park strip that screens the visual dredge of the built environment around them. The decomposed granite driveway is metered by wiry and sculptural Sonoran Desert trees. The drive ends in a Luis Barragán-inspired blue wall in honor of the firm's trip to Mexico City to experience that architect's use of color. Two desert gardens flourish inside the masonry perimeter, the tinkle of a fountain ever animating the space. This infill lot, irrigated by harvested rainwater, is a mini oasis of desert inside the asphalt fields of Tempe.

Culling knowledge gained from their diverse body of work allowed the team to fine tune strategies for treading lightly on their home planet. In addition to the energy efficient systems embedded in the building—water harvesting, passive and active heating and cooling—the location in Tempe cut by an estimated 20% the distance traveled by the team, yet another way in which the building reduced the firm's carbon footprint.

Above Living units study sketches - Eddie Jones. **Opposite page** Entry sequence with scupper shade canopy at front door.

344 **Above** Eddie designing masonry "wrapper" wall with dominos on sister's dining room table. **Below** Elevation and section study sketches - Eddie Jones.

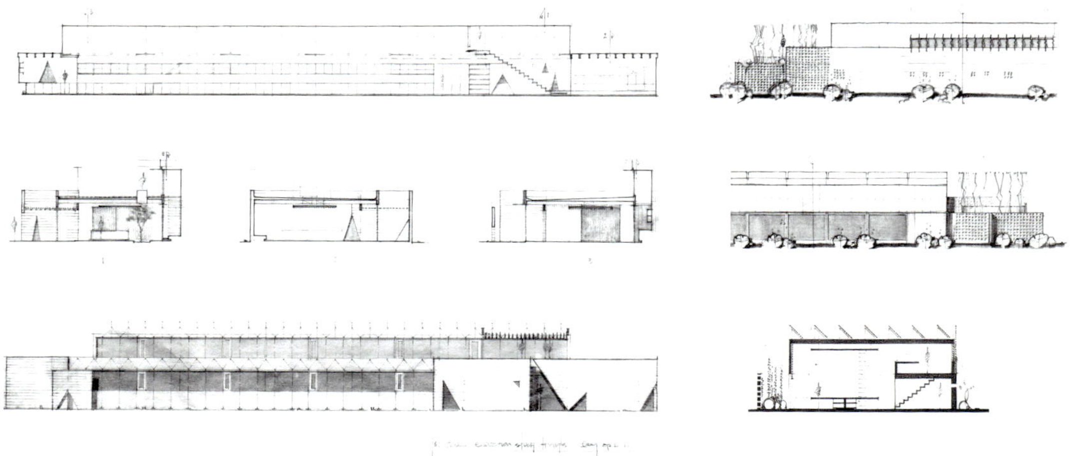

Family Table #3 is Eddie's *gesamkunstwerk*, an all-over art work. Bruce Goff, one of the most inventive practitioners of an American architecture and early influence on Neal and Eddie, noted that architecture is not just the building but the space inside—and the feelings evoked is the most important thing.[1] Eddie often speaks of his love for artists as diverse as early 20th century Austrian artist Gustav Klimt (for his use of shimmering gold leaf), 17th century Dutch painter Johannes Vermeer (for his translucent washes of color that capture light) and contemporary Arizona-based land artist James Turrell (and his use of land and space to focus light). Each of these artists, and many others besides, provided inspiration for Eddie's idiosyncratic and inspired design choices.

With origami-like ceiling planes, walls of glass, windows open to nature and fluorescent tubes tucked away in corners and sheathed in sleeves of colored gels, light conducts the swim of a typical day. The building itself tracks the sun with sprays of color that shape and dissolve across walls and ceilings, washes that change the very contours of the space. Eddie tamed the nearly 4,000 annual hours of Phoenix sunlight into cascading caresses, soft like the air of a tropical paradise, dense like a painted wall. Light is one of the most tangible and delicious sensations in the changeable atmosphere of the interior.

Family Table #3's nerve center is the long central table, floating on a carpet of cheery raspberry and capturing and distributing the charged passion of the team. Bodies entering the space gravitate to the open mosh pit of ideas after passing Neal's glass-encased lair. At the east end are open seats to foster conversation and speculation on projects and marketing strategies, often accompanied by beer from the built-in kitchen Kegerator. Jones Studio hosts high school and college classes, discussions by Nobel Prize winners, physicists, poets, journalists, artists and politicians, as if a bit of Vol'ume[s] bookstore had been preserved and transplanted to Tempe.

The sunken conference room is full of art rather than awards or images of their own buildings. Eddie is particularly proud of a painting by Goff-trained architect Herb Greene. Eddie had seen an image of this work, *The Crying Frenchman*, (see page 355) 40 years earlier in a photo of Greene's own house. The work features a famous *Life* magazine image of a man weeping as Nazis marched into Marseille during World War II. Eddie heard Greene was selling the painting, so he called, and the swampy, surreal painting now sits at the crown of the Jones Studio conference room. Propped along the concrete ledge are other treasures including drawings by Paolo Soleri, Brian Farling and Chuck Albanese, pictures of touchstone buildings by Greene and another Goff student, Bart Prince, with other treasures too. Mounted from the ceiling are the thousand small brass plates rescued from the Logan Residence, shimmering against the ceiling and set into motion by the movement of cool air.

A tiny fraction of the firm's awards *are* kept on the bottom shelf of a floor to ceiling built-in, the rest of the shelves holding the tchotchkes and fragments of masonry collected from places and architectural sites around the world. Fragments including a shard of concrete stair nosing from Paul Rudolph's Boston Mental Health Center, Frank Lloyd Wright's Imperial Hotel in Tokyo and a cobblestone from the streets of Florence hold pride of place. These objects reveal the architect as archaeologist, mining the past to help imagine the future.

Opposite page Sunken conference room and garden courtyard. **Above** Arizona Forward committee meeting at Jones Studio. **Below** Family Table #3 at Jones Studio office floor plan.

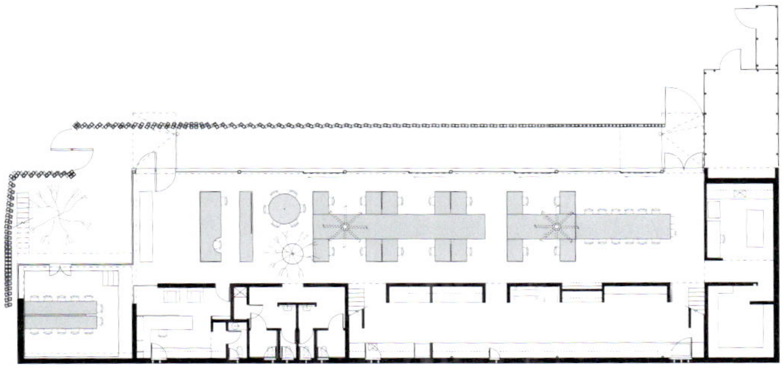

To complete the project with the level of quality and detail it deserved, Budd Conn, one of Jones Studio's earliest family members, joined the team as the onsite manager for Build Inc., the firm Rich Fairbourn formed when he left Construction Zone. With Budd and Rich orchestrating the onsite refinements, sensitively calibrated solutions would serve the demands of the busy firm while supporting their artistic ambitions. The structure's expressive volumes and resource-reducing strategies confounded the City's permitting folks. There was cajoling, browbeating and grandstanding to get Tempe's inspectors to understand the meaning, value and safety of these features. Once the occupancy permit was in place, Jones Studio put in place the final pieces of the structure's puzzle.

When Eddie was asked which project most reflects his dreams for making architecture to "help people live better" he did not hesitate: it is Family Table #3. Eddie's touchstones, and the images and ideas that animate everyone in the firm, make Family Table #3 one of the most buoyant and inspiring work spaces this author has ever seen.

Above Studio life with mezzanine above. **Opposite page** Gathering at east end of Family Table #3. **Following spread** Sunken conference room with table and courtyard sharing the same elevation, salvaged brass "leaves" from Logan House shimmering above.

Jones Studio Culture

Neal's "statement of philosophy" for Jones Studio has three core values: instill accountability at all levels, cultivate collaboration and teamwork and encourage initiative and innovation. He describes his job as nurturing the firm's culture and allowing family members to be playful, even childlike, so genius can bubble to the top. He is also very much the business bouncer for the firm; his business acumen has kept Jones Studio on firm financial footing despite turns in the economy. Eddie's job title is "Practice Visionary," always pointing to the end goal of creating excellent architecture. The "statement of philosophy" also describes the workplace environment as "zany," grounded in the belief that people who work well and play well together can be creative and innovate within a fun and safe environment. "Zany" also suggests an all-out embrace of the joys and ironies of the world in which the family works and lives.[2]

Of Eddie, Brian says it's not rose-colored glasses that tinge his thinking, it's his rose-colored senses that flavor the culture of the office. Neal pushes design and business together to strike the right balance for the firm's stability. Brian and Jacob's endless well of inventive design ideas, and Jacob's near perfect recall of events, places and people, create an elastic envelope that foregrounds experimentation through design thinking.

Eddie and Neal finagled their way into the good ol' boy network for their first jobs, but today the dynamics for qualifying for projects have changed. RFPs now require firms to have completed many works of the same typology (specialist versus generalist) in a short period of time, preventing new firms from cracking into and cracking open that typology, which has been a hallmark of Jones Studio's success. Kirstin Keane joined the team in the fertile 2018-2019 period, bringing with her marketing expertise to help tell Jones Studio's story effectively in this changed environment. Jones Studio excels at bringing clients along with compelling and meaningful stories that reflect their program goals; having back-up materials as reference and a dynamic outward facing web presence helps them tell their own story in a crowded marketplace.

Opposite top left AIA awards banquet for Mariposa - 2014. **Opposite top right** Happy hour in Al Beadle's 12th street courtyard - 2015. **Opposite middle** Studio retreat in Puerto Penasco, Mexico visiting Jones Studio's Casas De Las Balaustradas - 2019. **Opposite bottom left** Office photo in Al Beadle's 12th street courtyard - 2012. **Opposite bottom right** Jones Studio at Cosanti by Paolo Soleri - 2022.

Top Brian and Maria's 2016 UofA CAPLA Capstone studio visiting Michael Heizer's *Double Negative.* **Above** Jones Studio visiting Luis Barragan's *Satelite Towers* in Mexico City - 2001.

As Jones Studio continually grows and changes, adding new expertise is essential to help navigate a constantly shifting profession. Everyone is a lifelong learner, excited about absorbing ideas from their colleagues. And because of their collaborative work process, where all team members participate in brainstorming sessions and project presentations, every day is full of informal learning. This spirit of growth permeates the firm, so it is no surprise that so many of the family teach. This is another way that Jones Studio's beliefs and strategies permeate the infrastructures of the field.

Outlets for the family's teaching include the area's architecture programs—ASU and UofA—and the School of Architecture at Paolo Soleri's Cosanti and Arcosanti, where Eddie sits on the Board of Governors. (The team also gives lectures across all types of forums both regionally and nationally as opportunities and time allow.) The School of Architecture program, founded at Taliesin by Frank Lloyd Wright, has found a new voice, energy and purpose after an unfortunate break between the Taliesin Foundation and the School. At ASU, Neal's teaching efforts to make real estate developers understand that "good architecture makes good business"—as was the case at NAI Horizon—could not compete with the dollar signs floating in his student's eyes. The quick buck turn-around for developers does not preclude thinking about place, people and the natural environment—there is just simply no reward big enough to slow down Phoenix's unstoppable gluttony of growth. Neal prefers to mentor colleagues and students from around the Valley whose outreach indicates they are inclined to be better stewards of their home.

Above UofA CAPLA studio visit to Jones Studio with *Crying Frenchman* Painting in background - 2022.

One of the biggest concerns for architecture firms anywhere is the disjunct between university curricula and the skills needed when students leave school. Finding ways to give students a taste of the real work of a design firm—through practicums or charettes—benefits everyone in the field, particularly the students. Everyone on the team promotes water consciousness through their work—but also a sensitivity to adjacent fields such as psychology, neurobiology, environmental psychology, neuroscience, anthropometrics, ergonomics, biophilia and wellness studies. Considering the human brain and its reactions to the world deepens how designers affect how we live in their structures. Of equal concern is the need for more diversity in design. Understanding how different cultural groups, and folks from different generations, of different genders and abilities use and perceive space is central if architects are to design buildings of welcome and equity.

The collective weight of these activities—teaching, learning, experimenting—are all supported in a commitment to the future of the firm and the community. Many companies would argue these outside activities and more experimental fields, untested in the design space, don't rack up billable hours. These activities by contrast continue Jones Studio's tradition of testing ideas through collaboration. By sharing their own higher standards for design of excellence and meaning, they inveigh their colleagues to reach higher too.

Reimagining a City Block

Post-World War II Phoenix saw yet another rebirth of this ashes-to-riches city. The depredations of the Depression yielded to a booming economy driven by the technical industries and military facilities needed to win World War II. After the war, Phoenix was able to satisfy the appetite of people like Al Beadle who served in the South Pacific and wanted a warmer climate with plenty of cheap land and available buildings where they could start new businesses. The Valley of the Sun became a destination for road trippers wanting to stretch their wallets through travel to exotic warm locales; it was a mark for mid-century America's wanderlust.

Unfortunately, downtown Phoenix was hobbled by the centrifugal force of the freeway system that flung residents towards the suburbs where they could enjoy big new houses, schools and golf courses. When Brian moved to the area in the early 1990s, he recalls the downtown being a ghost town, punctuated by the occasional new structure that stuck out against the residue of the mid-century boom cycle.

Phoenix is again seeing another economic rebirth after the country-wide disruptions of the 1970s and 1980s and again in 2008. This rebirth is driven by ASU and new types of technical industries meeting the needs of the population's growth. Local leaders are acutely aware of the increasingly dangerous legacies of global warming on the fragile Sonoran Desert ecology; concentrating population in sustainable buildings is a way to grapple with the climate change barreling down on the region.

This most recent rebirth is clear on a block where Jones Studio has helped ASU bring new energy and audiences downtown.Their new facility would become the Beus Center for Law and Society [BCLS]. Next door to BCLS is ASU's Thunderbird Global School of Management [TGSM], whose international outlook allows ASU to expand its offerings and capture Thunderbird's alumni to offer future business leaders an urban environment like those found at competitor campuses.

This specific downtown block is emblematic of Phoenix's rise-and-fall economy. Until 2010, it was

Above left Sahara Motor Inn aerial - 1994. **Above right** Sahara Motor Inn postcard - 1962.

home to the sprawling Sahara Motor Inn, opened in 1955. The Sahara's celebrity investors and desert climate cachet brought movie stars and regular Americans alike to Phoenix.[3] Its resort-like amenities made the Sahara Motor Inn an emblem of America's mid-century optimism and industrial might turned from the war machine towards leisure experiences for an exploding middle class. But America is a restless country of first adopters willing to throw out the old for a taste of the new. Styles of travel shifted from the great car adventure to airplanes with longer reach into ever-more distant locales. A new style of tourism gave the region its current "playground for the rich" reputation; this new tourism is focused on carpets of green grass, resource-intensive swimming pools and luxury second homes in the far reaches of the Valley. Finding companies or institutions motivated by a modicum of public good would be required to reignite growth in downtown Phoenix.

ASU has been adept at using its resources to reanimate the City's downtown core by working with a willing local government and plenty of cheap land. ASU has filled in downtown's gap-tooth smile with teaching, research and meeting facilities and student housing that together have brought life to the streets. The light rail system, launched in 2008, exceeded all predictions by providing transportation across the central sections of the region, linking Tempe and other parts of the city to downtown to encourage mobility for a distributed student and workforce. The University's multilayered strategic plans will play out over time, but by planting buildings and people in an underutilized urban center, their imprint on the social and cultural life of the region is unmistakable and hopefully irreversible.

Downtown Phoenix is virtually unrecognizable today from the early aughts. Its sidewalks bustle with students and a reenergized and changing business community. Central Avenue, the north-south thermometer that gauges the social "temperature" of the city, has become a gathering point for residents and visitors alike. Jones Studio had the opportunity to influence and nurture 21st century Phoenix's development by winning two adjacent ASU buildings sharing a block, partnering with highly regarded firms with experience in law or management schools respectively.

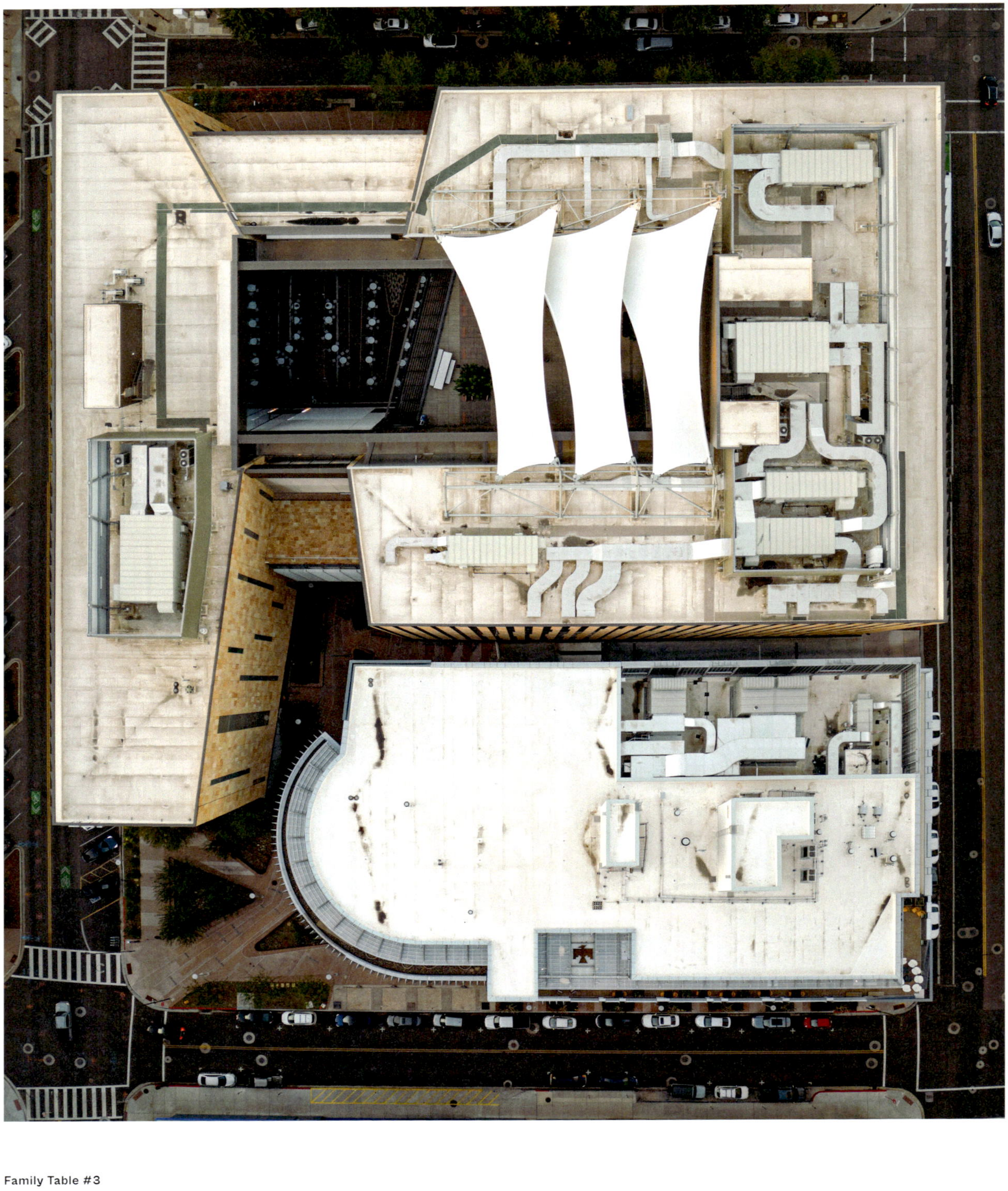

Family Table #3

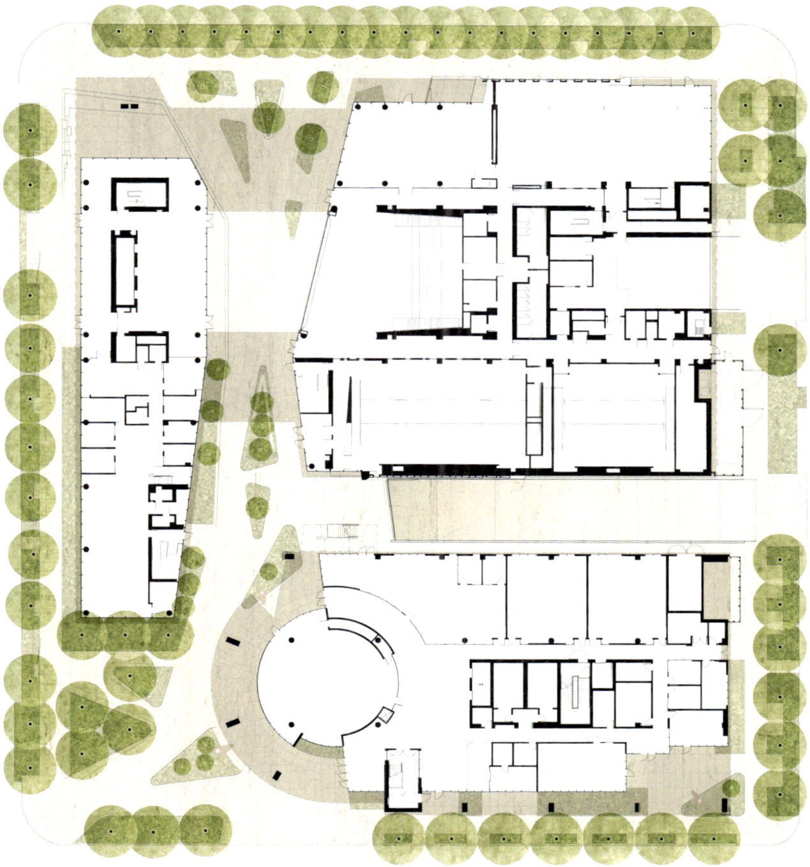

Opposite page Aerial of ASU Beus Center for Law & Society (upper left) sharing block with ASU Thunderbird School of Global Management (lower right). **Above** Site & ground floor plan of Beus and Thunderbird.

Shawn Swisher, who grew up in the Valley of the Sun and witnessed firsthand the evolution of its downtown, guided the Thunderbird project for his first undertaking with the studio. The team would contribute to this intentional refashioning of the city by applying its sensitivity to the aesthetics and natural life of the desert and a commitment to generous, connected public spaces which serve the conceptual goals of the University. Through Beus and Thunderbird, Jones Studio has the chance to monitor their design solutions over time, to observe how they evolve with changing demographics, social concerns and technologies.

Arizona State University Beus Center for Law and Society

Phoenix, Arizona, 2016

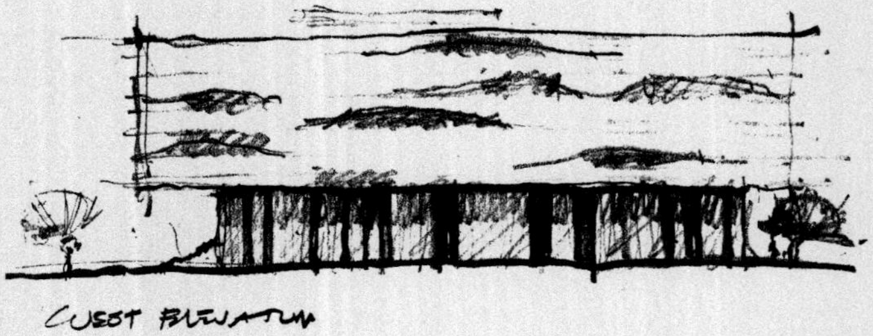

The premier school in the Beus Center for Law and Society is the Sandra Day O'Connor College of Law, named after the first woman to serve as a United States Supreme Court Justice.[4] By honoring Justice O'Connor, ASU not only claims a piece of history, it signals its intention to crack open the rigid legal structures designed to exclude women and people of color from the protections enshrined in the constitution. The College of Law is designed to change the standards for legal practice and processes for writing laws that have national and international ramifications. ASU's faculty will inculcate a sense of shared responsibility for the social contract at the heart of our democratic ideals that are under assault. BCLS exemplifies how architecture can fulfill those goals.

Jones Studio partnered with Ennead Architects of New York to develop a facility dedicated to educating students and citizens on the importance of law in shaping a civil society. Brian led the design for Jones Studio's team which focused on the interior development, working closely with Dean Doug Sylvester and Associate Dean Tom Williams of the College of Law. The two remarkable client collaborators led with clarity, vision and determination to ensure Beus expressed the dreams of the College.

One of the design drivers for Beus was connecting the school to the public realm for a new type of civic space. To achieve this, the design team cracked open the 270,000-square-foot building with a canyon at the ground plane, allowing students, faculty and citizens to have unimpaired access to the building and its capsules of knowledge. At the ground level, the "Great Hall" opens with a 50-foot-wide by 25-foot-tall airplane hangar style door (see page 365). Inside, a 250-seat auditorium faces the open slot canyon. The Hall can be informal, for impromptu study sessions, or formal, with presentations, projections and parties. Three stacked double-height spaces make up the core of the six-story structure. Finally, the fifth and sixth levels include a garden courtyard (see page 362) that allows light to penetrate deep into the building. This central stacked core is encircled by state-of-the-art classrooms, offices, meeting spaces, a working alumni law firm, campus bookstore and a restaurant in a protective outer shell of locally sourced Arizona sandstone.

Above Conceptual elevation study - Brian Farling. **Opposite page** Northwest corner.

FOR LAW AND SOCIETY

Opposite page Fifth floor courtyard. **Above** Executive conference room. **Below** Bookstore public art studies - Maria Salenger.

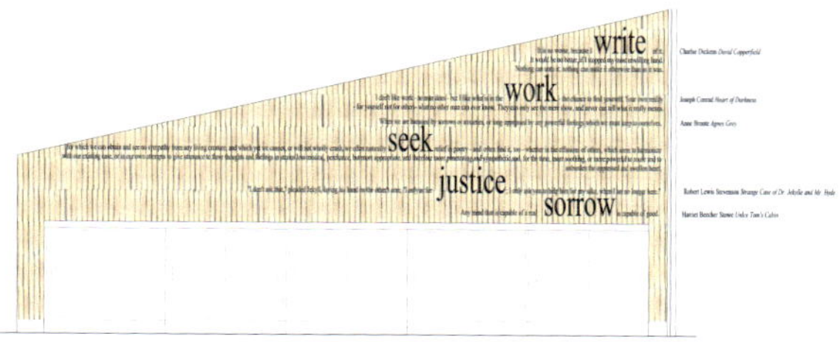

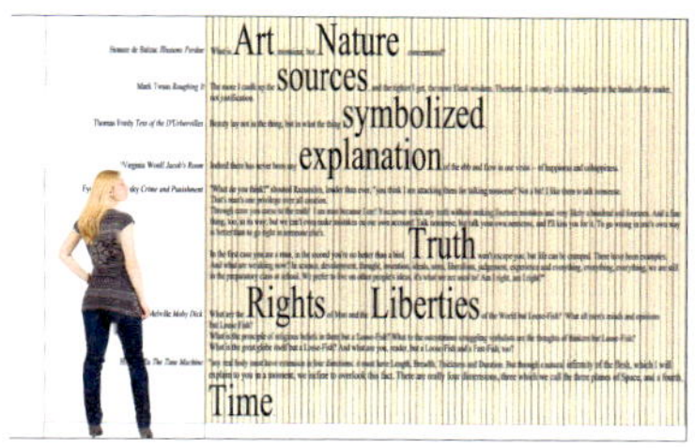

Maria worked closely with Brian on all aspects of the interior including a public art installation inside the bookstore. Against a background of many book fore-edges (the part that opens) in cream and white, Maria arranged 20 quotes from classic 19th century novels reflecting the various disciplines—law, journalism, visual art, nursing, health and letters—located in ASU's downtown campus. The idea was to show how academic disciplines affect lay people, and vice versa, through the quotes.[5] Maria's text-based work honors the prodigious intellectual labor that spins from universities, taking life in their communities as their theories become concrete.

Opposite page Third floor bridge. **Above** "Hangar" door at Great Hall. **Below left** Great Hall event. **Below right** Private stucy rooms.

Family Table #3

Opposite page Student reading room. **Above** Lobby reception. **Below left** Seminar rooms at top of Great Hall. **Below right & following spread** Library "Living Room" with skylight diffusers.

Arizona State University Thunderbird School of Global Management

Phoenix, Arizona, 2021

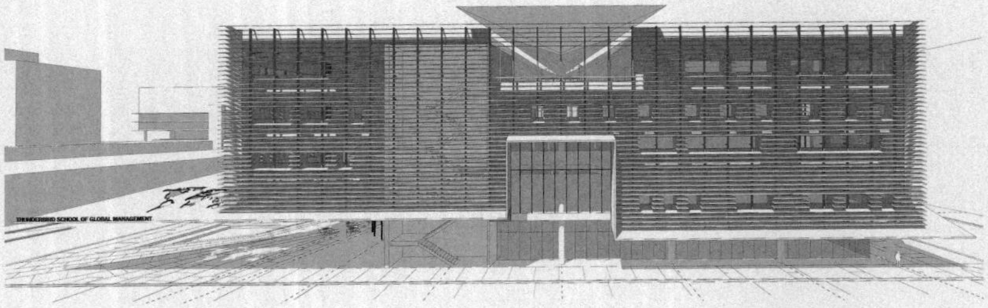

The Thunderbird School of Global Management, the first graduate management school focused on global business, was founded in 1946 on a deactivated wartime airfield in Glendale, Arizona. The school's founding mission statement, "Borders frequented by trade seldom need soldiers," was a call for the globalization of commerce to prevent future world-shaking conflict.[6] ASU purchased Thunderbird in late 2014 with the intention to move it to the downtown campus. With Thunderbird refreshed and renewed under ASU's leadership, ASU was able to plant a foothold in the global market for students by connecting to Thunderbird's 13 Centers in North and South America, Africa, Europe, Asia and the Middle East. Thunderbird allowed ASU to solidify its international connections and compete with other American schools building campuses abroad. Thunderbird sits on the remaining third of the old Sahara Motor Inn block to the south of Beus. The goal for this 110,000 square foot, five-story building was to create a seamless connection to local and global conversations in the Fourth Industrial Revolution.[7]

In contrast to Beus, Jones Studio led the exterior design for Thunderbird with partners at Moore Ruble Yudell, Los Angeles, who brought their experience designing business and management schools to the interior. This dedication to diminishing distance and borders with technology, with an ethical approach to our shared humanity, is brought alive in the ground level Global Forum. The Forum is shaded from the Arizona sun by deep overhangs and vertical shade fins. The Global Forum's two-story cylindrical volume opens with a sliding wall of glass to the public canyon, complementing Beus' Great Hall. The Hall connects digitally to international thought leaders, demonstrating what diverse, dispersed leadership looks like. Surrounded by a balcony ring of high-resolution displays, touch screen interfaces and a suspended 16-foot-diameter digital globe, the Forum is a step into the future of education, global communication and commerce.

Above Conceptual elevation study - Shawn Swisher. **Opposite page** Interior Global Forum extending to exterior with vertical shade fins above. **Following spread** Southwest corner of Thunderbird and Beus from above.

F. Francis & Dionne Najafi
Thunderbird Global Headquarters

ASU

401

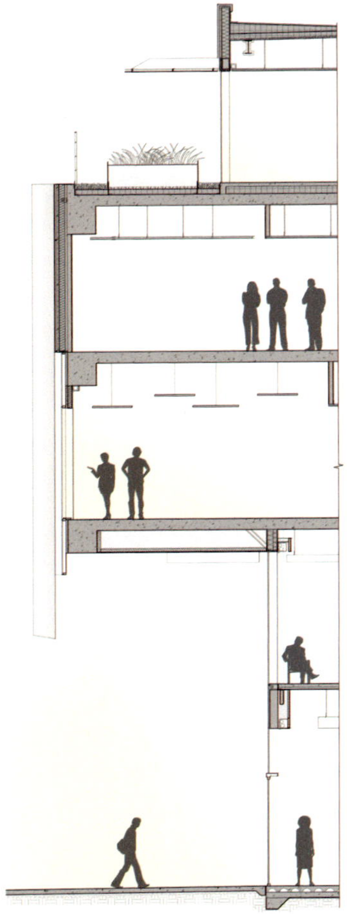

Above left Pedestrian "canyon" connecting Beus and Thunderbird. **Above right** Wall section at Global Forum and shade fins. **Below** Thunderbird roof drain drawings and inspiration image. **Opposite page** Thunderbird roof drain screen "wings".

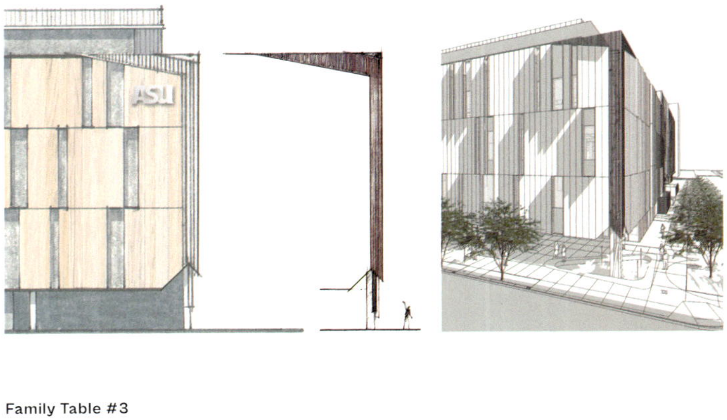

The exterior is a composition of silver metal, glazing and Arizona sandstone, extending the local geological references from BCLS to distinguish the entire block. In contrast to the high-tech of the Global Forum, a long-cherished, low-tech tradition of the Thunderbird Pub was built on the roof. The high-tech digital world is brought down to Earth over a drink and views of the Phoenix skyline and the desert's distant mountains, reminding us that business can still be conducted in-person.

Water consciousness was realized by a passive harvesting strategy that also honors the various Indigenous stories of the Thunderbird. Roof drains are expressed at the northwest and southeast corners of the building, carefully guiding rain down the building to a series of interlocking sunken rain gardens in the ground level canyon. At the roofline, 40-foot-tall custom grills at each drain flare like wings in honor of the building's namesake. The technologies of the Fourth Industrial Revolution allow us to connect to people elsewhere while these crucial design structures remind us that ancient communities were first gathered by their shared natural resources like water.

Above Lobby and cafe. **Opposite page** Global forum with continuous curved digital display and digital globe display. **Following spread** Southeast corner.

ership for the Fourth Industrial Revolution

ASU
N 400
2nd St

120

Return to the Border

Jones Studio has had the unique opportunity to address the complex needs and meanings of the U.S.-Mexico border. They have forged with the General Services Administration a positive and trusted working relationship that allows the design team to tackle complex processes with transparent accountability and feedback mechanisms. But in dealing with the United States at its edges, Jones Studio is drawn into real (and ginned-up) geo-political strife. Between 2016 and 2020, over 472 changes were made to U.S. immigration policies.[8] These granular changes shift how visitors come across the border to shop, and impact workers who enable a constant flow of food and goods that support both economies. These changes cause whiplash for the employees of the Ports and their contractors, like Jones Studio, who help to fashion efficient and equitable spaces of exchange.

Above Jones Studio team in Nogales, Mexico on BorderLinks tour with border wall art in background. **Opposite page above** Commercial truck queuing in Mexico at Otay Mesa Land Port of Entry. **Opposite page right** Otay Mesa LPOE collage of aerial and existing conditions - Brian Farling.

RODRIGUEZ

San Luis Land Port of Entry North Annex Building

San Luis, Arizona, 2016

Since the 19th century, Americans have needed labor from south of the border to build, harvest, clean and nurture, but it has always been an uneasy relationship, with immigration quotas and threats of deportation boomeranging back at our neighbors to the south as thanks.[9] America makes her borders firm but needs help managing the land captured inside them. In response to America's desperate call for help in harvesting food, César Chávez founded the United Farm Workers in 1962 to demand rights (equal and hazard pay and establishment of heat standards) for the migrant farm workers who answered that call.[10] Chávez was born near Yuma, Arizona, and died in San Luis, Arizona in 1993, making San Luis an historic site of struggle for equity along the southern border.

By the 2010s the existing 1980s San Luis border facility was inadequate to handle current pedestrian traffic. Day laborers who harvest produce in the fields that supply 80% of the leafy greens used by Americans during the winter months were experiencing long wait times, lining up at two in the morning to get to the fields by sunrise. Jones Studio won the GSA contract to design a small annex building that would accelerate cross-border pedestrian traffic. By imagining a more comfortable experience, Jones Studio would create a moment of positive interaction to support these hard-working agricultural workers while maintaining the high safety standards required by the Port's federal agencies.

San Luis sits on the border south of Yuma at the southwestern-most corner of Arizona "as the Colorado River turns to dust and there's no water left."[11] Yuma receives about three inches of rainfall per year (by contrast Phoenix gets about seven and Tucson luxuriates, by desert standards, with almost fourteen). Solving the technical needs of the Port was straightforward, but the designers wanted to capture the life and movement of the water that is central to the region's life.

Above Sawtooth section sketch - Brian Farling. **Opposite page** Pedestrian path and shadows.

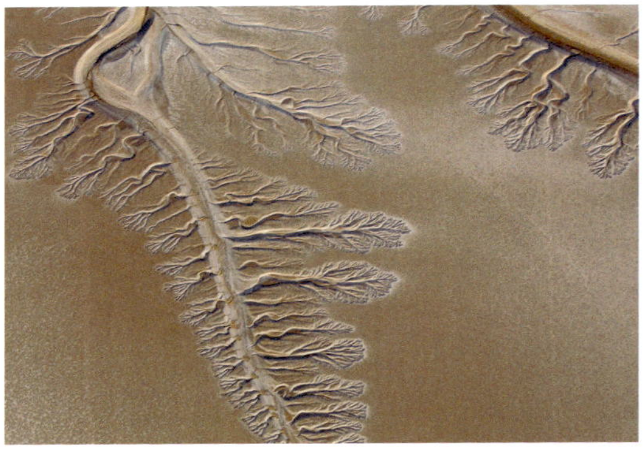

Top left Aerial photo of dry Colorado River delta. **Top right** Agriculture fields of the Yuma Valley. **Above left & right** Lettuce fields and sawtooth furrows.

In his book *Landscape and Western Art*, Malcolm Andrews observes that architecture is about controlling the relationship between people and the landscape.[12] At San Luis, Jones Studio found ways to connect the two by honoring the symbols and resources that fuel the regional economy. The primary image of the Port is inspired by the linear rhythm of the sawtooth furrows that funnel water to the plants in the nearby fields. An extruded sawtooth pattern cuts across the facility, skylights at the high points flooding the space with light (see page 382). Visitors are pulled through the building by the channels of sun, like water following the troughs that guide water to the greens outside. Jones Studio has created a lovely visual feedback loop connecting humans to the plants that feed them.

Harvesting graywater can be expensive because it must be gathered, filtered and stored while awaiting reuse. For this small 8,000-square-foot glass, galvanized metal and steel building, there was an outsized number of drinking fountains, sinks and showers, making a graywater system an appropriate investment to give water a second life. The team also channeled water coming off the roof to irrigate the native trees and plants that replaced non-native growth, but not before the water does a small dance by the public exit before it goes back to work. An expandable photovoltaic array was installed, so along with abundant daylighting and precise control systems, the building sees 41% energy savings over traditional systems.

Above Migrant agricultural workers of San Luis Rio Colorado, Mexico. **Following spread** Primary pedestrian entry with "safety yellow" canopy.

As with many Jones Studio projects, color plays many roles, from wayfinding to the creation of an emotional experience in shared space. At San Luis the color choice was prompted by observations at Mariposa, where even before the building was completed, splotches of safety-yellow paint would bloom. The staff's do-it-yourself bright yellow safety program covered curb edges in officer work areas and the protective bollards surrounding the scanning equipment. At San Luis, safety-yellow is not an afterthought, but an important design element used to identify wayfinding elements while denoting the primary safety function of the site.

The San Luis North Annex Building served as a "seed" building in anticipation of a future overall redevelopment of the facility. In 2022, with newly approved government funding, Jones Studio teamed up with Hensel Phelps, the contractor that built Mariposa, to apply for the massive redesign project. Jones Studio won the project based on their skills designing high-functioning, landscape-sensitive facilities that support dignified work and travel. As with Mariposa, redesigning the traffic patterns to expedite private vehicle traffic and pedestrian processing while using the desert to connect the two sides are the umbrella goals for the redesign. San Luis, Arizona, and its border twin San Luis, Rio Colorado, will be reunited through design with Alberto Ríos's stitched together border in mind.

U.S. Customs and
Border Protection

U.S. Customs and
Border Protection

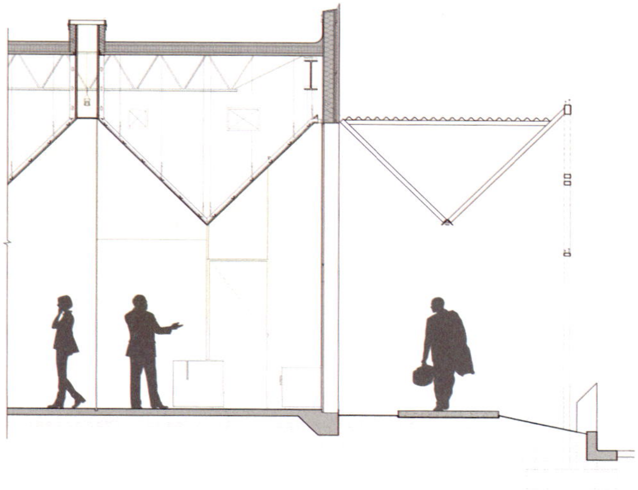

Opposite page Sawtooth ceilings and strip skylights. **Above left** Section drawing of sawtooth at interior and exterior. **Above & below** Pedestrian processing lobby and "safety yellow" booths.

Above Custom wedge shaped mullion extrusion and glazing system. **Below** Recessed glazing sill in concrete slab edge. **Opposite page** West elevation at dusk. **Following spread** Southwest corner at dusk.

Otay Mesa Land Port of Entry

San Diego, California, 2023

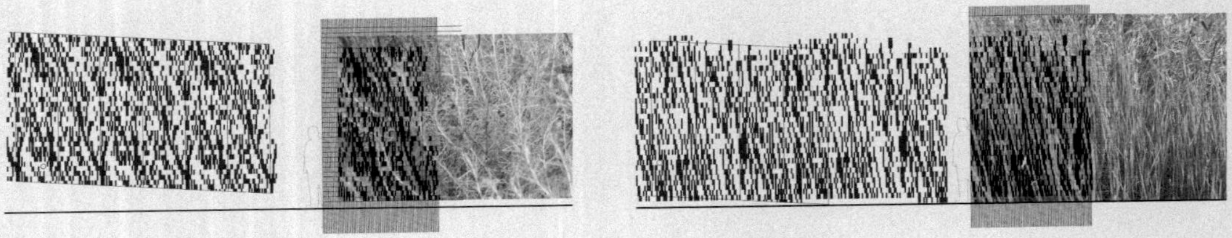

Like other southern land ports of entry, Otay Mesa represents the conflicting goals of American immigration and trade policies. Californians are uniquely connected to Mexico since the entire state was wrested from Mexican hands in the Treaty of Guadalupe Hidalgo in 1848.[13] The 1990s San Diego "tortilla" wall that extends west from Otay Mesa into the Pacific Ocean counters Californians' sense of equity and mutual dependence with their neighbor. Finding an architectural vocabulary that would bring to life the communities' aspirations for a collective response to issues of mutual benefit would be Jones Studio's animating goal.

For this Design/Build project, Jones Studio teamed with Gruen Associates, Los Angeles, and builder Atkinson/Clark Construction's San Diego office. In pursuing the Otay Mesa project, the team resolved the conflict between operations and truck circulation rather than abiding by the requirements in the RFQ. This was a calculated risk that luckily paid off—they won the job. They have reimagined the commercial side of the Otay Mesa Land Port of Entry [OMLPOE] to speed up inspection times and ease the flow of traffic between the U.S. and Mexico.

The traffic pattern of the existing Port was oddly convoluted. Enormous, lumbering trucks were forced to weave across traffic, dancing around other gigantic vehicles before being released. Using their experience at Mariposa, Jones Studio developed a range of solutions to support the Port's goals of easing trade bottlenecks, unblocking pedestrian flow, integrating the new technologies used to implement government regulations, reducing the environmental footprint in the fragile coastal desert and creating a positive work and travel environment for employees and visitors alike. Jones Studio commandeered a nine-acre open field to the east of the existing Port to improve traffic flow while the existing Port could lumber on. A central docking building for heightened checks was preserved, but the flow smoothed and flattened out to the east, allowing for the bulk of truck movement to always circulate in the same direction.

Above Sun scrim pattern study - Maria Salenger. **Opposite page** Stainless steel custom perforated sun scrim at main north edge public entry. **Following spread** Canopied courtyard at pedestrian gathering area.

WELCOME TO THE
UNITED STATES
ESTADOS UNIDOS
THANK YOU FOR
YOUR COOPERATION
GRACIAS POR SU COOPERACION

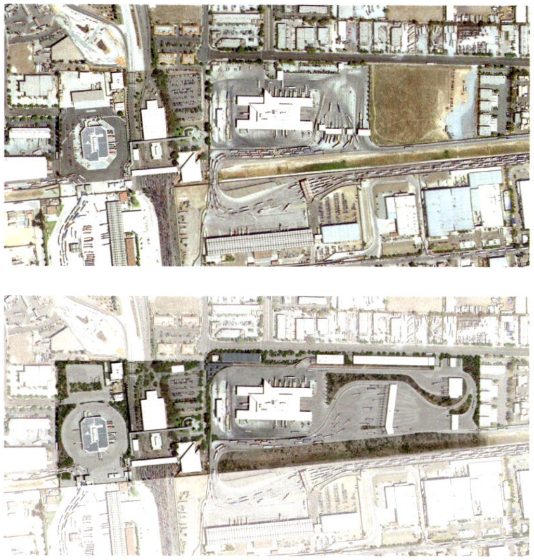

Opposite page Curved masonry wrapper wall with perforations. **Above left** Before and after aerials stacked. **Above right** Eddie and Jacob on construction site.

Another pillar of the development was to connect to the community surrounding the facility. The OM-LPOE forms the southern edge of the small community of Otay Mesa, with retail shops, restaurants, offices and warehouses across the street from the Port (see page 400). To respond to this existing commercial neighborhood, Jones Studio designed a new building, positioning it along the northern border of the site to support and permit a range of public-facing activities for the traveling public. A wrapper wall weaves in and out of, across and through the campus, capturing and controlling the site's beehive of movement while presenting a cohesive architectural face for the facility. Inspired by Jones Studio's own office building, the patterned masonry wall opens and closes to let light in or out, curves to embrace pedestrians and straightens up to help support the building's roof.

This building's primary public entrance is situated at a new pedestrian plaza designed as a desert garden to shade visitors and staff using custom canopies and a gauzy curtain of landscaping. The plaza, located partly inside the secure compound and partly in the public area, expresses the complex reality of the border. Public amenities were placed closest to public traffic flow, shaded by the blur of plants and shade structures that diminish the effects of the heat island. Exterior circulation pathways for Port personnel are capped with photovoltaic panels. California's natural white light feeds the campus with its abundance. The gardens soften the hard contours of the Port, wandering between public and private realms, stitching people together as Alberto Ríos imagined.

All land ports of entry are like the mythical Roman God Janus. They surveil and support, look forward and back, oversee beginnings and endings. The technologies supporting federal regulations execute the surveillance role of the port, monitoring and controlling who enters and leaves. But it is Jones Studio's design that makes the Port's beginning and endings more humane.

Above Public access building and existing port art work - *Spirit of the Earth*, Bob Haozous, 1995. **Below** Main entry of United States Department of Agriculture building. **Opposite page** Custom perforated walkway. **Following spread** Public lobby and dappled daylight.

CBP CAJERO
CBP CASHIER
TRUSTED TRAVELER
CHECK IN / CASHIER

10
11
12
13

Pacific Highway Land Port of Entry

Blaine, Washington, 2023

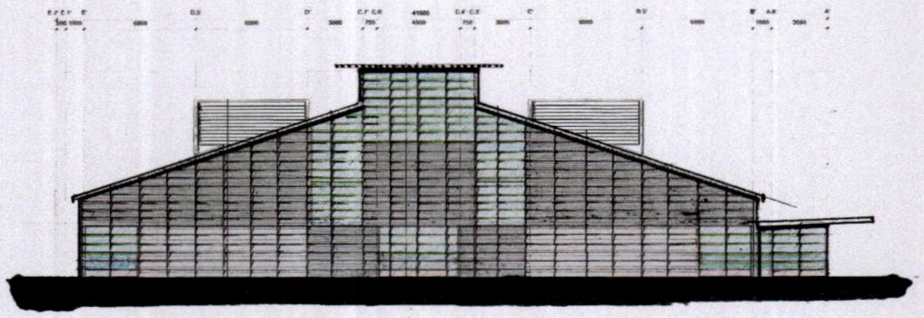

Jones Studio was awarded their first GSA Land Port of Entry project on the U.S.-Canada border, the world's longest international border, stretching 5,525 miles with over 100 border crossings. Blaine, Washington, is the northernmost town on the Interstate 5 highway. The nearby Peace Arch Monument, marking friendship between the two countries, suggests the radically different attitude we have towards Canada than Mexico. Blaine has the same political and safety mandates as the users of the Ports at Nogales, San Luis and Otay Mesa—minus a wall—but the climatic conditions pose drastically different problems. Blaine sees precipitation 159 days for a total of nearly 38 inches of rain per year, with about eight inches of snow thrown in for good measure. Jones Studio was moving from drought to deluge.

The original Pacific Highway LPOE was built in the early 1990s and leaked from the start due to poor construction. For this Design/Build project Jones Studio partnered with Hensel Phelps' Seattle office. The primary goal was to resolve long-term water infiltration and air leakage by elevating the building envelope's moisture control while also addressing performance issues such as energy efficiency. Repairing the facility while it stayed open would be risky, requiring a carefully phased sequence of temporary protection then demolition of the existing façade and roof followed by construction of the new wrapping. Jones Studio would also renovate canopies and shade structures to protect visitors and staff from the abundance of water. The building's long wood-clad shapes are reminiscent of Northwest Indigenous longhouses, homes for extended families to share daily living

Top Conceptual elevation study - Eddie Jones. **Above** Construction photos of new envelope. **Opposite page above** Existing commercial cargo building. **Opposite right** Perspective drawing of reimagined envelope - Eddie Jones.

Bus
Inspection

BUS

chores and social and political gatherings. Jones Studio preserved this building type to reinforce the Pacific Highway Port's relationship to its community.

Jones Studio enjoyed the challenge and contrast of addressing 30 plus inches of annual rain as compared to their local seven inches of rainfall, providing the opportunity to focus more on the building envelope in this very wet part of the world. Learning about too much water was educational as the firm simultaneously continued their work to salvage every drop in the Southwest.

Jones Studio's work with the GSA has come full circle. The GSA took a chance on the firm with the Mariposa Land Port of Entry, but today, the GSA, like many clients, is looking for firms with experience in specific building types. Jones Studio has been successful with their "we've never done that before" and "we'll bring a fresh perspective" attitude, but with the Land Port of Entry typology, they are now the 300-pound gorilla. How ironic.

Above left Mural study drawing - Maria Salenger. **Above right** Existing auto and pedestrian building. **Below** Perspective drawing of reimagined envelope - Eddie Jones.

Focused Future

Unbuilt and Conceptual Projects

The unbuilt projects explored in *STRIVE* exemplify Jones Studio's passion for architecturally inventive, emotionally fulfilling and systems-changing projects, even when the structures may never come alive. Jones Studio has designed several significant water-focused programs that confirm the team has always been on the right path for a sustainable future; the more difficult issue is finding the right funder, politician or organization to commit to a vision that will require sacrifice and change. These speculative projects allow creatives to unlock new ideas that will find an outlet elsewhere, no ideas are wasted, no moment of brilliance forgotten even when the source project never makes it off the paper.

Occasionally there are those speculative opportunities that seem simply too good to be true. It's easy for an organization or individual to reach out to an architect always eager to give expression to someone's hopes and vision. It is *much* harder for that resource-rich person or group to face the difficult realities when building something that will shock and awe clients and competitors alike. These projects are harder to bear when they disappear like some desert mirage, like a figment of the designer's imagination. Eddie would put a recent private home commission into the "too good to be true" column, and although the project will never be built, he cherishes the process of thinking and drawing. His knows his ideas are meaningful, and he has the patience to wait for the right opportunity to come along to let them sing.

Opposite page Phoenix Tower concept model.

Monroe Street Abbey

Phoenix, Arizona, fundraising phase

Eddie, Chris Winters and architect Michael Johnson, who in his eighties is still making pristine Miesian homes, spent a morning in early 2011 searching for an older building to test mutual friend and inspiration Herb Greene's theory of architecture as a community "Armature" for art installations, performance and other social activities. The trio spent the day rooting out possibilities but were disappointed by what they did not find. Although they were tired and looking forward to happy hour, Chris offered one last idea. They stopped by what appeared to be an abandoned church, still intact except for boarded up doors. They took turns peering into the interior through the widest crack in the fencing. All three knew they had come upon a perfect opportunity to test Greene's idea of cultural Armature in the former place of worship missing its roof and with a secret garden growing inside. The transformation of this once sacred space downtown would give Jones Studio the chance to be part of historic preservation and revitalization in the city. Monroe Street Abbey is, like the Pauson Chimney, another of Eddie's personal passion projects, honoring the buildings, and thus the people, who have shaped Phoenix.

Relative to other large U.S. cities, Phoenix is young and therefore short on buildings that tell the city's modern history, and its building stock from the late 19th and early 20th century has largely been erased from the landscape. Even the buildings of Frank Lloyd Wright and other significant mid-century modern architects are continuously under threat unless well-loved and used, like Valley Presbyterian Church. Most of the area's older masonry, bow string truss warehouses were demolished to make room during the 20th century's boom periods. Things have been changing, however; between 1989 and 2006 the City developed bond and grant programs to encourage preservation of historic structures and neighborhoods to provide some stability in the housing market and reduce the impact of tearing down newer structures.[1] Local leaders were slowly understanding that repurposing the past provides guiderails for the future.

Above Section sketch - Eddie Jones. **Opposite page** Former First Baptist Church of Phoenix - future Monroe Street Abbey.

Above Existing conditions with structural stabilization interventions. **Opposite page** Concept perspective drawings - Chris Winters.

Architect Herb Greene's "Armature" concept inveighs architects to work with artists, citizens, builders, developers, craftspeople and others not normally included in the design and construction of their communities to treat historic structures as "permanently renewable buildings." Greene's philosophy asserts that architects have the chance to revive their communities through sensitive interventions and resuscitations that preserve cultural memory.[2] The Monroe Street Abbey allows Eddie, Maria and Chris Winters, along with Greene's niece, architect and filmmaker Lila Cohen, the chance to engage with one of Phoenix's few modern "ruins," which has kept the team's excitement high despite years of funding fits and starts.

The Phoenix First Baptist Church was founded in 1883. The congregation's new Monroe Street building, by architect George Merrill, New York with local firm Fitzhugh and Byron, was begun in 1903.[3] In 1929 the old church was leveled for a larger, more modern structure that opened in 1930, with another addition in 1950. The last service there was 1968, before the congregation moved out of downtown. In 1982 the building was placed on the National Register of Historic Places [NRHP]. Unfortunately, a 1984 fire gutted the interior and roof of the church, and the city declared the building a hazard in 1992. The First Baptist Church was saved by the non-profit Housing Opportunity Center, founded by former City of Phoenix Mayor and Arizona Attorney General Terry Goddard.[4] The group bought the Church and built low-income apartments next door to protect the complex from new development encroachment.[5]

The First Baptist Church was unique because the congregation wanted "evangelism through staged presentation," not just a top-down, or rather pulpit-to-pew, delivery of the day's homilies. The Church's architecture signaled a shift from traditional organized religion to ritual through community performance, which is why the building is listed on the NRHP. New design elements included a screen that rose out of the stage, a radio broadcasting booth, a lighting switchboard, chairs rather than pews for flexibility and a flat ceiling to draw the 1,500 worshipers' attention to the stage. The

First Baptist Church represented a shift in how Phoenicians perceived religion in a rapidly urbanizing and modernizing America. Religion had to catch up to the technical innovations of radio and the movies if it wanted to stay relevant to its flock.

Jones Studio's goals for the decommissioned Church, now called the Monroe Street Abbey, include attracting different communities to the space to perform their versions of contemporary secular life. Construction priorities include inserting safety systems and public amenities and conceptualizing portable audio visual and sound systems that can capture sounds from inside while rebuffing noise from outside. They anticipate the building will hold a unique combination of conditioned and unconditioned spaces to support future tenants providing food, entertainment and other cultural activities in spaces ranging from a secret basement hideout to a rooftop bar with a fireplace and views of the city. Jones Studio has overseen the rebuilding of internal structures with bracing for safe access while awaiting resources to build out more robust infrastructure elements.

The studio is working with Chris Winters to expand the sanctuary courtyard's secret garden, a refuge from the concrete hardscape of downtown. Water harvesting strategies include a tank integrated into the underground systems that will keep the gardens vibrant throughout the year. There is a lovely textural difference in the open courtyard between the stone walls and arches, the "melting" strip pilasters and the gleaming aluminum and steel beams. The contrast of old and new promises to make the Abbey an enchanting place, and perhaps one day, it will be part of the pulsing central core.

This slow-moving preservation project shows Jones Studio expanding its reach as a creative, arts-focused firm. Teaching the next generation how to care for their inheritance and consider social good drives Jones Studio's care for the property. Through the Abbey project, Jones Studio is reviving and restoring architecture of public value while avoiding the waste of history destroyed.

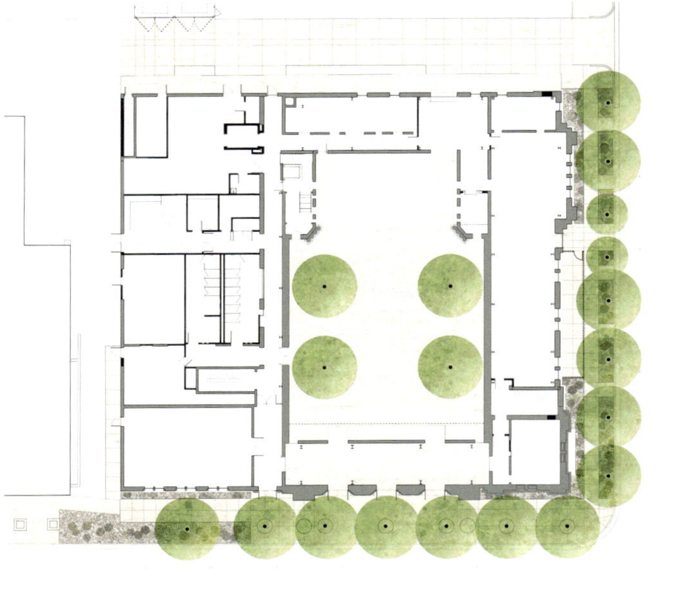

Above Floor and site plan. **Below** Section perspective. **Opposite page** Section perspective rendering.

Lake Havasu Environmental Learning Center

Lake Havasu City, Arizona, concept completed 2019

There are Two Easy Ways to Die in the Desert: Thirst and Drowning.
Craig Childs[6]

The Environmental Learning Center [ELC] was born of the 2017 America's Best Communities Competition sponsored by Frontier Communications, DISH Network, CoBank and The Weather Channel to revitalize small towns and rural communities.[7] Lake Havasu's leadership received the $2 million second prize to invest in "future-proofing" the town known for its spring break parties, retirees and kids who leave after they graduate. Lake Havasu's City's Vision 20/20 plan prioritized better schools, a coworking space and a water education "eco" center to reverse the demographic starvation that threatens the area's future.[8]

Lake Havasu, created by Parker Dam, is one of many reservoirs on the stressed and over-allocated Colorado River system that supplies water to over 40 million westerners and irrigates over 5.7 million acres of agriculture.[9] The Colorado River keeps America in carrots and lettuce all winter long.[10] Lake Havasu and Parker Dam are key elements in the overall system supplying water to Arizona and California. It is the nexus of water issues in a region challenged by antiquated water law, climate change and drought. City leadership understood their unique position to promote water resource awareness and stewardship and turned to Jones Studio to craft a vision for the Environmental Learning Center.

In the ELC, Jones Studio found a project where they could apply their evangelical fervor for conscious water design. The facility, envisioned as a regional model for sustainability, a community educational resource and a celebration of water in the desert, encourages engagement by highlighting complex water issues. Educational spaces like classrooms and observable water quality laboratories—where researchers discover alongside visitors—reinforce the Center's aspiration to be the premier water research institution in the Southwest. The environment for discovery includes experiential learning in physical and

Above Distant mountain sketch - Maria Salenger. **Opposite page** Arrival sequence rendering.

Above Interior exhibit and water quality lab rendering. **Below** Colorado River watershed map with Lake Havasu at the water nexus. **Following spread** Event center (at left) rendering with early morning sun.

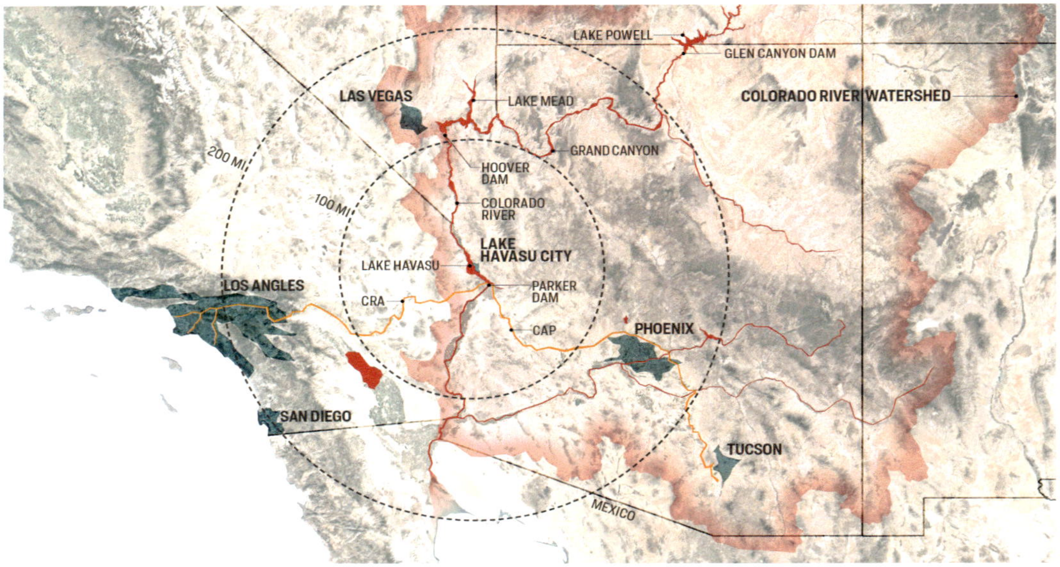

digital forms and utilizing immersive technology to better communicate research. Multi-purpose spaces of various scales support local partnerships and outreach, highlighted by the large, flexible event space overlooking the site. These areas are stitched together by galleries communicating the importance of water through different media with the goal of inspiring viewers to activate their own water-saving behaviors.

The ELC building, mirroring the geology and erosion of the desert, sits seamlessly in the site at the peak of the hillside, a staged gateway from the City to the rugged vistas beyond. Its fractured shapes frame views and carve paths across the desert. Cresting roof planes, recalling the jagged fragments of the adjacent hills, bring daylight and natural ventilation deep into the building while gently guiding rainwater to the ground below. Supporting concrete walls are cast with a face of loose stone quarried from the site in a tactile recognition of place.

In looking for a collaborator for the overall site, Brian turned to Los Angeles-based Mia Lehrer and Studio MLA to work on the project. Brian observes that, since Arizona and California have their straws deep into Lake Havasu, residents of both states have a stake in protecting it. Their innovative water management systems are activated through the harvesting gardens on site, most prominently in the central Living Machine Garden that illustrates how natural ecosystems can process blackwater for reuse. The grounds are a laboratory for discovery, visitors are invited to explore the flora native to the desert biome. A trail network leads from the ELC through the surrounding 280-acre park and nature preserve that includes exterior public gathering spaces, an amphitheater for on-site classes and outdoor performances as well as gardens for botanical research. Amenities like playgrounds and habitat towers, which shelter a diversity of displaced animals, invite learning through play and observation. The ELC's halo of desert gardens carry equal value to the learning spaces inside the structure. With reverence and joy, nature is yet again the teacher.

Inside the ELC, the cafe will serve local, sustainable food made from ingredients grown in the indoor hydroponic farm. Plants will root in sand and be fed with water and a nutritious drip solution, using a fraction of the water needed for traditional agriculture. Both inside and outside gardens illustrate the potential for sensible agriculture in the desert.

Jones Studio's water strategies provide the structure to help the ELC blossom with new thinking about the desert's own boom-and-bust—or drought-and-flood—cycles. Engaging visitors through varied adaptive uses underscores the importance of water in their lives. Through the informative interventions with the building's sustainable design strategies and on-site photovoltaics, the ELC holds the promise to transform the future of water in the desert.

Water issues are everywhere—either there is too much, as in Blaine, or there isn't enough, as in the entire Southwest. A project like the ELC requires an acute connection to our common problem, a scientist's ability to anticipate consequences and an architect's skill in shaping spaces that visualize these urgent and concrete issues. The ELC becomes an ecosystem that moves from source to use to reuse, from lake to food to toilet and back to lake. We must face this cycle squarely if we are to truly address the water crisis triggered by population growth and climate change. Humans and technology have accelerated this climate crisis; humans and technology should be harnessed to solve it.

 Above Main entry rendering with bioremediation fountain and Lake Havasu beyond. **Below** Wood study model of massing and immediate site. **Opposite top left** Site plan. **Opposite top right** Fractured rock found on site inspired plan organization. **Opposite bottom left** Floor plan. **Opposite bottom right** Concept plan sketch - Brian Farling. **Following spread** Inside event center rendering.

Upper Colorado River Basin
Lower Colorado River Basin
UTAH
Glen Canyon Dam
Page
COLORADO RIVER
LITTLE COLORADO RIVER
Las Vegas
Hoover Dam
Davis Dam
Parker Dam
CALIFORNIA
Phoenix
Imperial Dam
GULF OF CALIFORNIA

Above South Living Machine garden rendering. **Below** North and south elevations. **Opposite top** Section at water quality lab, Living Machine garden and rain water harvesting tank. **Opposite middle** Conceptual roof drainage drawing study - Brian Farling. **Opposite bottom** Conceptual elevation study - Brian Farling. **Following spread** Aerial rendering of overall facility at sunset.

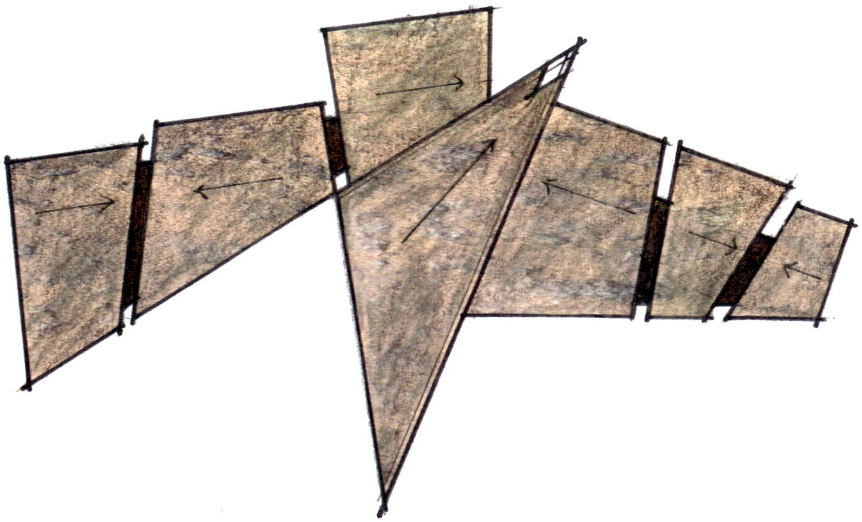

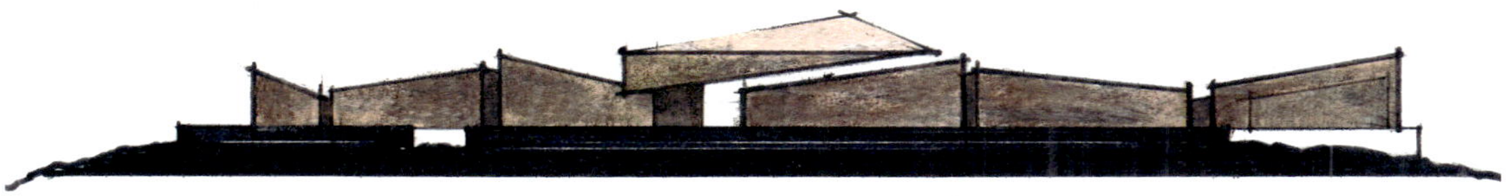

NORTH ELEVATION 1"=100'

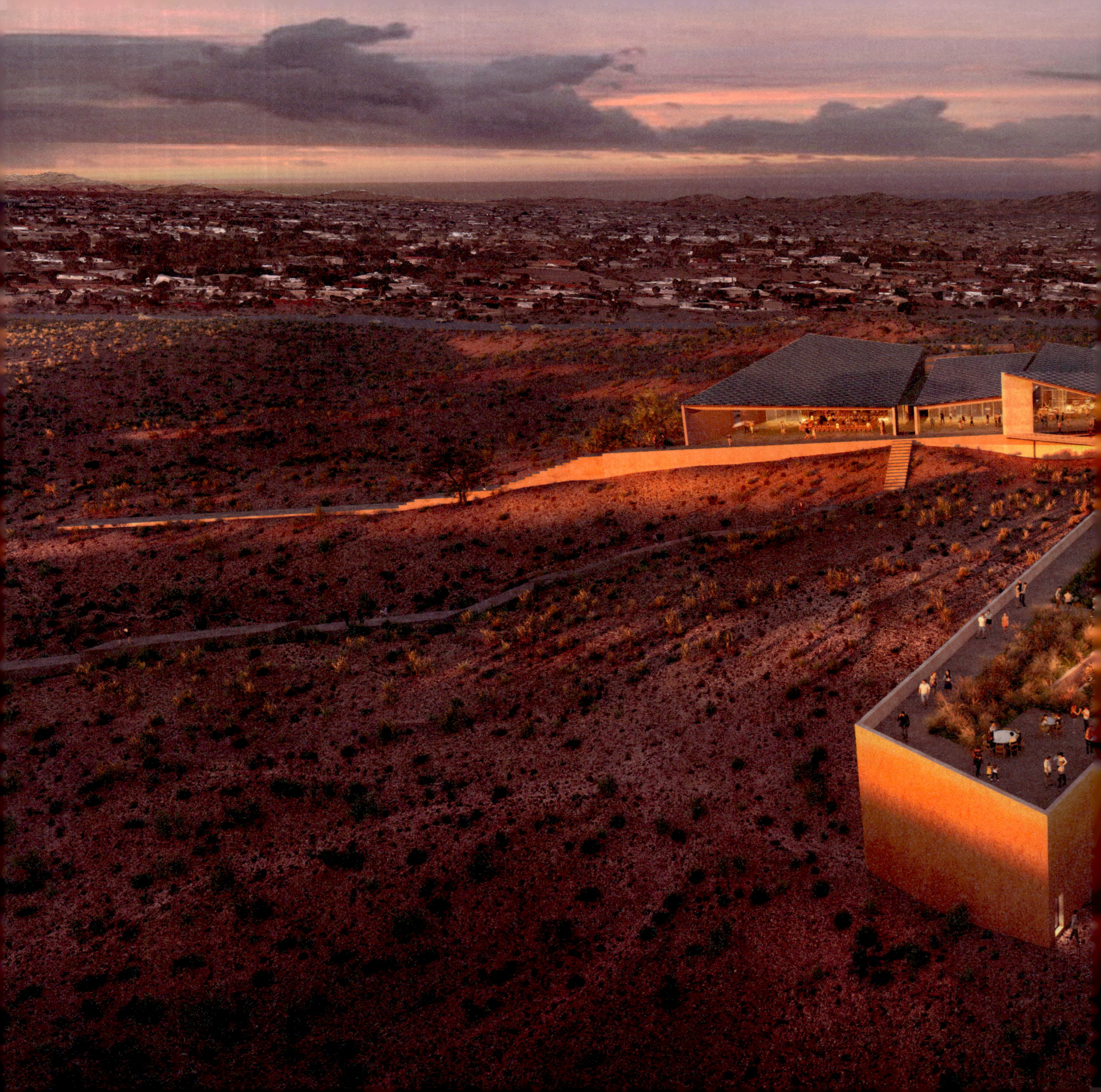

Phoenix Concept Tower Competition

Phoenix, Arizona, 2019

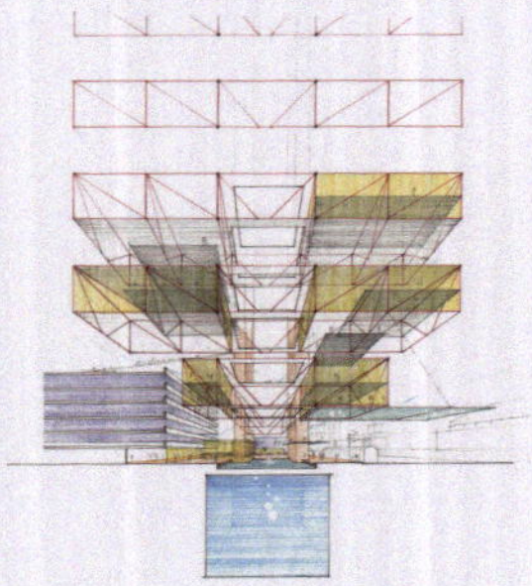

The 19th century invention of skyscrapers, pioneered by Louis Sullivan and Dankmar Adler, was an exuberant manifestation of America's newfound might during its youthful growth spurt. Skyscrapers represented the country's ability to amass wealth founded on a flood of new immigrants extracting resources from the land. Skyscrapers would thus appear to be an appropriate building type for Phoenix given its bouts of growth and boastful claims to big city status, but this tall building type is relatively rare in the city's downtown. Jon Talton, former journalist for the *Arizona Republic*, observed proximity to Sky Harbor airport and lack of corporate headquarters suppressed downtown building height. It seems a hit-and-run lifestyle facilitates an in-pouring of people but out-pouring of wealth that stops corporate and political leaders from investing in their own city.[11]

Yet we must consider multi-family housing as one strategy in managing our problems with sprawl. Cost-effective multi-family skyscrapers may be a way to in-fill downtown and encourage densification, words anathema to the country's mania for single-family houses. With downtown slowly being filled in by ASU, appropriately sized parcels for big projects have become scarce. Navigating the economies of the high-rise typology is an intriguing challenge, one Jones Studio was invited to consider. The goal was to create an efficient building that made business sense for the developer as well quality-of-living sense for its residents.

Unfortunately, the competition's developers could not assemble the three parcels needed because of a two-story building on the National Historic Register of Places, so the thought exercise was cancelled. But Eddie kept thinking about how a tall building could have enough leasable space to be profitable despite being on a hemmed-in, postage-stamp sized lot. He designed a building that would rise above those adjacent by creating a cantilevered structure, increasing the floor size once they cleared the neighboring rooflines. The huge cantilevers would require extremely deep trusses which would define the architecture's form and identity. Eddie would apply water harvesting

Above Perspective sketch - Eddie Jones. **Opposite page** Photo montage of tower in downtown Phoenix.

Alliance Bank
Bank of America

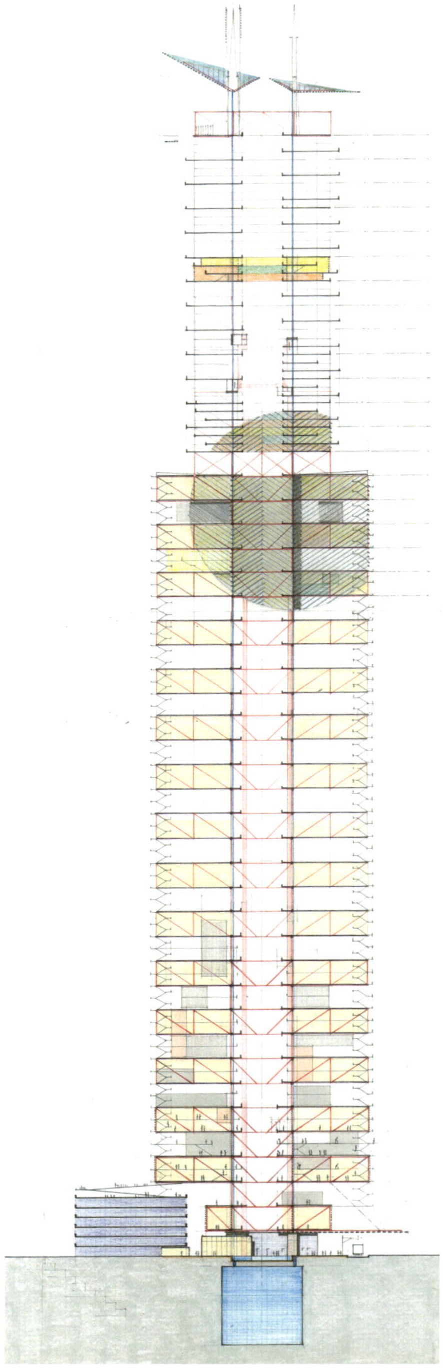

strategies to the miles of mullions, channeling rainwater to underground cisterns that would recirculate water for landscaping and other reuses. This would have been the tallest waterfall Eddie had ever designed. The cisterns would provide ballast to the building, perched on the lot like a giant flamingo with only one leg touching the ground.

The cost of multi-family housing—and the lock bankers, developers and inspectors have on processes and materials that reinforces an undistinguished sameness—prevents large-scale experimentation in this typology. Al Beadle created multi-family housing with good design but never with a developer for just that reason. Affordability is the sticking point for good architecture—is it only for the rich, especially in the sky? Just as revitalizing existing buildings will be key to halting the short build-tear down cycle, tackling multi-family housing could slow sprawl. The alarming rate of habitat loss, and animal, bird and insect extinction, needs to be reversed, and grappling with our insistence on individualized spaces may be the price paid to address these environmental problems.

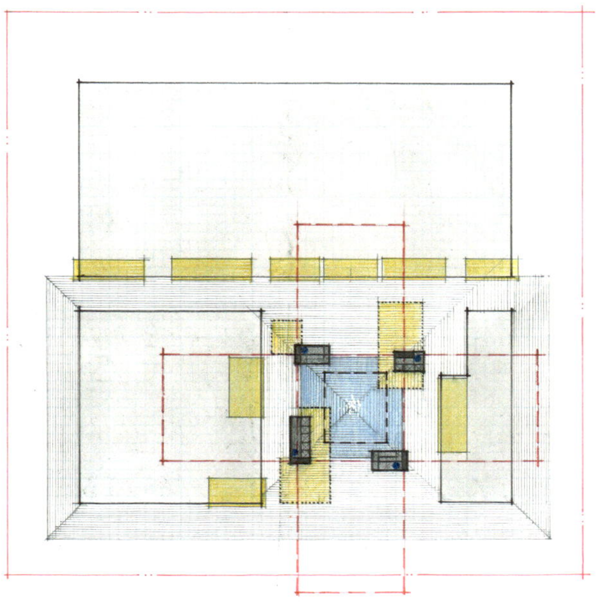

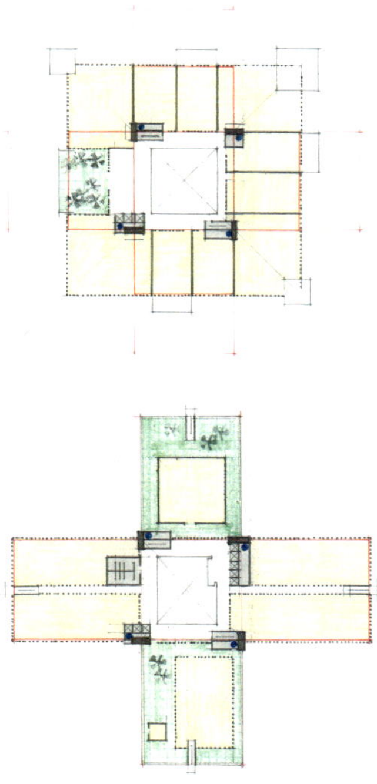

Opposite left Concept model. **Opposite right** Section drawing - Eddie Jones. **Above** Plan drawings at street level and above - Eddie Jones.

Rio Unido

Phoenix, Arizona, concept completed 2019

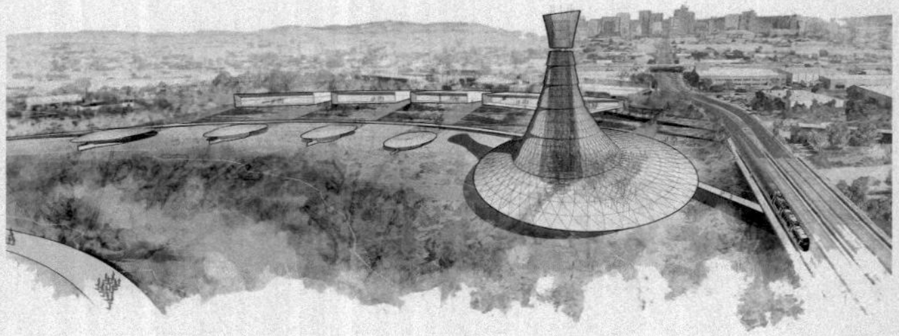

Cities can *only* exist when they have reliable access to water. The extraordinary expansion of urbanized spaces during the industrial revolution left our waterways degraded, and in America we buried rivers and canals underground to make way for roads, tearing up ancient water sources and wetlands as if nature did not use them. Communities across the country are reorienting themselves towards water for high end real estate and recreation, but more important, to reestablish an equilibrium and broad access to water that is at the core of our survival. Conservation is important, but water consciousness must be introduced to transform minds and thus transform systems as well.

Phoenix was born of the Salt River or *Rio Salado*. The Salt River hosted the West's largest irrigation system north of Peru, built by the Hohokam 1,000 years ago. Between 1906 and 1908, the U.S. Bureau of Reclamation built the 29-foot-tall Granite Reef Diversion Dam 22 miles northeast of Phoenix, with aqueducts used to control the Salt River's flow towards the gulf. Today the region's canal system, overlaid on the Hohokam's water system, rivals those of Venice in scale and scope. Cultural thinkers like Andrew Ross have explored the forces that led residents and speculators to prize growth over equity, single family homes over density, and other missteps in his 2011 book *Bird on Fire: Lessons from the World's Least Sustainable City*, decrying the short-sighted decisions that have brought us where we are today.[12] Yet there have been many changes in thinking in the region. Even though Arizona has ballooned in size from under a one million residents in 1957 to seven million in 2017, water usage has stayed steady or has even slightly dipped.[13] Decades of educational efforts, building process improvements, water use control and other individual and structural changes have had some impact. But it's not enough.

Jones Studio's Rio Unido proposal was in response to a "Rio Reimagined" competition call put out by a consortium of political and educational leaders in the region. The conceptual design

Above Alternate conceptual study for this site - Shawn Swisher. **Opposite page** Master plan drawing.

TO DOWNTOWN
URBAN FARMING
RESILIENT ZONE
RIO SALADO
OVERBANK TRAIL
OVERBANK TRAIL
RIO SALADO SCENIC DR
RESILIENT ZONE
URBAN FARMING
FARMING
FARMING
PUBLIC PLAZA
TO SOUTH PHOENIX

exercise was meant to stimulate thinking across social, cultural and economic boundaries of the Valley as the area faces increasing pressure to re-imagine collective water use. Jones Studio's vision was nothing less than a far-reaching effort to update, upgrade and upscale the celebration and preservation of water for the region's very existence. Brian, Shawn and Miles Foster led Jones Studio's response to the challenge of considering how 58 miles of the Salt River, flowing through six metro cities, two tribal communities, government properties and ASU, might again become the lifeblood of the city. This was another opportunity for the team to use their passion and professional goals to imagine, and perhaps drive, broad-based change that would affect millions of citizens for decades to come.[14]

Brian, Jones Studio's most avid water crusader (a prolific reader on the subject who even took a university level water law class), wants to consider water at its source, beyond one building and one client, and for public benefit, not just private profit.[15] He is sensitive to the elegant efficiency of the desert that is minimal *and* maximal in its forms and spaces. He notes we must radically change our acculturated way of existing on this planet. We've been programmed to turn the faucet on and not worry how the flowing water came to us, nor where it will go next. Water's life-giving cycles have been designed out of our experience. The conceptual Rio Unido project would bring together all of Jones Studio's thinking around Arizona's water opportunities, expressing water's preciousness and elevating how we engage with it.

During their deep analysis of the Salt River's meander, Brian, Shawn and Miles saw that the economically under-resourced South Phoenix was hidden behind a dirty wall of industrial buildings, enforcing a geographic segregation and environmental racism while changing the river's ecology. The studio recognized the need to apply a robust equity and inclusion lens to reverse decades-long actions by the few that have disrupted a disproportionately larger group of citizens. How could design reverse this equation?

For Rio Unido, the team created a multi-layered proposal that held overt political meaning by rebuking the casual degradation of our shared environment justified by our extractive lifestyles. Jones Studio proposed that citizens can, and must, understand that public benefit (community gathering spaces, walkable pathways, restoration of habitat, the breaking up of heat islands and protection of water) has clear and tangible private benefits (lower public health impacts and costs, improved quality of living and restoration of degraded industrial landscapes). Using the political space of water, the team also pointed out the irony that Phoenix has many "food deserts" in a state that helps feed the rest of the country with its bounty. Jones Studio's Rio Unido proposal takes advantage of existing infrastructure as well as the Rio Salado Habitat Restoration and Gateway Project designed by their frequent collaborator Christy Ten Eyck. Ten Eyck's project is south of Interstate 17, the sharp edge that slices through the city's cultural, social and ethnic groups. This additive action recognizes the work already accomplished by the region's creative thinkers and administrators while insinuating new layers of infrastructure and art into the mix.

Opposite page Existing conditions at the Rio Salado and Central Avenue.

As with Jones Studio's other work, water and sun are partners in linking ideas to place. The visual centerpiece is the spiraling Forum, built so its conic top reaches the same height above sea level as the Granite Reef Diversion Dam located miles up the river. At ground level much of Phoenix is unremarkable and monotonous; go up a story or two and the power of water on desert life erupts before us. The Forum's main purpose is to give viewers perspective from the air with views of the vast Valley of the Sun and the watershed that has shaped, and has been shaped by, the Salt River.

Finally, as part of a larger master plan, the design team created programmatic "rings" with practical ideas linked to social functions. The first ring is the Resilient Zone, providing recreation, conservation and education where the desert's inhabitants coexist. The natural cycles of drought and flood become actors in the desert's narrative. The next ring acknowledges the history of urban agriculture and the potential for rethinking our methods of food production. Finally, interpenetrating layers of mixed-use development, commercial and light industrial spaces are re-engineered away from the existing brittle buffer zone into more supple, subtle, environmentally and economically interconnected spaces demonstrating the possibilities for smarter city growth. The project encourages residents to reconsider what constitutes a holistic quality of life in the Valley.

This environmental reality in Phoenix's rear-view mirror is closer than it seems. The Hohokam's disappearance was long ago, but it was not far away. Historians and archaeologists tell us that civilizations do not build in deserts, rather deserts swallow civilizations. Nearly 30 years after Jones Studio showed suburbanites how they could live more responsibly in the Valley through the APS House, a broader swath of political, cultural and educational leaders are looking to the future through the blue of water, not the present green of money. In the face of environmental change triggered by human activities, the public must rely on—or force—its leaders to face the consequences of their inaction and take steps to blunt the coming changes to their communities. Rio Unido provided the studio the chance to synthesize their passions for sustainability and environmental equity and to describe real strategies to help the region avoid an environmental bust cycle.

Opposite page Conceptual look-out tower rendering.

NORMAL RIO

MONSOON RIO

FLOOD RIO

ZONES

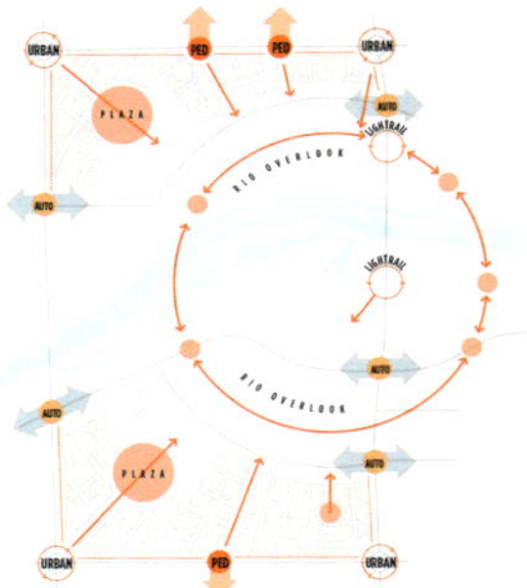

NODES
+
ACCESS

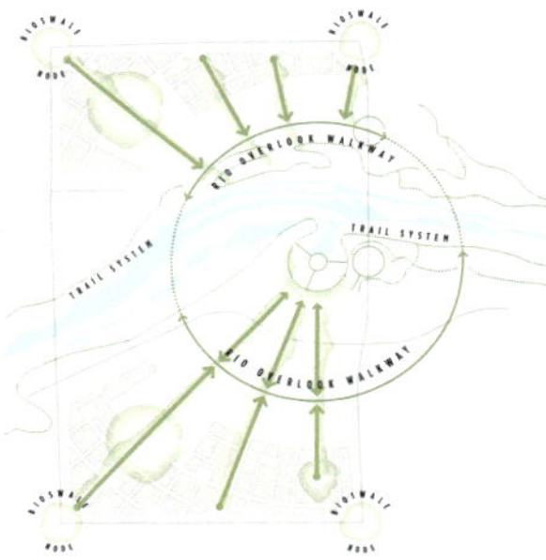

BIOSWALES
+
GREENWAYS

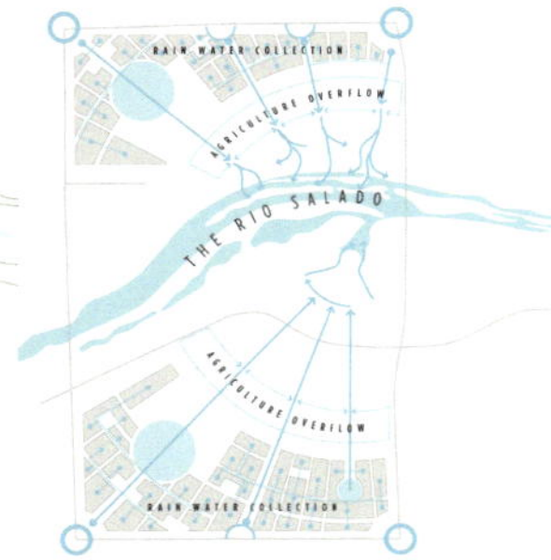

WATER
+
DRAINAGE

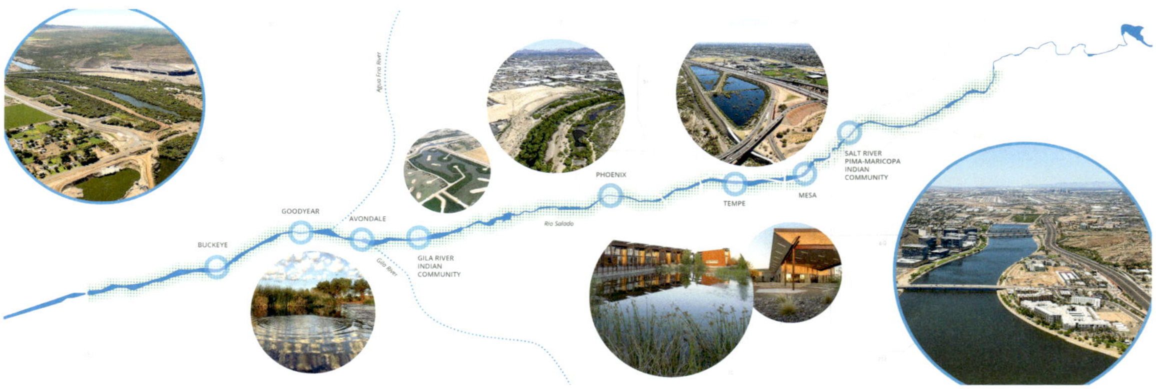

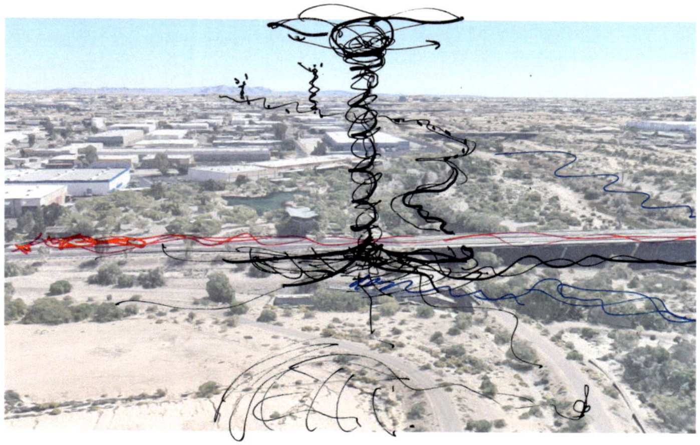

Opposite top Diagrams of normal, monsoon and flood conditions at Rio Unido. **Opposite middle** Planning diagrams. **Opposite bottom** Rio Reimagined on the Rio Salado - University City Exchange. **Above** Conceptual look-out tower sketch - Brian Farling. **Below** Conceptual tower study drawing - Shawn Swisher. **Following spread** Civic amphitheater at the river bottom, with views north to Downtown Phoenix.

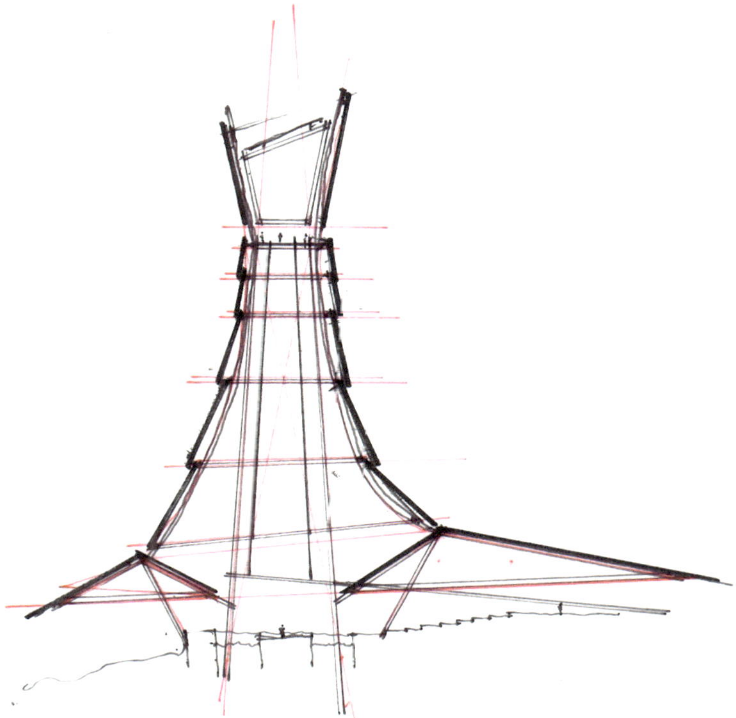

Bushidō Kanji

Phoenix, Arizona, concept completed 2020

Eddie was hired by a Los Angeles-based orthopedic "doctor to the stars" to design a home on a prime parcel of land on Camelback Mountain with an unobstructed view of the Valley and Phoenix's now-impressive skyline. The steep parcel was cut into thirds by two millennia-old washes that created organic negative spaces Eddie was eager to embrace in his design. Like an ancient, fortified structure, Eddie used boulders as support and frame to screen the home from the neighbors. The long, low structure sliced across the hillside, like a samurai's sword, deftly parsing solids and voids into spaces for living and viewing.

Eddie named this plan the *Bushidō Kanji*. *Bushidō*, or Way of the Warrior, is the ancient code of fealty and justice of the Japanese samurai; kanji are the ancient ideograms the Japanese borrowed from the Chinese and enhanced to capture their written language.[16] *Bushidō Kanji* is Eddie's building-sized ideogram that declares his devotion to the nature that nourishes his work. The rhythmic forms guide our restless eyes across the hide-and-seek home, receding so the mountain remains the star.

This project opportunity was too good to be true. The doctor had engaged, but rejected, an earlier design from John Lautner's legacy firm; Eddie became part of the doctor's collection of architects paid to imagine what might crown Camelback Mountain.[17] A year later Eddie got a call from a colleague who, like Eddie, took the bait. He predicts the doctor's pile of important architect's drawings would get higher and one more architect's heart would be broken by the opportunity that was a mirage.[18]

Throughout *STRIVE* there are hints about the gap between client aspiration and reality; perhaps schools should add an educational unit around "taming egos" to weed out the faint-of-heart idealists who think architecture is just about playing with other people's money. Architecture is a rough-and-tumble field that requires sharp elbows and a firm grasp of reality so when projects evaporate, the designer still has their feet on the ground. Eddie's biggest pleasure came from defining the rich seeds of the project and creating his elegant drawings of vast potential.

Above Elevation study drawing - Eddie Jones. **Opposite page** Plan drawings - Eddie Jones. **Following spread** Perspective drawing of house engaged with Camelback Mountain - Eddie Jones.

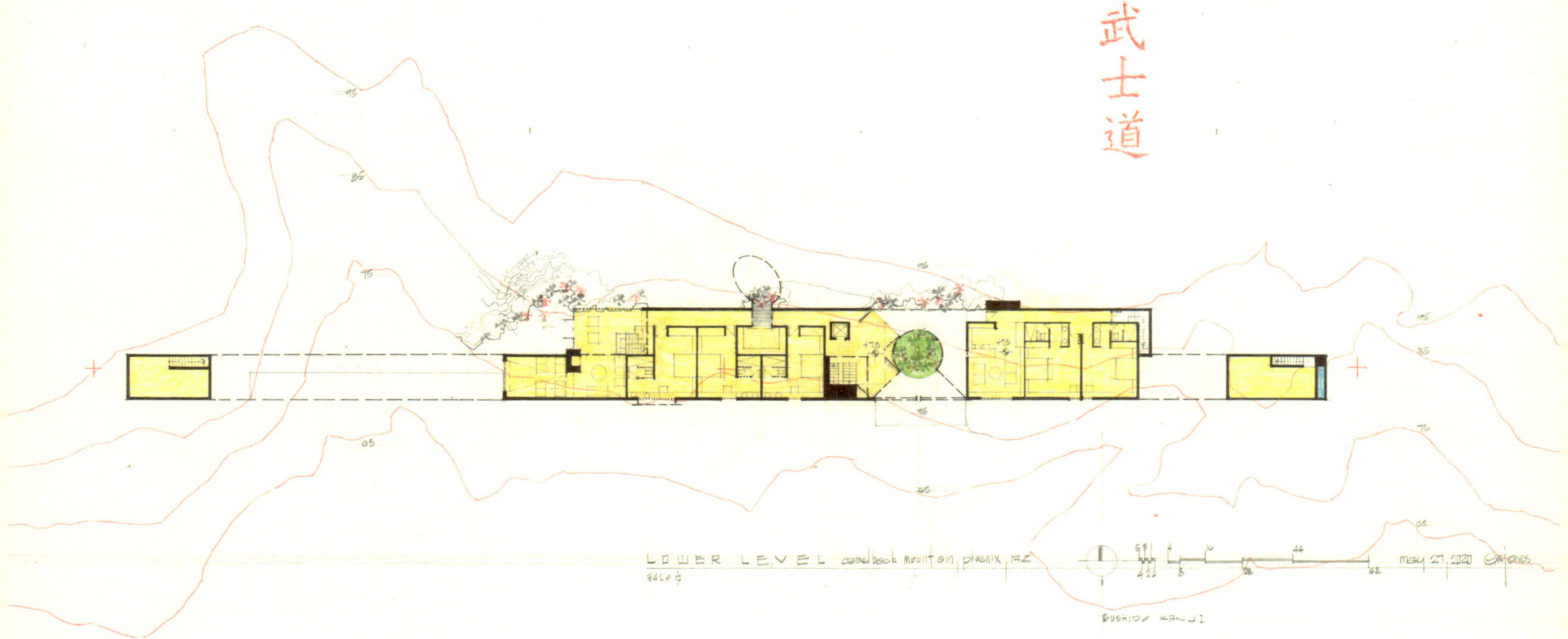
武士道
LOWER LEVEL camelback mountain, phoenix, AZ
may 27, 2020
BUSHIDO KANJI

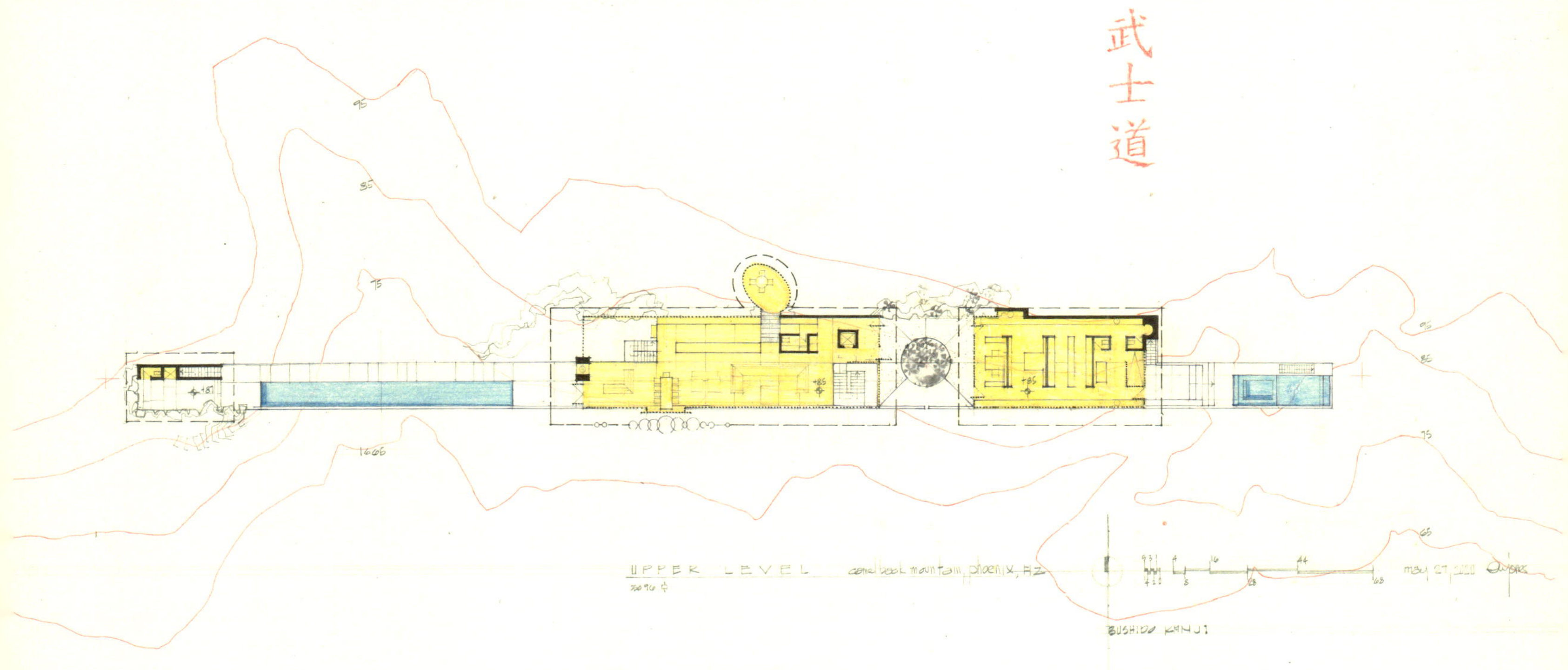
武士道
UPPER LEVEL camelback mountain, phoenix, AZ
may 27, 2020
BUSHIDO KANJI

武士道
camelback mountain phoenix, az
BUSHIDO KANJI
6.8.20

Bird's Fort Cultural Center

Arlington, Texas, concept completed 2022

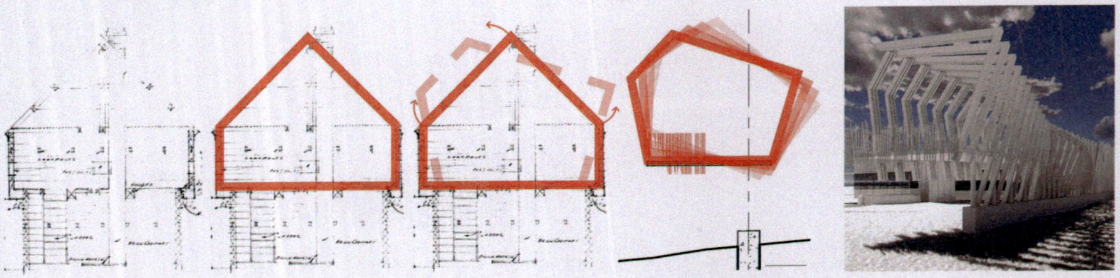

Jones Studio was contacted by the leadership at Bird's Fort Cultural Center at the recommendation of their neighbors at the River Legacy Parks Living Science Center. The Viridian Municipal Management District was charged by the state legislature to manage the natural assets of the 2,000-acre subdivision by building and managing infrastructure and cultural assets nestled amongst lakes, green spaces and wetlands. Bird's Fort's leadership commissioned Jones Studio to create an education facility because of their effective reading of landscape, for their proven sustainability strategies and for their expansive thinking about place.

Bird's Fort was a private fort named after General Jonathan Bird and established in 1841, the first attempt by white settlers to colonize north Texas.[19] Several small buildings were surrounded by a picket stockade and blockhouses, protection and jail in one. Indigenous tribes in the area attacked the invaders stationed at Bird's Fort; the settlers quickly abandoned the site to move south to help found Dallas. The stockade served as the site for the 1843 negotiations between the Native Nations of Texas and Oklahoma to cease hostilities with the colonizers.[20] The land was eventually purchased and turned into a private hunting and fishing club. The land also played host to oil and gas drilling and gravel mining, all leaving deep scars on the land. The addition of a public, educational non-profit amenity to the site would allow the developers to pose questions about the site's history while making it accessible for enjoyment.

During an initial site visit, Eddie and Neal noticed that the suburbs were easily masked by the forest, allowing Jones Studio to focus on the ghosts of the site's past. The buildable area—above the base flood elevation located along Meadow Hawk Drive and within the natural crescent of Calloway Lake—was deemed "sacred ground" by the design team. They would respect and preserve those ghosts while addressing the myths and realities of American history and the fight over land ownership. The design would make visible the Cultural Center's programming balance between historical reenactments bringing the mid-19th century alive while leaving open-ended opportunities for critical assessment of the past.

Above Block house transformation study. **Opposite page** Roof terrace rendering.

Above Site plan. **Below** Elevation study drawing - Eddie Jones.

The primary design strategy unapologetically uses the image of a 19th century stockade to launch the visitor's interpretation of history. The threshold stockade has many functions: it is the identity of the project and visually connects the visitor to the story of Bird's Fort. The stockade acts as a wrapper, protecting the discovery that lies within. It defines the outdoor spaces, from the welcoming outdoor plaza area and re-enactment space, with a release to the "sacred ground" of the site, guiding visitors on their journey through the sometimes tragic, sometimes uplifting story. The stockade slowly dematerializes as viewers move into the sacred grounds of the ruins lost to history.

Jones Studio applied a range of environmental and cost-saving systems to return water to the site, daylight across the main building's spaces to reduce energy consumption and sit lightly on the rich forest grounds. Sensitively-placed walkways provide opportunities to pause and appreciate the site, allowing nature to tell its own story.

Bird's Fort is nestled in the landscape and focused on history. The nearby River Legacy Parks Living Science Center is focused on nature and her changing habits. Both highlight the rich living assets of the region. Both facilities use natural materials but are radically different design responses driven by the mission and programming goals of each organization. Jones Studio's restoration and celebration of the two facilities' forested spaces continue the firm's work providing public good through thoughtful integration of landscape. The two Centers are part of a "cultural necklace" along the Trinity River that promotes, protects and interprets the Texas landscape and its human histories. Jones Studio has applied their critical thinking about place to influence those interpretations for generations of visitors looking for answers about our past and ideas for our future.

Above Stockade courtyard rendering. **Below** Approach at sunrise. **Opposite page** Exhibit hall. **Following spread** Chapel on the lake rendering.

WERNER
DELTA
DELTA

Central Arizona Project Visitor Center

Phoenix, Arizona, concept completed 2023

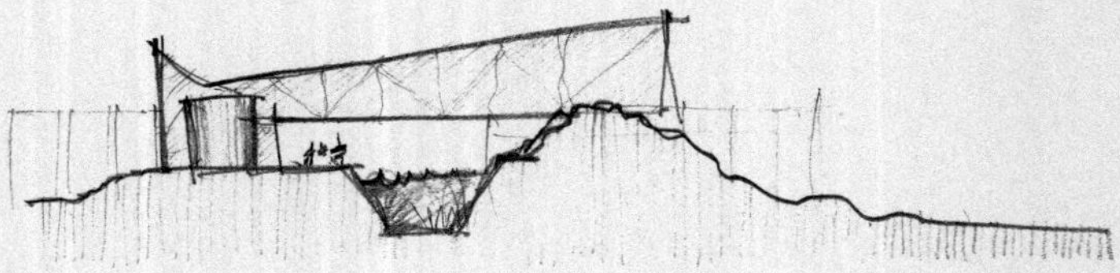

The earliest Jones Studio projects were at the edges of the state, where the glory of Arizona's ancient peoples, prickly plants and primordial stones were unified under washes of water and sun. Over the next four decades the team has become embedded in the conurbation of the Phoenix metropolitan area, shaping plots and platens with their unparalleled designs and high wattage energy born of passion and commitment to the social contract at the heart of architectural practice. The team's growing ambitions to design for the most precious element of life—water—are laid out in the conceptual designs for Rio Unido and the Environmental Learning Center and exemplify their big picture ambitions to influence water systems beyond a single structure. They thirst for influence over the invisible mechanisms that bring water to Arizona's farms, homes and businesses by expanding into the spaces where those decisions about distribution are made.

In their design for a Visitor Center for the Central Arizona Project [CAP], Jones Studio returns to their wild roots at the edges of development while tossed into the very heartbeat that makes development possible. CAP's canals have supported Arizona's industrial boom-and bust-cycles and their attendant mushrooming populations since the 1970s, the very moment when Eddie moved to Arizona to start the firm. CAP's draw from the Colorado River maintains the green fields of food, imported lawns of bermudagrass and wet fixtures of Arizona's buildings that house five million residents, or nearly 80% of the state's population.[21] A Visitor Center would need to represent the enormous scope of this giant earthwork, running 336 miles to mete out liquid blue gold, and embrace this giant spigot of life while educating the public on its fragility in an era of shifting weather patterns.

As experts in designing with all of nature's assets, Jones Studio's elegant steel, stone, wood and glass boat-like form floats above and across the canal, using four enormous tanks as anchors to demonstrate ways in which water can be used, and reused, to conserve water. The giant oculus

Above Concept section sketch - Brian Farling. **Opposite page** Visitor's arrival in rain and sun. **Following spread** Shaded bridge spanning the aqueduct.

O VALLEY
TWIN PEAKS
SANDARIO
BRAWLEY
PIMA
TUCSON
PIMA MINE ROAD

Tier 1 Shortage:
CAP Reductions
CAP Supply

Opposite page Site and floor plan. **Above** View from north canal bank. **Following spread** Early morning over the aqueduct.

links sky to water and focuses the energies of the site so visitors can feel and see water's tangible and intangible power. Like Homolovi, River Legacy and Bird's Fort, the CAP Visitor Center will be a beacon of knowledge about human management of earth's resources, alerting visitors to their own responsibility and agency in future environmental changes. The Visitor Center brings together the "warts and stars, the prospect of utopia and the specter of dystopia" that is the contemporary arid West.[22]

Just as Arizona built CAP to stop draining the non-renewable aquifer beneath the state's land, the frail Colorado River seems less like a renewable resource than ever, which has great consequences for the CAP system and for Arizona's residents and visitors. Marc Reisner has written that only one ancient desert civilization has survived to today—Egypt—and only by using a radically different irrigation system than those used across America.[23] The question for Phoenix remains: what can residents expect if they do not heed the lessons of the past? Jones Studio is part of a cultural movement, one committed to the urgency of a sustainable future that must be served by politicians, corporations and industry. Jones Studio's innovations are to serve the sustainability of their place.

Opposite page Colorado River watershed paving inlay at entry. **Above & below** Sections. **Following spread** Aerial rendering at sunrise.

Jones Studio: Next

Principles don't mean very much…unless we say something with them.
Bruce Goff[24]

Jones Studio is thriving well into the 21st century, integrating ideas from an expanded array of fields that allows the team sharpened tools for forward-looking creative adventures. They continue to design projects big and small, understanding how history and climate change are shifting the meaning and value of their work.

The team is also at a pivot point: as Jacob and Brian continue to expand their roles, Neal and Eddie are digesting their experiences from the middle of the country and the middle of the last century to scan ahead to the middle of the 21st. What does fearlessness look like in today's cultural atmosphere? As the 21st century beckons, Jones Studio is defining their priorities and opportunities to shape and protect Arizona's unique land and history.

Since the late 1970s, Jones Studio has pursued a philosophical goal for transparency and not just by using glass. Transparency here suggests an open dialogue with society, a committed relationship to the Earth and its glorious forms and creatures, and honest communication with partners, clients and each other. Jones Studio's underlying aesthetic is shaped by a moral response to the desert Southwest's water and light, creating architectural forms for the future. Like Goff, the designers believe that their architecture says something about our place and time. They have done hand-to-hand combat with rigid industry standards to introduce new design solutions, particularly when harvesting water to feed and sustain the desert and its residents. A rich pemmican of experience and speculation feeds the firm's work. Jones Studio has a passionate youthful drive with the gravitas of a mature firm. This combination underpins a striving ambition, buttressed by a finely calibrated willingness to push beyond their own boundaries.

From the start, Eddie and Neal shared the ambition to make great and meaningful architecture no matter its scale. Much of their early work was around the wilderness edges of the state, enhancing our appreciation for the ancient desert by making important contemporary buildings no matter the location, or perhaps *because* of the location. Neal explains that Jones Studio's success comes from the recognition of their regionalism, and how they have adapted their architecture to it: "Our practice is about materiality and texture. We look at the context of site and let the context influence the architecture. Regionalism is not about being modern or contemporary, it's about the historical influences of the past, of that region, and of local climate demands."[25]

The golden thread that links Jones Studio's projects to the other global architectural communities is their celebration of the living platform beneath them. Until the Industrial Revolution's inventions allowed us wholescale extractive capacity, architecture was always a matter of place. Materials were drawn from ancient rock formations and sea beds, shaped by jet streams or siroccos, monsoons or typhoons. It is Jones Studio's foundational sensitivity to site that makes them part of the continuum of architects building for place.

Designing architecture is like peering through a kaleidoscope. One minute the assembled elements resolve into a graceful solution, but with the slightest jiggle, that image deconstructs, awaiting the next iteration of aspiration. It should be obvious throughout *STRIVE* that intentional, perceptive, empathetic design can be knocked out of alignment by changing regulations, new materials hitting the market or updated client demands. Tumbling ideas about, adding in ever-more interesting or challenging elements, technologies or sites, helps Jones Studio polish their projects to achieve an elegantly precise fit.

Architects are artists, creating new images and experiences through material and spatial experimentation. Even on holiday, seeing architecture in new places, they bring back with them ideas that can be transformed for the desert. Eddie and Jacob traveled with a group on an architecture-intensive trip to India in 2007. Seeing ancient, rammed earth forts insulated against the sun and their enemies, as well as 20th century buildings by Louis Kahn and Le Corbusier, gave them a new appreciation for volume.

Although structures of the past inspire the team—ancient Anasazi, Roman baths, Indian step wells—they also look at their contemporaries' work for inspiration. More modern inspiration comes from elegant European minimalists like Alvar Aalto and Eero Saarinen and maximalists like Antoni Gaudí. More recently, the work of Brooks + Scarpa of Santa Monica, California, Marlon Blackwell of Fayetteville, Arkansas, and Peter Zumthor of Switzerland, among others, play point/counter-point through the firm's thinking, demonstrating the designers' polyglot taste for architectural lessons.

Arizona too has an important and supportive architecture community that includes colleagues Wendell Burnette, Rick Joy, Will Bruder (now in Oregon), the DeBartolos, Jim Richärd and Michael Johnson, with many more besides. Jones Studio has been challenged through the boundary-defying work of these colleagues, many of whom were also included in the 2002 article by Lawrence W. Cheek where he first named the Arizona School. Comparing and contrasting ancient with modern allows the designers to constantly stretch their ideas about how and why architecture fulfills Eddie's primary goal "to help people live better," or, perhaps, to tell the truth about our inescapable connection to one another and thus our mutual responsibility for our shared home.

The Arizona School moniker continues to evoke conflicting responses. Brian quotes John Wesley Powell's idea that rather than the artificial borderlines of states, each region should be defined by its watersheds to prevent the kinds of water wars we are seeing today. Brian proposes Arizona, and the architects who work within the region, be part of the Colorado River Watershed School, not the Arizona School.[26] School implies a rigid orthodoxy; adding "watershed" removes human intention and replaces it with nature's design, a more intelligent way of connecting residents of the region. Colorado River Watershed School also suggests that the river is the teacher, a thought that Jones Studio already embraces and celebrates.

Jones Studio seeks to return the desert to itself—working at a high level to ensure native plants twine across their projects indoor and out, setting the stage for a biodiversity that allows the desert's other creatures to thrive. (They carry this principle of native plant diversity to their increasingly frequent projects outside the desert Southwest as well.) Through his deep and unending dive into water issues, Brian believes a 21st century solution to agriculture that uses 80% of the Earth's available freshwater may be tied to indoor hydroponic systems that use 10% the amount of water instead. This is but one example of how architects and designers can help integrate solutions that would support living gently with the Earth.

Since architecture mediates the relationship between humans and their landscape, architects must grapple with the impending changes in that relationship. But *everyone* in the construction field must commit to reducing their carbon footprint by adopting the kinds of sustainable strategies Jones Studio has been using since the 1970s. In discussing their energy and cost-efficient buildings Brian notes concrete's capacity to perform many functions—as frame, surface and support, bulletproof and long-lasting—though the process of creation makes it one of industry's biggest polluters.[27] Even the best solution carries its own challenges. Capitalism, a fevered system that has infected every vein of American life, means net financial profit is always privileged over net social benefit. Only when large clients—governments, universities, municipalities, developers—understand their role in the preservation of resources for long-term sustainability will others catch up to Jones Studio.

As a mature firm with a substantial and diverse body of work in its portfolio, Jones Studio wants to grow the intellectual scope and public reach of their buildings. Everyone in the family returns to the inspirational lodestar—to make great architecture—and every project must align with that goal. The team will not diminish their sterling-silver reputation by sacrificing quality, so they often sacrifice hours and income to satisfy themselves. Jones Studio considers being on time and on budget as a bottom-line expectation for everyone in their field. It is not good enough to merely do the required; expectations must be exceeded if one is to achieve excellence.

Brian believes architecture is more "tree time" than "human time." Architecture plays out over generations, buffeted by the droughts and deluges and human folly that swamp the cultures that create them. Architecture, like any art form, alerts us to the stresses and traumas of history; we often learn about other cultures from their ruins and remains. Buildings are more durable than just about any other art form since even small dwellings can leave traces thousands of years later. It is up to us to divine the lessons our forebears have left us—what lessons, in turn, are we leaving for the future?

The world has molted and remade itself many times since Jones Studio was founded in 1979 and even again since 2020. We take architecture for granted until we don't have it. The complexity of finding a sense of home, of being anchored to place, is a right for some and a dream denied to others. Architecture has been enlisted in the fight for human survival, and Jones Studio uses their skills, resources and opportunities to help in that fight. It turns out that Eddie's quote from Kurt Andersen, about being of and from the middle of the country, has led the entire firm to recognize the benefits of being in the middle; that is, to mediate conflicts between humans and nature, between past and future.

No one can accurately guess how the shrinking Colorado River will reshape the West and its cities, towns, suburbs and villages and the industries, workplaces, farms and ranches that draw life from it. We might look to other desert cultures in that "stripe of the Earth" for a hint. Middle Eastern countries continue to build fantastical cities in the desert, yet global desertification is accelerating, with dust storms affecting whole regions. In 1994, the United Nations adopted the Convention to Combat Desertification [UNCCD].[28] Perhaps Phoenix's boom-and-bust cycles are simply the human mirror for the desert's drowning-or-dying-of-thirst cycles.[29] Since the West's weather and water woes have put the rest of the country on notice about the rolling sustainability crisis, Emily Eliza Scott's observation that that the invention of the desert is the very invention of America feels truer every day.[30] These civil and environmental rights struggles echo the tumultuous social environment of the 1960s that shaped Jones Studio's commitment to saying something with their architecture. Jones Studio has met that commitment in every way possible.

STRIVE could have a silent subtitle: *Spark*. Since the firm's founding, Eddie and Neal have used the spark of curiosity to lead them into new arenas for action. Brian and Jacob bring sparks of knowing spritzed by a willingness to find unique solutions for their buildings. Like a sparkler, their collective spirit of inquiry shoots tiny pricks of heat as it flickers and shimmers. When the process works, the results are enchanting, intense, magical. In the whirlwind that is our present, we are all looking for those moments of inspiration, of light, of hope. Jones Studio's family wakes up every day to start again creating buildings of joy and significance as their contribution for our collective future.

Appendix

Family

The following list has been developed by **Neal**, **Eddie**, **Jacob** and **Brian**. This represents the Partners' best recollection of Jones Studio family members, both former and **current**, who have contributed to the firm's success for more than four decades. If anyone has been left out, it is certainly not intentional. The Partners blame it on "senior moments" crowded out by priceless experiences and rewarding friendships.

Abdullah Aldakheelallah
Jay Atherton
Tanya Bartels
Spencer Bates
Wyatt Beard
Brandusa Bularca
Andy Byrnes
Amiee Chan
Patricia Chen
Daniel Childers
Kira Collins
Matthew "Budd" Conn
Tom Connor
Lisa Cressy
Edwin Curiel
Isabella Day
Richard Fairbourn
Melissa Farling
Aaron Forbes
Kim Foster
Rena Foster
Miles Foster
Alex Gino
Cynthia Godinez
Tom Hahn
Richard Hofmeister
Doyle Hostetler
Rob Huff
Mary Jones
Lexie Jones
Kevin Jones
Kirsten Keane
Chris Kelly
Ashley Kenneally
Amanda Kizer
Brian Lee
Ora Mae Leffard - RIP 2009
Yesenia "Jenny" Leon
Burt Little - RIP 2013
Sandy Long
Brett Marinoff
Logan Matos
J. Barry Moffitt
Christiana Moss
Rebekah "Becka" Nash
Nick Nevels
Joanna Noonan
Bill Osborne
Claudia Parker
Tony Pensiero
Gailyn Porter
Jena Rimkus
Deborah Roe
Maria Salenger
Matthew "Matt" Salenger
Krista Shepherd
Shawn Sheppard
Shawn Swisher
David Takeuchi
Mark Tate
Brianna Tsatskin
Amit Upadhye
Rob Viergutz
Connor Von Holten
Eric Watson
Eric Weber
Mike Whalen
Harold Williams - RIP 2019
Amie Zemer

Jones Studio family - January 2023

Bibliography

Books

Archaeologies of Placemaking: Monuments, Memories, and Engagement in Native North America. Patricia E. Rubertone, ed. Walnut Creek, CA: Left Coast Press, Inc., 2008.

Andersen, Kurt. *Fantasyland: How America Went Haywire: A 500-Year History.* New York: Random House, 2018.

Andrews, Malcolm. *Landscape and Western Art.* Oxford, UK: Oxford University Press, 1999.

The Art of Architecture Exhibitions. Kristen Feireiss, ed. Rotterdam, The Netherlands: NAi Publishers, 2001.

Banham, Raynor. *Scenes in America Deserta.* Cambridge, MA: The MIT Press, 1989.

Blake, Peter. *No Place Like Utopia: Modern Architecture and the Company We Kept.* New York and London: W.W. Norton, 1993.

Blueprints for Modern Living: History and Legacy of the Case Study Houses. Elizabeth E. T. Smith, ed. Los Angeles: The Museum of Contemporary Art, 1989.

Childs, Craig. *The Secret Knowledge of Water: Discovering the Essence of the American Desert.* Boston, New York, London: Little, Brown and Company, 2001.

CONSTRUCTIONS: Buildings in Arizona by Alfred Newman Beadle. 2nd ed. Bernard Michael Boyle, ed. Cave Creek, AZ: Gnosis Ltd., 1993.

Curtis, William J. R. *Modern Architecture Since 1900.* 3rd ed. London: Phaidon Press Limited, 1982.

Deutsche, Rosalyn. *Evictions: Art and Spatial Politics.* Chicago and Cambridge, MA: Graham Foundation and MIT Press, 1996.

Diamond, Jared. *Collapse: How Societies Choose to Fail or Succeed.* New York: Viking Penguin, 2005.

Domin, Christopher and Kathryn McGuire. *Powerhouse: The Life and Work of Judith Chafee.* New York: Princeton Architectural Press, 2019.

Eero Saarinen on His Work. Aline B. Saarinen, ed. New Haven, CT and London: Yale University Press, 1962.

Goff on Goff: Conversations and Lectures. Philip B. Welch, ed. Norman, OK: University of Oklahoma Press, 1996.

Graeber, David and David Wengrow. *The Dawn of Everything: A New History of Humanity.* New York: Farrar, Straus and Giroux, 2021.

Hitchcock, Henry-Russell and Johnson, Philip. *The International Style.* rev. ed. New York and London: W. W. Norton & Company, 1932.

The Invention of the American Desert: Art, Land, and the Politics of Environment. Lyle Massey and James Nisbet, eds. Oakland, CA: University of California Press, 2021.

Jacobs, Jane. *The Death and Life of Great American Cities.* rev. ed. New York: Random House, Inc., 1961.

Johung, Jennifer. *Replacing Home: From Primordial Hut to Digital Network in Contemporary Art.* Minneapolis, MN: University of Minnesota Press, 2012.

Jones Studio Houses: Sensual Modernism. Hong Kong: Oscar Riera Ojeda Publishers, 2021.

Landscape and Power. W. J. T. Michell, ed. Chicago: University of Chicago Press, 1994.

Landscape Painting Now: From Pop Abstraction to New Romanticism. Todd Bradway, ed. New York: D.A.P./Distributed Art Publishers, Inc., 2019.

Leaves of Iron: Glenn Murcutt: Pioneer of an Australian Architectural Form. Philip Drew, ed. Sydney: Angus & Robinson, 1994.

Lesser, Wendy. *You Say to Brick: The Life of Louis Kahn.* New York: Farrar, Straus and Giroux, 2017.

Limerick, Patricia Nelson. *Desert Passages: Encounters with the American Desert.* Albuquerque, NM: University of New Mexico Press, 1985.

The Legacy of Conquest: The Unbroken Past of the American Desert. New York and London: W.W. Norton & Co., 1987.

McKay, George. *Radical Gardening: Politics, Idealism & Rebellion on the Garden*. Toronto: Frances Lincoln Limited, 2011.

Morris, Christopher. *The Big Muddy: An Environmental History of the Mississippi and Its Peoples from Hernando de Soto to Hurricane Katrina*. New York: Oxford University Press, 2012.

PHX: Phoenix 21st Century City. Edward Booth-Clibborn, ed. United Kingdom: Booth-Clibborn Editions, 2006.

Pijawka, K. David and Kim Shetter. *The Environment Comes Home: Arizona Public Service's Environmental Showcase Home*. Tempe, AZ: Herberger Center for Design Excellence, College of Architecture and Environmental Design, Arizona State University, 1995.

Recovering Landscape: Essays in Contemporary Landscape Architecture. James Corner, ed. New York: Princeton Architectural Press, 1999.

Reisner, Marc. *Cadillac Desert: The American West and Its Disappearing Water*. New York: Viking Penguin, 1986.

Renegades: Bruce Goff and The American School of Architecture. Luca Guido, Stephanie Pilat and Angela Person, eds. Norman, OK: University of Oklahoma Press, 2020.

Ross, Andrew. *Bird on Fire: Lessons from the World's Least Sustainable City*. Oxford, England: Oxford University Press, 2013.

Solnit, Rebecca. *Savage Dreams: A Journey into the Landscape Wars of the American West*. Berkeley, CA: University of California, Press, 1999.

Articles

Aguirre, Jessica Camille, "How to Recycle a 14-Story Office Tower," *The New York Times*, October 6, 2022, https://www.nytimes.com/2022/10/06/headway/office-tower-carbon-emissions-amsterdam.html?smid=nytcore-ios-share&referringSource=articleShare.

Bolter, Jessica, Emma Israel and Sarah Pierce, "Four Years of Profound Change: Immigration Policy during the Trump Presidency," Migration Policy Institute, February 2002, https://www.migrationpolicy.org/research/four-years-change-immigration-trump.

Cheek, Lawrence W., "The Making of the Arizona School," *Architecture* magazine, May 2002, p. 87-127.

Cornelius, Keridwen, "Bard of the Border," *Phoenix* magazine, June 1, 2014, https://www.phoenixmag.com/2014/06/01/bard-of-the-border/.

Estabrook, Rachel and Michael Elizabeth Sakas, "The Colorado River is drying up — but basin states have 'no plan' on how to cut water use," *CPR News*, September 17, 2022, https://www.cpr.org/2022/09/17/colorado-river-drought-basin-states-water-restrictions/.

Hudson, Hitsati, "The Sahara Motor Inn: From Landmark to Law Building," *Salt River Stories*, n.d., https://saltriverstories.org/items/show/399.

Náñez, Dianna M., "A border tribe, and the wall that will divide it" from The Wall, azcentral/*USA Today Network*, n.d., https://www.usatoday.com/border-wall/story/tohono-oodham-nation-arizona-tribe/582487001/.

Petersen, Christian, "Rainfall in Deserts," *Sciencing*, updated November 22, 2019, https://sciencing.com/rainfall-deserts-6632010.html.

Pavlakovich-Kochi, Vera, "Nogales Port in the Post COVID-19 Recovery of U.S.-Mexico Trade," University of Arizona Eller College of Management, June 12, 2022, https://azmex.eller.arizona.edu/news/2022/06/nogales-port-post-covid-19-recovery-us-mexico-trade.

Sisson, Patrick, "Judith Chafee: Dean of desert architecture," *Curbed*, August 10, 2017, https://archive.curbed.com/2017/8/10/16120726/judith-chafee-midcentury-architect-tucson.

St. John, Rachel, "The Raging Controversy at the Border Began With This Incident 100 Years Ago," *Smithsonian Magazine*, July 2018, https://www.smithsonianmag.com/history/raging-controversy-border-began-100-years-ago-180969343/.

Talton, Jon, "Phoenix and skyscrapers," *Rogue Columnist*, April 12, 2019, https://www.roguecolumnist.com/rogue_columnist/2019/04/phoenix-and-skyscrapers.html.

Wright, Frank Lloyd, "In the Cause of Architecture," *The Architectural Record*, Vol. XXIII, March 1908, no. 3, 4+.

Film

Louis Sullivan: The Struggle for American Architecture, Mark Richard Smith, dir. Chicago: Whitecap Films, 2010. YouTube, 2020, https://www.youtube.com/ watch?v=aAZEM-hloTM.

Endnotes

Introduction: Jones Studio: The Urgency of Now

1. Brian Farling, unpublished interview with the author, August 19, 2021.

2. Luca Guido, "The School of Architecture at the University of Oklahoma" in *Renegades: Bruce Goff and the American School of Architecture*, eds. Luca Guido, Stephanie Pilat and Angela Person (Norman, OK: University of Oklahoma Press, 2020), 57.

3. Eddie Jones, unpublished interview with Chad Schwartz, June 2, 2021. Schwartz is currently writing a book that examines the architecture of Arizona, the notion of the Arizona School and the responsiveness of this architecture to its place in the Sonoran Desert.

4. Farling, unpublished interview with the author, August 19, 2021.

5. For more information on the Sonoran Desert see Christian Petersen, "Rainfall in Deserts", *Sciencing*, updated November 22, 2019, https://sciencing.com/rainfall-deserts-6632010.html, accessed April 4, 2022.

6. Wendy Lesser, *You Say to Brick: The Life of Louis Kahn* (New York: Farrar, Straus and Giroux, 2017), 55.

7. Christopher Morris, *The Big Muddy: An Environmental History of The Mississippi and Its Peoples from Hernando De Soto to Hurricane Katrina* (Oxford, United Kingdom: Oxford University Press, 2012), 7.

8. David Graeber and David Wengrow, "Wicked Liberty: The indigenous critique and the myth of progress" in *The Dawn of Everything: A New History of Humanity* (New York: Farrar, Straus and Giroux, 2021), 27-77.

9. Raynor Banham, *Scenes in America Deserta* (Cambridge, MA: The MIT Press, 1989) quoted in Lyle Massey and James Nisbet, "Introduction" in *The Invention of the American Desert: Art, Land, and the Politics of Environment*, eds. Lyle Massey and James Nisbet (Oakland, CA: University of California Press, 2021), 8. Massey and Nisbet go on to explore how Banham's post-modern thinking allowed him to turn the "empty" desert into an "open" space, shifting away from early colonizer cliches about the American desert.

10. Patricia Nelson Limerick, *Desert Passages: Encounters with the American Desert* (Albuquerque, NM: University of New Mexico Press, 1985), 82, 88.

11. Emily Eliza Scott, "The Desert in Fine Grain" in *The Invention of the American Desert*, 160.

12. Jacob Benyi, unpublished interview with the author, August 25, 2021.

13. Rebecca Solnit, *Savage Dreams: A Journey into the Landscape Wars of the American West* (Berkeley, CA: University of California Press, 1999).

14. For more information on the Hohokam, visit the Arizona Museum of Natural History, https://www.arizonamuseumofnaturalhistory.org/plan-a-visit/mesa-grande/the-hohokam, accessed March 31, 2022.

15. Jared Diamond, *Collapse: How Societies Choose to Fail or Succeed* (New York: Viking Penguin, 2005), 4.

16. For more information on the City of Phoenix history see https://www.phoenix.gov/pio/city-publications/city-history, accessed March 31, 2022.

17. Lawrence W. Cheek, "The Making of the Arizona School", *Architecture* magazine, May 2002, 91.

18. For Phoenix Metropolitan area population growth see https://www.macrotrends.net/cities/23099/phoenix/population, accessed October 4, 2022.

19. Marc Reisner, *Cadillac Desert: The American West and Its Disappearing Water* (New York: Viking Penguin, 1986.)

20. George McKay, *Radical Gardening: Politics, Idealism & Rebellion in the Garden* (London: Frances Lincoln Limited, 2011).

21. American geographer Carl Sauer's work quoted in Chip Colwell-Chanthaphonh, T.J. Ferguson and Roger Anyer, "Always Multivocal and Multivalent: Conceptualizing Archaeological Landscapes in Arizona's San Pedro Valley" in *Archaeologies of Placemaking: Monuments, Memories, and Engagement in Native North America*, ed. Patricia E. Rubertone (Walnut Creek, CA: Left Coast Press, Inc., 2008), 66.

22. Jennifer Johung, *Replacing Home: From Primordial Hut to Digital Network in Contemporary Art.* (Minneapolis, MN: University of Minnesota Press, 2012), 9.

23. Aaron Betsky, "Questions Concerning the American School", in *Renegades*, ix

24. Cheek, "The Making of the Arizona School", 92.

25. William J.R. Curtis, *Modern Architecture Since 1900*, 3rd ed. (London: Phaidon Press Limited, 1982), 30-31.

26. I am grateful for the City of Tempe, AZ's Native American Land Acknowledgement, and have left their spelling of O'Odham (written elsewhere as O'odham) in place, https://www.tempe.gov/government/community-development/historic-preservation/native-american-land-acknowledgement,accessed March 31, 2022.

Jones Studio: The Early Years

1. Eddie Jones quotes Kurt Andersen in his book *Fantasyland: How America Went Haywire: A 500-Year History* (New York: Random House, 2017), 150, in unpublished notes to the author, August 2, 2021.

2. Stephanie Pilat, "People, Place, Time, Materials, and Spirit: The Search for an American Architecture", in *Renegades*, 181.

3. Albert Narath, "Notes From Bioteknika" in *The Invention of the American Desert*, 61-78.

4. Solnit, *Savage Dreams*, 365.

5. Siegfried Giedion, "*Space, Time and Architecture"* in *Leaves of Iron: Glenn Murcutt: Pioneer of an Australian Architectural Form*, ed. Philip Drew. 5th ed. (Sydney: Angus & Robinson, 1994), 42.

6. John Meunier, "Foreword" in *The Environment Comes Home: Arizona Public Service's Environmental Showcase Home*, eds. K. David Pijawka and Kim Shetter (Tempe, AZ: Herberger Center for Design Excellence, College of Architecture and Environmental Design, Arizona State University, 1995), xii.

7. Lesser, *You Say to Brick*, 55.

8. Robert W. Preucel and Frank G. Matero, "Placemaking on the Northern Rio Grande: A View from Kuaua Pueblo" in *Archaeologies of Placemaking*, 91.

9. Patrick Sisson, "Judith Chafee: Dean of desert architecture", *Curbed*, August 10, 2017, https://archive.curbed.com/2017/8/10/16120726/judith-chafee-midcentury-architect-tucson, accessed September 16, 2021.

10. Eddie Jones, unpublished interview with Chad Schwartz, June 2, 2021.

11. For a broader exploration of the architects named as part of the Arizona School see Cheek, "The Making of the Arizona School", 87-127.

12. For a broad understanding of Al Beadle's work see *CONSTRUCTIONS: Buildings in Arizona by Alfred Newman Beadle*. 3rd ed. ed. Bernard Michael Boyle (Cave Creek, AZ: Gnosis Ltd., 2008.)

13. Cheek, "The Making of the Arizona School", 90.

14. Reed Kroloff, "The Architecture of Alfred Newman Beadle" in *CONSTRUCTIONS*, 29.

15. For an overview of the Case Study House program see Elizabeth E. T. Smith, "Introduction" in *Blueprints for Modern Living: History and Legacy of the Case Study Houses*, ed. Elizabeth E. T. Smith (Los Angeles: The Museum of Contemporary Art, 1989), 13.

16. Eddie Jones, unpublished notes to the author, August 2, 2021.

17. For more information on Homolovi and the Hopi culture, see https://azstateparks.com/homolovi/hopi/cultural-sites, accessed April 8, 2022.

18. *Eero Saarinen on His Work*, Aline B. Saarinen, ed. (New Haven and London: Yale University Press, 1962), 6

19. Aaron Betsky, "Hover: The Architecture of Eddie Jones" in *Jones Studio Houses: Sensual Modernism* (Hong Kong: Oscar Riera Ojeda, 2021), 16.

20. For more information on Black Canyon see https://www.blm.gov/programs/recreation/mountainbike/blackcanyon, accessed February 28, 2023.

21. Massey and Nisbet, "Introduction" in *The Invention of the American Desert*, 13.

22.Thomas Woodfin, "Bruce Goff: Master of the Intimate Design Context" in *Renegades*, 147.

23. Helen Searing, "Case Study Houses: In the Grand Modern Tradition" in *Blueprints for Modern Living, 106-128*.

24. K. David Pijawka and Kim Shetter, "From Idea to Design" in *The Environment Comes Home*, 9.

25. Lesser, *You Say to Brick*, 140.

26. Jessica Camille Aguirre explores how construction and demolition of buildings effect global emissions and raw mineral extraction, and the call for more circular uses and reuses of materials in countries across the globe, in "How to Recycle a 14-Story Office Tower," *The New York Times*, October 6, 2022, https://www.nytimes.com/2022/10/06/headway/office-tower-carbon-emissions-amsterdam.html?smid=nytcore-ios-share&referringSource=articleShare, accessed October 16, 2022.

27. Neal Jones, unpublished interview with the author, August 5, 2021.

28. Data on Coconino County can be found at https://www.census.gov/quickfacts/coconinocountyarizona, accessed February 11, 2022.

29. Brian's interest in Chafee and his passion for water, the desert and sustainable architecture is so mighty that he is quoted in Christopher Domin and Kathryn McGuire's *Powerhouse: The Life and Work of Judith Chafee* (New York: Princeton Architecture Press, 2019), 153.

30. William J.R. Curtis, "Principles and Forms: The Architectural Vison of Judith Chafee" in *Powerhouse*, 16.

31. *Louis Sullivan: The Struggle for American Architecture*, Mark Richard Smith, dir. (Chicago: Whitecap Films, 2010), YouTube, 2020, https://www.youtube.com/watch?v=aAZEM-hloTM, accessed June 22, 2022.

32. Frank Lloyd Wright, "In the Cause of Architecture," *The Architectural Record*, Vol. XXIII, March 1908, no. 3, 156.

33. Peter Blake, *No Place Like Utopia: Modern Architecture and the Company We Kept* (New York and London: W.W. Norton, 1993), 55.

34. Cheek, "The Making of the Arizona School," 92.

35. Malcom Andrews, *Landscape in Western Art* (Oxford, UK: Oxford University Press, 1999), 18.

Family Table #1

1. Cheek, "The Making of the Arizona School," 93.

2. For more information on BJ Krivanek's work at Lattie Coor see https://tours.asu.edu/tempe/lattie-f-coor-hall, accessed March 15, 2022.

3. For more information on South Mountain Community College see https://www.southmountaincc.edu/about, accessed April 18, 2022.

4. Thirteen Wright buildings of the eighteen he designed were built. For more on Florida Southern College see https://www.flsouthern.edu/frank-lloyd-wright/frank-lloyd-wright-history.aspx, accessed April 10, 2022.

5. For fuller information on CAPLA's mission and goals see https://directory.arizona.edu/colleges/college-architecture-planning-landscape-architecture, accessed February 3, 2022.

6. Corner, "Introduction: Recovering Landscape as a Critical Cultural Practice" in *Recovering Landscape: Essays in Contemporary Landscape Architecture*, ed. James Corner (New York: Princeton Architectural Press, 1999), 16.

7. James Corner, "Introduction: Recovering Landscape as a Critical Cultural Practice" in *Recovering Landscape*, 1.

8. Abdu'l-Baha, 1844-1921, was the Iranian religious leader of the Bahia' faith, https://www.bahai.org/abdul-baha/life-abdul-baha/, accessed May 2, 2022.

9. McKay, talking about the work of community gardens in New York's Loisaida (lower east side), *Radical Gardening*, 172.

10. Barry Schwabsky, "Painting with the Flow of the World" in *Landscape Painting Now: From Pop Abstraction to New Romanticism*, ed. Todd Bradway (New York: D.A. P. Distributed Art Publishers Inc., 2019), 22.

11. Patricia E. Rubertone, "Engaging Monuments, Memories, and Archaeology" in *Archaeologies of Placemaking*, 25.

12. Rosalyn Deutsche from her book *Evictions: Art and Spatial Politics* (Chicago and Cambridge, MA: Graham Foundation and MIT Press, 1996), quoted in Jennifer Johung, "Visibly Skinned" in *Replacing Home: From Primordial Hut to Digital Network in Contemporary Art,* ed. Jennifer Johung (Minneapolis: University of Minnesota Press, 2012), 110.

13. Jane Jacobs, "The uses of sidewalks: safety" in *The Death and Life of Great American Cities*, rev. ed. (New York: Random House, Inc., 1961), 29-54.

14. For information on Ralph Haver-designed Mayfair Manor, 1950, see Modern Phoenix's Haver archive, https://modernphoenix.net/haver/mayfairmanor.htm, accessed February 8, 2022.

Family Table #2

1. *PHX: Phoenix 21st Century City*, Edward Booth-Clibborn, ed. (United Kingdom: Booth-Clibborn Editions, 2006.)

2. Kristin Feireiss, "Introduction: It's not about art" in *The Art of Architecture Exhibitions* (Rotterdam, The Netherlands: NAi Publishers, 2001), 8.

3. For the full description of the GSA Design Excellence program see https://www.gsa.gov/real-estate/design-and-construction/design-excellence/design-excellence-program/guiding-principles-for-federal-architecture

4. W. J. T. Michell from *Landscape and Power* (Chicago: University of Chicago Press, 1994), p. 29-30, quoted in Corner, "Introduction: Recovering Landscape as a Critical Cultural Practice" in *Recovering Landscape*, 11.

5. For more information see Dianna M. Náñez, "A border tribe, and the wall that will divide it" from The Wall, *azcentral/USA Today Network*, n.d., https://www.usatoday.com/border-wall/story/tohono-oodham-nation-arizona-tribe/582487001/ and website of the Tohono O'odham Nation, http://www.tonation-nsn.gov/history-culture/, accessed February 4, 2022,

6. For more details on the early fencing at *Ambos Nogales* see Rachel St. John, "The Raging Controversy at the Border Began With This Incident 100 Years Ago", *Smithsonian Magazine* online, July 2018, https://www.smithsonianmag.com/history/raging-controversy-border-began-100-years-ago-180969343/, accessed September 30, 2022.

7. For an overview of 50 years of border and immigration policies in the U.S., including the 2006 Secure Fence Act and the beginning of construction on 650 miles of fencing, see the University of Arizona webpage https://mexico.arizona.edu/revista/brief-legislative-history-last-50-years-us-mexico-border, accessed February 4, 2022.

8. For comparative data on trade between the U.S. and Mexico through Nogales and other southern LPOE's, see Vera Pavlakovich-Kochi, "Nogales Port in the Post COVID-19 Recovery of U.S.-Mexico Trade", University of Arizona Eller College of Management, June 12, 2022, https://azmex.eller.arizona.edu/news/2022/06/nogales-port-post-covid-19-recovery-us-mexico-trade, accessed September 28, 2022.

9. This essay is based on the author's text for an exhibition on Jones Studio's Mariposa Land Port of Entry at ASU's architecture gallery in 2008, just as the team was gearing up for the final design work on the seven-years-long project. My original essay has been edited to reflect the final project's accomplishments. All subsequent work on other U.S. Land Ports of Entry is rooted in Jones Studio's experiences, successes and hiccups in managing the monolithic tasks of Mariposa.

10. Poem reproduced with permission of Alberto Ríos. For more information on Arizona's first Poet Laureate see Keridwen Cornelius, "Bard of the Border," *Phoenix* magazine, June 1, 2014, https://www.phoenixmag.com/2014/06/01/bard-of-the-border/, accessed October 24, 2022.

11. For a deeper understanding of BorderLinks' work, see https://www.borderlinks.org, accessed September 27, 2022.

12. To understand the scope of Moore's work, see the artist's website, https://matthewmoore.com/portfolio/, accessed April 11, 2022. 483

13. For a brief introduction to Baboquivari Peak see https://www.smithsonianmag.com/travel/baboquivari-peak-wilderness-180952519/, accessed April 11, 2022.

14. To explore how Kimsooja's work has featured acts of stitching people together, see the artist's website, http://www.kimsooja.com/projects/2013_An-Album-Borderlines.html, accessed October 3, 2022.

15. Henry-Russell Hitchcock and Philip Johnson, *The International Style*. rev. ed. (New York and London: W. W. Norton & Company, 1932), 42.

16. Source of the demographic data is from College Simply, https://www.collegesimply.com/colleges/arizona/mesa-community-college/, accessed January 20, 2022.

17. Heather C. Flores, *Food Not Lawns: How to Turn your Yard into a Garden and your Neignborhood into a Community* (White River Junction, VT: Chelsea Green, 2006) quoted in George McKay, *Radical Gardening*, 21.

Family Table #3

1. Philips B. Welch, "Goff's Creative Growth and Design Philosophy" from a private interview with Bruce Goff at the University of Oklahoma, March 11, 1953, in *Goff on Goff: Conversations and Lectures*, ed. Philip B. Welch (Norman, OK: University of Oklahoma Press, 1996), 17-38.

2. Neal Jones, unpublished Jones Studio "statement of philosophy", emailed to the author July 7, 2022.

3. For more information on the Sahara Motor Inn and the changes in downtown Phoenix see Hitsati Hudson, "The Sahara Motor Inn: From Landmark to Law Building", *Salt River Stories*, no date, https://saltriverstories.org/items/show/399, accessed September 30, 2022.

4. For a brief outline of O'Connor's career see *Oyez*, n.d., https://www.oyez.org/justices/sandra_day_oconnor, accessed April 17, 2022.

5. Maria Salenger, unpublished email to the author, February 8, 2022.

6. For more information and background on the Thunderbird School of Global Managements founding and motto, https://thunderbird.asu.edu/about, accessed February 7, 2022.

7. For specifics on the Fourth Industrial Revolution, and ASU's response by preparing business and government leaders to adapt ethical practices in the face of the changing tide of technology, see https://thunderbird.asu.edu/executive-education/individual/global-foundations-fourth-industrial-revolution, accessed September 29, 2022.

8. Jessica Bolter, Emma Israel and Sarah Pierce, "Four Years of Profound Change: Immigration Policy during the Trump Presidency", Migration Policy Institute, February 2002, https://www.migrationpolicy.org/research/four-years-change-immigration-trump, accessed February 9, 2022.

9. For more details on the United States' historical relationship to Mexican nationals see Patricia Nelson Limerick, "America the Borderland" in *The Legacy of Conquest: The Unbroken Past of the American Desert* (New York and London: W.W. Norton & Co., 1987), 222-258.

10. For a brief introduction to César Chávez see *Britannica*, https://www.britannica.com/biography/Cesar-Chavez, accessed October 3, 2022.

11. Farling, unpublished interview with the author, August 19, 2021.

12. Andrews, *Landscape and Western Art*, 4.

13. For more information on the Treaty of Guadalupe-Hidalgo see the National Archives, https://www.archives.gov/education/lessons/guadalupe-hidalgo, accessed August 17, 2022.

Focused Future

1. To understand more how citizens, business people and politicians have pressed for more logical and sustainable preservation to balance unbridled growth, see *Preservation Phoenix Style: A Study of the Impacts of Historic Preservation in Phoenix*, https://www.phoenix.gov/pddsite/Documents/Final%20Preservation%20Phoenix%20Style%20Report%20(1).pdf, accessed February 8, 2022, 5 & 49.

2. For more on Greene's "Armature" see brief descriptions and pdfs available at https://herbgreene.org/writing/, accessed August 18, 2022.

3. For specifics on the First Baptist Church see the nomination form to the National Historic Register, http://www.housingopportunitycenter.net/abbey/wp-content/uploads/2015/03/nationalregister.pdf, accessed March 21, 2022.

4. Terry Goddard was Phoenix Mayor between 1984 and 1990 when the city developed its historic preservation guidelines, https://www.goddardlawplc.com/our-attorneys, accessed March 21, 2022.

5. For a timeline on the Monroe Street Abbey see http://www.monroestreetabbey.org/history/, accessed March 21, 2022.

6. This phrase floats above the title of Craig Childs's book *The Secret Knowledge of Water: Discovering the Essence of the American Desert* (Boston, New York, London: Little, Brown and Company, 2001.) Childs, a naturalist who has retraced the steps of ancient peoples moving into North America from Asia and followed in the paths of the Pueblo peoples, explores the ways water shapes the desert. For more on Childs and his writings see http://www.houseofrain.com/bookdetail.cfm?id=1183863164364, accessed October 4, 2022.

7. For more information on America's Best Communities competition see https://www.lhcaz.gov/news/article/america%27s-best-communities-competition, accessed April 21, 2022.

8. See Lake Havasu's Partnership for Economic Development Vision 2020 overview, https://www.lakehavasu.org/vision-2020-projects, accessed April 21, 2022.

9. Rachel Estabrook and Michael Elizabeth Sakas, "The Colorado River is drying up — but basin states have 'no plan' on how to cut water use", *CPR News*, September 17, 2022, https://www.cpr.org/2022/09/17/colorado-river-drought-basin-states-water-restrictions/, accessed September 30, 2022.

10. The Nature Conservancy, "Coming Together for the Colorado River," March 19, 2020, https://www.nature.org/en-us/about-us/where-we-work/priority-landscapes/colorado-river/agricultural-partnerships-colorado-river/, accessed August 26, 2022.

11. Jon Talton, "Phoenix and skyscrapers", *Rogue Columnist*, April 12, 2019, https://www.roguecolumnist.com/rogue_columnist/2019/04/phoenix-and-skyscrapers.html, accessed February 8, 2022.

12. Andrew Ross, *Bird on Fire: Lessons from the World's Least Sustainable City* (Oxford, England: Oxford University Press, 2013), written while Ross was in residence at Future Arts Research (F.A.R.) @ ASU at the invitation of the author.

13. Andrew Nicla, "Does Arizona really use less water now than it did in 1957?", *azcentral*, https://www.azcentral.com/story/news/local/arizona-environment/2019/02/12/arizona-water-usage-state-uses-less-now-than-1957/2806899002/, accessed February 11, 2022.

14. For more information on the "Rio Reimagined" project, see https://rioreimagined.org/, accessed February 11, 2022.

15. Farling, unpublished interview with Chad Schwartz, December 15, 2021.

16. For more on *Bushidō*, or Way of the Warrior, see Britannica, https://www.britannica.com/topic/Bushido, accessed February 12, 2023.

17. John Lautner is one of the premier 20th century American architects merging landscape and architecture. See Lautner's 2011 biography by Melissa Matuscak at http://www.johnlautner.org/wp/wp-content/uploads/MatuscakBio.pdf, accessed February 12, 2023.

18. Eddie Jones, unpublished email to the author, February 10, 2023.

19. For more background on Bird's Fort see https://www.tarrantcounty.com/en/county/about-tarrant/history.html, accessed February 28, 2022.

20. Background on the "Republic of Texas Treaty with the Indigenous Nations of the Delaware, Chickasaw, Waco, Tawakani, Keechi, Caddo, Anadahkah, Ionie, Biloxi, and Cherokee" can be found at the Coppell Historical Society website, http://www.coppellhistoricalsociety.org/birds-fort-treaty.html, accessed February 28, 2022.

21. For background information on the Central Arizona Project, authorized in 1968 with construction starting in 1973, see https://www.cap-az.com/about/history-of-cap/, accessed January 19, 2023.

22. Farling, unpublished email to the author, January 19, 2023.

23. Reisner, *Cadillac Desert*, 3.

24. Philip B. Welch, "The New and Different in Architecture" from a lecture given by Bruce Goff at the School of Architecture, University of Oklahoma, October 28, 1953, in *Goff on Goff*, 90.

25. Neal Jones, unpublished interview with the author, September 15, 2021.

26. Farling, unpublished interview with Chad Schwartz, December 15, 2021.

27. Jessica Camille Aguirre reports that the "production of cement is alone responsible for eight percent of global emissions" alongside the 40% of climate emissions from raw material extraction to construction in "How to Recycle a 14-Story Office Tower" from *The New York Times*, October 6, 2022, https://www.nytimes.com/2022/10/06/headway/office-tower-carbon-emissions-amsterdam.html?smid=nytcore-ios-share&referringSource=articleShare, accessed October 16, 2022.

28. For more information on the United Nation's Convention to Combat Desertification see https://www.unwomen.org/en/how-we-work/intergovernmental-support/climate-change-and-the-environment/united-nations-convention-to-combat-desertification, accessed October 14, 2022.

29. Childs, *The Secret Knowledge of Water*, cover.

30. Scott, "The Desert in Fine Grain" in *The Invention of the American Desert*, 160.

Index

Image Credits

KEY

AFP A. F. Payne, **BF** Brian Farling, **BT** Bill Timmerman, **BW** Brad Wheeler, **EJ** Eddie Jones, **ET** Ed Taube, **IB** Inessa Binenbaum, **JC** Julian Clark, **LJ** Lisa Johnson, **LR** Lynne Rostochil, **MB** Mark Boisclair, **MW** Matt Winquist, **ND** Nic DiCarlo, **PG** Pedro E. Guerrero, **PM** Paul Markow, **QSS** Quantum Space Studio, **RR** Robert Reck, **RV** Rob Viergutz, **SB** Scott Baxter, *SZ* Scott Zimmerman, **TB** Tom Bonner, **TH** Tim Hursley, **TS** Thomas Story.

B bottom, **T** top, **L** left, **R** right, **C** center.

Front Cover Mariposa Land Port of Entry - BT
2-3 Rendering produced by QSS
4 BF
10 RR
15 ET
18T "Sonoran Desert National Monument (26426923160)" by the Bureau of Land Management (BLM) Arizona is dedicated to the public domain.
18C "Phoenix Dust Storm" by Alan Stark is licensed under CC BY-SA 2.0
18B "Rain Falling over Desert at Sunset" by Jessie Eastland is licensed under CC BY-SA 4.0
21T LR
21B "Taliesin Frank Lloyd Wright" by Christophe Krief is licensed under CC BY-SA 4.0
22 "View of Grape Orchards, Facing North. Camelback Mountain in the Background" by the National Park Service is dedicated to the public domain.
24-25 Prehistoric Irrigation Canals. Omar Asa Turney (1929), NAU.MAP.141. Northern Arizona University. Cline Library.
26L "View showing the demossing of Grand Canal…" is dedicated to the public domain.
26R Reg Manning Editorial Cartoon - AZ Republic, Feb 23, 1947, © Arizona Republic – USA TODAY NETWORK
28 "Lake Mead at Hoover Dam – 3" by APK is licensed under CC BY-SA 4.0
34 "The Work of a Great American Architect." Compton's Pictured Encyclopedia, vol. 15, F.E. Compton & Company, Chicago, 1956, pp. 308.
35TL "Where fortunes are made and lost overnight…" by Underwood & Underwood is dedicated to the public domain.
35TR LR
35B "2021 Arcosanti at Golden Hour" by Beyond My Ken is licensed under CC BY-SA 4.0, 3.0, 2.5, 2.0, and 1.0
36T "Canyon de Chelly 7-27-09 (11 cropped)" by Yoopernewsman aka Greg Peterson of Negaunee, MI is licensed under CC BY-SA 3.0
39 EJ
42L Photo of JSI Founder at 1st job - AZ Republic, pg 167, Phx, AZ Sunday, Sept. 26, 1983 - Photo credit in clip "Charles Krejcsi/Republic" © Arizona Republic – USA TODAY NETWORK
42TR "Rose Pauson House 1979 cropped" by Perry E. & Myra Borchers is dedicated to the public domain - PD-US-GOV-INTERIOR-HABS.
42BR PG
43 EJ
47T Modern Phoenix, LLC
47B MW
49-50 PM
53 Jones Family
55B EJ
56-57 BF
59-65 SZ
66 EJ
67-69 PM
70-71 SZ
72L Rendering produced by Julian Clark
73-75 SZ
77-78 SZ
79L SZ
79R BF
80-81 SZ
82 EJ
83-84 TH
86-89 TH
91-92 TH
93L EJ
93C "Melhok ki (ocotillo house), O'odham dwelling" by the National Park Service is dedicated to the public domain.
93R "Kare-sansui zen garden, Ryōan-ji, Kyoto 20190416 1" by DXR is licensed under CC BY-SA 4.0
94-97 TH
99 MB
100 Google Aerial Image
101-103 MB
105 Drawing by BF
106 MS Art Project
109 BT
111-112 MW
113 A.F Payne
114-117 MW
118-119 BT
121T ET
121B TH
122 TH
123 Google Aerial Image
124-127 TH
129 BT
132-135 BT
137 BF
140 Modern Phoenix
141 BT
142-143 PM
145 RR
147 TH
149 TS
150 TH
152-169 MB
171-175 RR
176 BF
177 RR
178-179 RR
181-182 RR
184 BT
186 BF
187 BT
188T BT
188BL BF
188BR BT
189T BT
189B BF
190-191 BF
192T RR
192C BW
192B RR
193-195 RR
197 ET
199-203 RR

204 BF
205 RR
206TL BF
206TR RR
206BR RR
206BL RR
207-209 RR
211 ET
212 RR
213-214 ET
215 RR
216-218 ET
219-221 RR
223 MW
225-227 BT
229-233 BT
235-239 MW
243-246 BT
248T SMoCA
248BL SMoCA
248BR BF
249 Photo of the top 1/2 of Section front page featuring JSI Office as living SMO-CA Exhibit - AZ Republic, Tue, May 30th, 2006, © Arizona Republic – USA TODAY NETWORK
250-251 BT
253 BF
255-257 BT
258 Google Aerial Image
259 BT
261T “Nogales Arizona 1910-1920” by the United States Army is dedicated to the public domain in the United States.
261BL “Nogales AZ-Mexico border in 1899” from the Arizona Historical Society is dedicated to the public domain.
261BR “Mexican-American border at Nogales” by Sgt. 1st Class Gordon Hyde is dedicated to the public domain in the United States.
263 “Industria maquiladora en Tlaxcala 06” by Isaacvp is licensed under CC BY-SA4.0
264TL “Nogales Border Wall and Concertina Wire” by the U.S. Customs and Border Protection is dedicated to the public domain in the United States.
264TR “Nogales CBP Officers Seize $924K in Marijuana” by the U.S. Customs and Border Protection is dedicated to the public domain in the United States.
264B BF
267 “360° Panorama Zocalo Mexico City” by Uwebart is licensed under the GNU Free Documentation License and CC BY-SA3.0 2.5 2.0 and 1.0
269 Google Aerial Image
270 “Oasis de Huacachina, Ica, Perú, 2015-07-29, DD 18” by Diego Delso, delso.photo, is licensed under CC BY-SA
272 BT
273TL-TR BF
273B BT
274 BF
275 BT
276-277 BT
279-286 BT
287 BF
289-291 BT
292T BF
292B BT
293-329 BT
330-331 MW
332-343 BT
344 LJ
346 MW
347 BF
348-351 MW
353-354 Jones Studio Family
355 BF
357L Google Aerial Image
357R Arizona Historical Society, AHS Postcard Collection, PP PC 250, B4/Phoenix Hotels & Resorts, 2004.55.988
358 Above AZ
361-364 BT
365T BT
365BL ASU Sandra Day O’Connor College of Law
365BR BT
366-369 BT
371 IB
372-373 Above AZ
374TL IB
374BR “Thunderbird on Totem Pole” by Dr. Haggis is licensed under the GNU Free Documentation License and CC BY-SA3.0
375-379 IB
380 Jones Studio Family
381T Image from US Customs and Border Protection, US-Mexico Border at Otay Mesa Land Port of Entry dedicated to the public domain.
383 MW
384TL “Colorado River Dry Delta” by Pete McBride, U.S. Geological Survey is dedicated to the public domain.
384TR “NRCSAZ02080” by Jeff Vanuga is courtesy of USDA Natural Resources Conservation Service and is dedicated to the public domain.
384BL “NRCSAZ02032(347)” by Jeff Vanuga is courtesy of USDA Natural Resources Conservation Service and is dedicated to the public domain.
384BR “NRCSAZ02010 – Arizona” by Jeff Vanuga is courtesy of USDA Natural Resources Conservation Service and is dedicated to the public domain.
385 SB
386-393 MW
395-397 TB
398 BF
399L Google Aerial Image
399R TB
400 TB
401 BF
402-403 TB
404 RV
405-407 EJ
411 MW
413-414 BF
415 Drawings produced by Chris Winters
419-424 Renderings produced by QSS
425 BF
426-431 Renderings produced by QSS
434 MW
438 TL TR CR B BF
438CL Google Aerial Image
442B Map below by ASU University City Exchange
451 Rendering produced by QSS
454-469 Renderings produced by QSS
477 ND
492-493 BT
494-495 ET
Back Cover (left to right, top to bottom): RR, TH, ET, MB, QSS, BT, TH, RR

Book credits

Graphic Design by Lucía B. Bauzá.
Art Direction by Oscar Riera Ojeda.
Copy Editing by Kit Maude and Michael W. Phillips Jr.

Front Cover Cast footprints in concrete tilt wall - Mariposa Land Port of Entry, Nogales, Arizona. **Pages 2-3** Sunrise over the aqueduct - Central Arizona Project Visitor Center, Phoenix, Arizona. **Page 4** Living sun screen at roof level - University of Arizona College of Architecture, Planning & Landscape Architecture, Tucson, Arizona. **Pages 492-493** Cornell Cookson Door Manufacturing Facility, Goodyear, Arizona courtyard view from manufacturing. **Pages 494-495** Logan Residence, Scottsdale, Arizona. **Back cover top left to right** House of Five Dreams, Paradise Valley, Arizona; River Legacy Parks Living Science Center, Arlington, Texas; University of Arizona College of Architecture, Planning & Landscape Architecture, Tucson, Arizona; South Mountain Community College Performing Arts Center, Phoenix, Arizona. **Bottom left to right** Lake Havasu City Environmental Learning Center, Lake Havasu City, Arizona; Mariposa Land Port of Entry, Nogales, Arizona; NAI Horizon Corporate Office Building, Phoenix, Arizona; Arizona State University Polytechnic Interdisciplinary Science and Technology Building 3, Mesa, Arizona.

OSCAR RIERA OJEDA
PUBLISHERS

ISBN 978-1-946226-66-2
Published by Oscar Riera Ojeda Publishers Limited
Printed in China

Oscar Riera Ojeda Publishers Limited
Unit 1331, Beverley Commercial Centre,
87-105 Chatham Road South, Tsim Sha Tsui, Kowloon, Hong Kong

Production Offices
Suit 19, Shenyun Road,
Nanshan District, Shenzhen 518055, China

International Customer Service & Editorial Questions: +1-484-502-5400

www.oropublishers.com | www.oscarrieraojeda.com
oscar@oscarrieraojeda.com